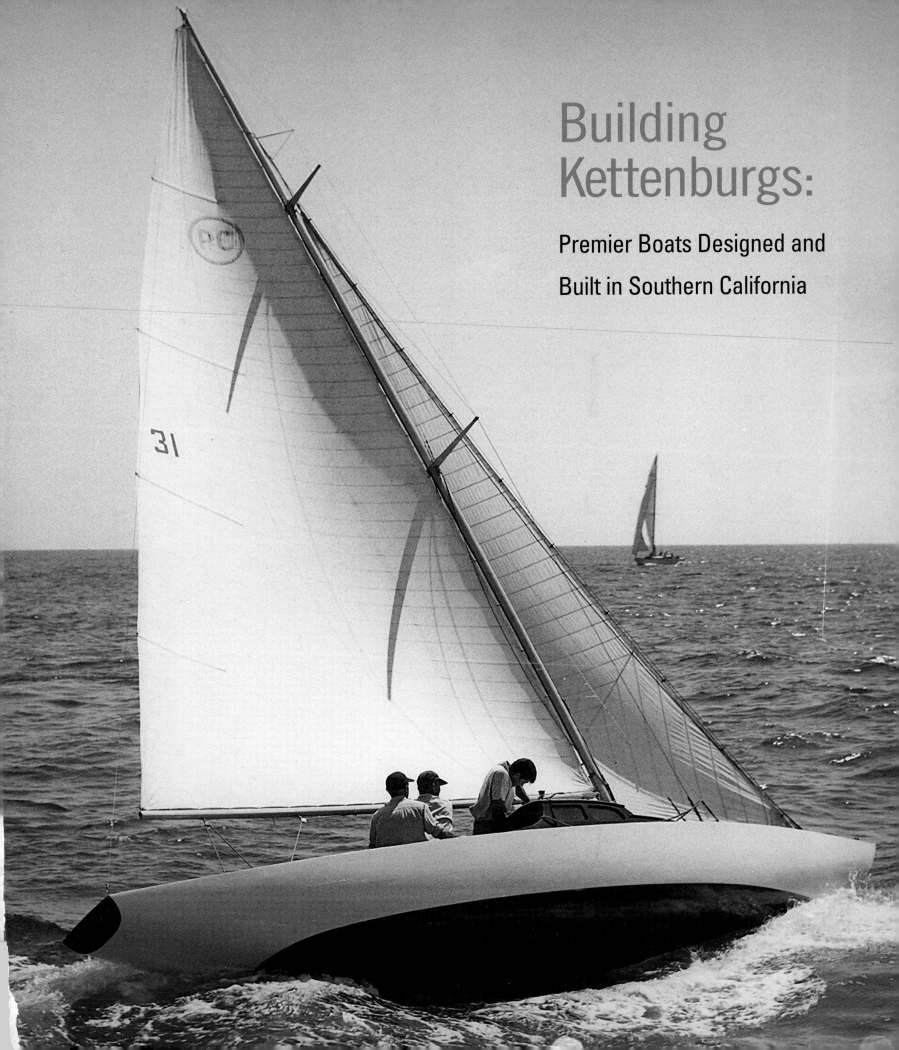

Building Kettenburgs:

Premier Boats Designed and

Built in Southern California

Building Kettenburgs:

Premier Boats Designed and Built in Southern California

By Mark Allen

MARITIME MUSEUM OF SAN DIEGO, SAN DIEGO, CALIFORNIA
AND MYSTIC SEAPORT, MYSTIC, CONNECTICUT, 2008

Mystic Seaport
75 Greenmanville Ave., P.O. Box 6000
Mystic, CT 06355-0990

 Published 2008
First edition

Designed by Clare Cunningham, Essex, CT

Manufactured in China

ISBN: 978-0-939511-26-6

Cataloging-in-Publication Data

Allen, Mark, 1966-
Building Kettenburgs : premier boats designed and built in southern California / Mark Allen.—San Diego, Calif. : Maritime Museum of San Diego ; Mystic, Conn. : Mystic Seaport, 2008.
p. : ill., ports. ; cm.
Includes bibliographical references and index.

1. Kettenburg, George W., 1904-1952. 2. Kettenburg Boat Works -- History. 3. Boatyards -- California -- San Diego -- History. 4. Sailboats -- Pacific Coast (North America). 5. Sailboat racing -- United States. I. Title.

VM321.52.U6 A45 2008

Page 1: The DeLuxe PC *Skylark* works to windward in a good racing breeze.
Page 2: George Kettenburg's pride, *Eulalie*, PCC 1, sets her spinnaker in this 1952 painting by Kipp Soldwedel.
Page 6: George Kettenburg navigates.

To George and Paul, to Bill Kettenburg, and to Charlie and Jim Jr.,
whose artistry is celebrated in these pages

Contributors

The Publishers wish to express their appreciation to the following
who have provided financial support for this book:

FOR MYSTIC SEAPORT

The Kyle Endowment for Intellectual Property Development at Mystic Seaport
The Olin Stephens Fund for Yachting Publications

FOR THE MARITIME MUSEUM OF SAN DIEGO

PLATINUM SPONSORS
John and Nonnie Barbey
Thompson and Jane Fetter
Gary and Gayle Gould
Vance Gustafson
Tom and Nancy Hurlburt
Thomas E. Kettenburg
Bob and Laura Kyle
George C. and Mary C. Jessop

DIAMOND SPONSORS
Neil Atwood
Steve Barber
Karan Cooper and Bennet Greenwald
Doug and Celeste Holthaus
Jane and Geves Kenny
Robin and Andy LaDow

GOLD SPONSORS
Bud and Mary Jane Caldwell
Diane Schneider and Dave Grundies
George and Pamela Lindley
Jim and Beth Oberg
Blake Oversmith
Barry Worthington

Table of Contents

Preface

"A man builds the best of himself into a boat," wrote California author John Steinbeck in *Sea of Cortez*. But can a family do the same? Today, Kettenburg-built sailboats remain fast and beautiful, but, oddly enough, the fact that so many are still with us is due to an almost unrelated quality. These boats were built to *last*, and built solidly—despite the fact that this family firm pioneered building race-winners of exceptional lightness. Call them "boats of integrity," if you like. In the interviews upon which this book is based, "integrity" was the word that came up most often to describe George and Paul Kettenburg, their partners, and their employees.

What follows springs from a series of afternoons I spent in the home office of Paul Kettenburg, then an owlish, patient man in his eighties who favored plaid shirts, and who graciously endured the questions I put to him—most of which were, in retrospect, ill-informed about how to build or sail a wooden boat. Above Paul's head as I asked my halting questions hung a huge model he had built of a Curtiss Jenny (the airplane that gave him his first ride aloft), while the walls around us were decorated with color photos of antique cars he had restored to life. Among the items filling the walls, the most interesting to me at the time were a dozen or so half models of sailboats that he, his brother, or their partner Charlie Underwood had designed and built. Among the models and celebratory plaques hung a nondescript little sign from a local bank. The significance of the phrase it bore was pointed out to me much later. "People Matter," it says.

Today, the company that bore the name of the Kettenburg family has a special kind of regional fame among people who know sailboats, and most agree that their work deserves to be much more widely known. In the early 21st century, there are still moments when the products of the long-defunct firm turn up in national news. Picture yourself for a moment as a Kettenburg owner walking into a bar along the Eastern Seaboard, perhaps in Newport, Rhode Island—American yachting's "Holy Land." If you drop the fact that the handsome sailboat you just steered into port is a Kettenburg, you may well draw blank stares from the others along the bar. If you explain that your sloop was built of wood in 1948, they may smile and lift their glasses, saluting you indulgently with the traditional show of envy, respect, and pity that owners of fiberglass-hulled boats display toward those lucky (or unlucky) enough to have to keep their wooden holes-in-the-water afloat. If you further insist, however, that your almost-sixty-year-old PCC raced a fleet of 14 fiberglass yachts around Block Island, overnight, into the teeth of a 25-mile-per-hour headwind, and beat them all, you may very well be shown the door. The indulgence of the owners of fiberglass-hulled sailboats toward the farfetched tales of their wooden-hulled brethren has its limits—even when the tales are true.

But you would at least have Olin Stephens on your side. Stephens, perhaps the most successful 20th-century yacht designer, recalls today that "I think my introduction to the Kettenburg name was via Hank duPont" when that well-known Eastern yachtsman bought a PCC after the Second World War. Olin remembers that she "seemed a surprisingly good all-around boat." In San Diego more recently, Stephens took the helm of the best-known Kettenburg design, the venerable Pacific Class (PC) sloop, and was still more impressed: "I thought her behaviour in a puffy afternoon breeze was exceptionally good, always easy to control with a nice light, slight weather helm, good stability and quick acceleration." Not bad, for a sailboat designed in 1929 by a man never educated past high school.

Kettenburg Boat Works was truly a San Diego phenomenon, and therefore a sort of open secret. When the firm began, its hometown was an unimportant but shamelessly self-promoting wide spot in the road, perched proudly if insignificantly on the lower-left-hand corner of the American map. (For several years after Mr. Kettenburg founded his company, there were fewer San Diegans than there were residents of Peoria, Illinois.) While their sailboats and their regional fame spread along the West Coast and out to Hawai'i fairly early, their handiwork is still mostly unfamiliar in the world beyond. Aside from traditional accusations of "East Coast bias" in boating matters, perhaps the main reason for this was the intervention of the Great Depression and Second World War, which prevented the popular and economical PC design from spreading as widely as it might have. Another is the fact that the extraordinary George Kettenburg Jr. completed only two original sailboat "class" designs before passing the designer's tools over to his equally unschooled (and equally highly skilled) brother Paul, and so never gained the fame of more prolific designers. And since many of the sailboat designs subsequently created by Paul and his partner Charlie Underwood balance postwar cravings for comfortable cruising against the bare-bones racing orientation of prewar designs, these fine boats still sail somewhat in the shadow of their elders. And they all, of course, were overshadowed by the wave of fiberglass-hulled boats that washed unwary wooden sailboat builders overboard into bankruptcy in the 1960s. Fiberglass sailboats—derided unfairly by Paul Kettenburg and others as "Tupperware"—opened up the possibility of sailboat ownership to a far wider group of men and women. But something was lost along the way, and today the Kettenburgs' wooden boats are cherished for qualities like those that Olin Stephens felt at the PC's tiller. They certainly deserve to be at least well known enough to permit any Kettenburg owner to walk into any sailor-frequented bar in the country and be saluted appropriately.

In the Kettenburg story, an ambitious, dedicated, and talented founder struggles to make a name for himself building wooden boats, succeeds (achieving even greater success in more commercially reliable aspects of this tricky business), and passes on an evolving design and production operation that dodges a near-mortal blow from the coming of fiberglass only to founder on the shoals of shifting business fortunes. It represents the story of many another 20th-century American recreational boatbuilding firm. But the Kettenburgs' story also represents a particular tack in the course of American sailing: George, his brother Paul, and their partner Charlie Underwood were perhaps the last "amateur" yacht designers, builders, and racers to gain a following based on the quality of their work alone, rather than on an academic pedigree. They were sailors first, designers after.

One reason for their success was Southern California itself. Neither Newport, Rhode Island, nor the other capitals of American yachting saw anything like the urban growth that cascaded across coastal Southern California. Demand for fast boats from the swelling local professional class drew young George into his craft, learning by "feel" as had Eastern predecessors like "Captain Nat" Herreshoff and W. Starling Burgess. The San Diegans' designs are rooted in an almost instinctual awareness that if a slender, lightly constructed hull looked fast, it probably was. But if their sun rose rapidly, its setting came equally quickly. Southern California was growing a new generation of yacht designers equipped with graduate degrees and the abilities to perform calculations well beyond anything for which San Diego's high schools had prepared the Kettenburgs. Even while George and his little crew were building PCs in a metal-roofed shed with simple tools, in the East Starling Burgess and MIT-educated Olin

Stephens were performing sophisticated tank tests on hull models that enabled their J-boat *Ranger* to capture the 1937 America's Cup. The Kettenburgs succeeded thanks to the lucky fact that their lives overlapped with this specific moment in the life of rapidly urbanizing Southern California. Unlike the way things might have turned out a few years before, or after, San Diego's exploding population of boat-lovers gave them the opportunity to rise to the level that their talents made possible.

The firm thrived for 68 years, long after their boat design and construction had faded from the scene. They outlasted competitors thanks primarily to a wise strategy of diversifying to meet boaters' needs. Kettenburg Boat Works grew organically from designing and building boats into repairing them, and selling the marine hardware to fix them. Along the way they filled the needs of the U.S. Navy—San Diego's major growth engine for much of the 20th century.

And all the while, the recreational potential of the bay just outside the boatyard's back door was gradually dawning on city planners, as promoters discovered how vividly pictures of sailboats illustrated their city's other magical key to economic development—climate. Those year-round recreational opportunities that lure tourists and winter-weary transplants alike were (and are) advertised by images of sailboats, a particularly effective tactic when the hardy sailors lie basking on deck on a 70-degree January afternoon. In the idealized picture that Southern California has tried to draw of itself as a kind of earthly, accessible paradise, Kettenburg boats made photogenic (if anonymous) icons. As the most historically significant of Southern California's recreational boatbuilders, they have always been important—if little known outside the boating community—to the smiling image the region projects to the world.

If a man can build the best of himself into a boat, then perhaps a family, and a family business, can too. "Integrity" informs the best of craftsmanship as a lasting consequence of choices made by living human beings. A surprising amount of the Kettenburgs' wooden architecture survives, still afloat on the Pacific. This isn't to say that other builders' work lacked quality. It's just that integrity was synonymous with Kettenburg Boat Works—from the sailboats themselves on up. Perhaps there is a hint of this in the sign Paul hung on his office wall, the one that says "People Matter."

Acknowledgments

The spirit of this book derives from the spirit of Kettenburg people—family, employees, and enthusiastic boat owners–who shared their stories for the book's creation. My intention throughout has been to tell a "people" story, not to write a dry business history or to compile a technical catalog of Kettenburg boat designs. Of course, people interpret situations differently and remember "facts" subjectively, so I have tried to be judicious and careful in weaving their stories together to create the narrative fabric. I take responsibility for any flaws that may appear in the finished product.

Of course, one cannot undertake such a work without a tremendous amount of support. I owe a debt of gratitude to Bob Kyle, this project's patient prime mover in Connecticut and California, who also, as librarian of the San Diego Yacht Club, opened the historical resources of that institution to me. Dr. Raymond Ashley of the Maritime Museum of San Diego also backed this project from the first, as did the administration at Mystic Seaport.

As a principal repository for Kettenburg material, the MacMullen Library & Research Archives at the Maritime Museum of San Diego contains photographs, copies of Kettenburg documents, and 40 taped interviews and partial transcripts used in this study. The San Diego Yacht Club Library and the San Diego Historical Society Research Archives also contain important material and were extremely cooperative.

As the voices of the participants are so central to this story, I benefited greatly from numerous interviews conducted by earlier researchers, as documented in the endnotes. At the same time, I was thrilled to conduct a number of oral history interviews in the course of my research. Whatever little I've learned about interviewing I picked up from Bob Wright of the Maritime Museum of San Diego.

Members of George Kettenburg's family—especially his children Tom, Bill (George W. III), and Jean; his brother Paul, who, sadly, didn't live to see this book in print; and Jean's husband, Morgan Miller—were most welcoming, generous, and encouraging in my telling of their family tale. They shared stories, photographs, and memorabilia, and they helped keep me on course.

"Oldtimers" who shared freely their stories of working at Kettenburg or sailing Kettenburg boats included Alex "Bud" Caldwell, Tom Fetter, Doug Giddings, Dick Hershey, Gary Keller, Art Miley, Wallace Springstead, Gene Trepte, Charles A. Underwood, Charles R. Underwood, and Jim Underwood Jr.

I also benefited greatly from the work of earlier Kettenburg researchers, especially Robert Smith, Chares La Dow, and Paul Lazarus.

Two prominent members of the present generation of Kettenburg owners contributed greatly to this work. Richard "Rish" Pavelec provided much information and perspective on his special passion, the Pacific Class (PC). Neil Atwood did the same for his specialty, the Pacific Cruising Class (PCC), and continues to broaden the Kettenburg story through his comprehensive Web site, www.kettenburgboats.com. Jack Sutphen and Steve Barber also contributed perspective on the resurgence of interest in Kettenburg boats.

I thank Patricia Nelson Limerick, who taught me that history books need not be boring. In that line, the first half of this manuscript benefited from the skills of a superlative critical reader, Dr. Raymond Starr; the second half benefited from my fear that he was looking over my shoulder. Expert racer and insightful yachting historian Tom Skahill provided valuable support, as well as occasional out-of-the-blue gifts. And I appreciate the collaborative effort of my editor in Mystic, Connecticut, Andrew German.

Visually, as documented in the photo credits at the back of the book, many individuals and institutions contributed to make this such a rich pictorial record. John Wright's skill in photographing the paintings reproduced here, and his hand with Photoshop, were invaluable. Designer Clare Cunningham, in Essex, Connecticut, then put it all together in stunning fashion, making this a true celebration of the Kettenburg story.

Finally, my enduring thanks to Laura, Everett, and "Hollisito" for putting up with me and my distractions during the years required to complete this book.

✛ Opposite: The restored *Wings,* PC 8, sails again, with the restored bark *Star of India* under sail in the background. The Maritime Museum of San Diego preserves both historic vessels.

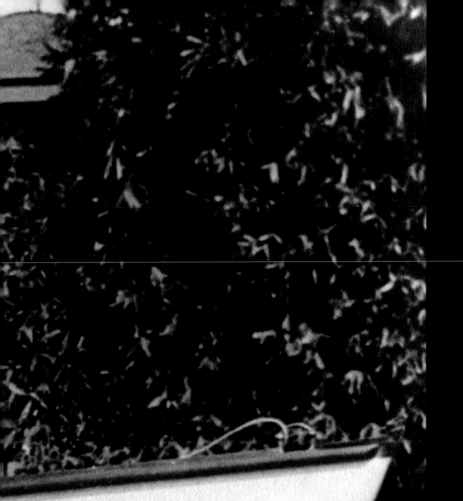

Chapter One

The Bulb
Blinks On

Opposite: George Kettenburg (center) and his crew pose in front of the
Kettenburg home with one of their Sun boats in 1926. Inset: Aerial
impression of Point Loma and San Diego Bay, ca. 1920.

George and Amelia
Kettenburg, ca. 1930.

Mr. George William Kettenburg seems to have spent many of his happiest hours with wrench in hand, smoothing the stutter from the voice of a balky engine, or peeling shiny metal curls off a new part he was turning on his lathe.

n a sense, it was Thomas Edison who launched the first Kettenburg boats. That inventor's incandescent light bulb and electric generating system illuminated new possibilities for American entrepreneurs in the 1880s and '90s, inspiring men like Pittsburgh's George William Kettenburg to start their own small electric plants. Young George was a confident, dapper, mustachioed electrical engineer, and the first boats to bear the family name grew out of seed money from the sale of his pocket-sized utility to a far bigger firm.

For a dozen years, Kettenburg Electric had generated DC power for the residents of about six blocks of Pittsburgh, Pennsylvania; Mr. Kettenburg would, upon request, even arrange to replace customers' burned-out light bulbs. In about 1911, the Duquesne Light & Power Co. made him an offer too tempting to refuse. So, in his early forties, Mr. Kettenburg suddenly found himself living the American dream, with a comfortable retirement income, mechanical skills and entrepreneurial talents, and nothing whatsoever to do.

Although he loved to travel, his temperament left him unsuited for taking an endless vacation or for sitting idly on his hands. The reserved-seeming former utility owner was actually a passionate tinkerer of the same stripe as Henry Ford and Edison himself. Mr. George William Kettenburg seems to have spent many of his happiest hours with wrench in hand, smoothing the stutter from the voice of a balky engine, or peeling shiny metal curls off a new part he was turning on his lathe. "An inventor," is how his grandson Bill Kettenburg remembered him: "He was a good mechanical man—an engineer type of person." Later, Mr. Kettenburg contented himself with stepping into the background, to become the financial backer and sometime machinist for his talented namesake son. If he ever regretted moving out of the municipal electricity business and into the boat business, or felt qualms at leaving Western Pennsylvania snow for Southern California sun, he never breathed a word of it.

His grandfather had emigrated from Germany

in 1832, and Mr. Kettenburg's own father, like many another German-American, answered the call when war came between the states in 1861. George W. Kettenburg and his friends enlisted in Company C of the 63rd Pennsylvania Infantry, suffering severe casualties on the battlefields at Fredericksburg, Gettysburg, and Petersburg. Back home, he set up as a plumber in yet another "burg": the heavily German-American city of Pittsburg. His son, also named George W. Kettenburg, grew up quietly loathing his father's prosperous but dull career. "My dad *hated* plumbing," remembered youngest son Paul, but his grandfather insisted that Paul's father learn the trade. The young man, however, discovered within himself an aptitude for tinkering with engines and electricity. "So, the minute his father died, he closed that plumbing business down— *boom*! No way was he gonna be a plumber."

As his neighborhood electrical generating utility prospered, the plumber's son took his budding family for extended vacations. In Palm Beach, Florida, George and his family—his wife Amelia, eldest son Robert, girls Ella and Julia, and little George Jr.—motored about in rented powerboats, nattily dressed in the starched whites that boating fashion demanded. In 1908, he rented a new Southwestern-style cottage near the extreme southwestern corner of the United States, at a windy San Diego-area seaside village called La Jolla—a name whose Spanish pronunciation frequently confounded fellow Easterners. The newly retired former businessman left his family there temporarily to indulge his love for ocean travel, departing by steamship for an excursion around the Pacific. The Kettenburgs' permanent move west four years later occurred with what family tradition records as surprising spontaneity. Paul said that his father was about to transplant the family south, where he planned to buy an existing electrical generating plant: "They were going to take a ship to go to Florida with all the furniture and everything, because they had sold out everything in Pittsburgh. So, they had everything all packed up and ready to go—and they put the

ship in drydock for awhile. So he said, 'The heck with that—let's go to California.'"

Perhaps partly in frustration at the projected two-week delay required by the steamship company, George took the family west instead. The six Kettenburgs and their crated possessions boarded a train for the Pacific coast. Among their possessions was proof, if any was needed, of Mr. Kettenburg's mechanical passions: the engine he had recently extracted from the family's 1907 Daimler rode along with them in its own crate. In 1912, they rented a house just inland from San Diego in the village of La Mesa, and he began searching methodically for the right location in

which to settle. In the late summer of 1913, as Amelia was pregnant with Paul, they moved into a handsome two-story house designed for them in the Arts and Crafts style, on the lee side of Point Loma in the growing San Diego neighborhood of La Playa. "After he arrived," explained Paul, "he decided to build a home here on Point Loma, after looking at La Jolla and deciding it was too cold and windy, and after looking at La Mesa and deciding that it was too hot and dry."

When the family settled in thinly populated Point Loma in 1913, San Diego was a tidy town with a distinctly Midwestern feel—and with only 39,600 citizens, was 13 times smaller than their

Center, the Kettenburg's Arts and Crafts style home at La Playa, on the lee side of Point Loma, ca. 1915.

Butcher Boy, the "meat boat" turned yacht, in the early 1900s.

Pittsburgh hometown. Despite San Diego's famously ideal weather, its bay was less than ideal for boaters. Ringed at low tide by foul-smelling mud flats, it had been snubbed as unsuitably shallow four years earlier by the U.S. Navy.

That snub had occurred in 1907 when, to the embarrassment of the town's more farsighted boosters—who were practically tumbling over the representatives of other West Coast cities in their eagerness to court the navy—not a single capital ship from the "Great White Fleet" had ventured past Point Loma, their bay's threshold. The stung local boosters used this slight to begin drumming up support for dredging, to make their port more welcoming to the navy's federal dollars in the future.

The town's handful of recreational boaters kept most of their craft moored near the San Diego Yacht Club, whose name and supposedly long pedigree belied reality. The club had endured the ignominy of bankruptcy and reorganization, and had moved several times, most recently into a makeshift clubhouse aboard an old ferryboat. This experimental screw-driven ferryboat had embarrassed local builders a quarter-century earlier by smashing uncontrollably into the pilings at ferry landings, earning it the unhappy nickname of "the pile-driver's friend."

Many local pleasure boats at the club were still little more than fancy workboats. One such dual-purpose craft survives today along the waterfront—generally overlooked by visitors craning their necks to better see the iconic square-rigger *Star of India*. The 29-foot sloop *Butcher Boy* was launched in 1902 as a "meat boat" intended to beat the competition out to greet arriving ships and sell them "Boss" Hardy's assorted meat products. By the time the Kettenburgs came to town, *Butcher Boy* had been adapted for pleasure use as, not entirely coincidentally, the harbor's commercial prospects had dwindled. The tonnage of cargo arriving in San Diego by sea had dropped to about half that of Los Angeles, now served by a new port built virtually from scratch at San Pedro.

The mountains that walled San Diego off from the east also sealed it off from the cheaper railroad freight rates enjoyed by that much-envied and loathed northern neighbor, whose transcontinental rail connection facilitated its development as California's biggest working port. "Steamship

The 29-foot sloop *Butcher Boy* was launched in 1902 as a "meat boat" intended to beat the competition out to greet arriving ships and sell them "Boss" Hardy's assorted meat products.

officials seem to consider it a favor to San Diego to come in here with their ships," huffed their Chamber of Commerce.

The seven little boatbuilding firms scattered around the bay in 1913 served a mixture of recreational and commercial customers. Joe Fellows, for example—who in 1903 opened what became the vast Fellows & Stewart yard in San Pedro—expanded to San Diego with local builder Willis "Clem" Stose in 1912; their San Diego shop produced a class of distinctive little sailboats. To meet commercial demand, however, Stose turned his company towards serving commercial fishermen. The other local firms—Campbell's Machine Co., Rask, Lynch, and later, National Steel & Shipbuilding—would grow into major shipyards with the expansion of San Diego's marine commerce in the 1920s.

Butcher Boy's builder Manuel Goularte turned to constructing fishing boats for his fellow Portuguese immigrants, most of whose families lived in La Playa and whose children attended school alongside the Kettenburg kids. Many of the Kettenburgs' comparatively impoverished Portuguese-born neighbors would soon begin ascending to prosperity thanks to a new product: canned tuna. Introduced shortly after 1900 as an outgrowth of the phenomenally productive canned salmon industry, the new tuna industry

had followed the fish to San Diego by the time the Kettenburgs arrived. This boom in catching and canning tuna created a product that few housewives, and certainly not the refined Mrs. Amelia Kettenburg, had yet tried in 1913. As San Diego's fishermen pursued ever-larger catches,

clambering to the summit of the world's tuna industry—where they perched proudly if briefly after the Second World War—commercial boatbuilders pursued tunamen and neglected yachtsmen.

American pleasure boat construction was centered along the eastern seaboard and in lakeside cities like Chicago. In these distant places, a "Who's Who" of wealthy clients commanded the talents of talented and increasingly famous naval architects, the younger stars among whom had been trained at MIT and other eastern universities. American yachting had first bloomed in the outpouring of industrial wealth that characterized the "Gilded Age" after the Civil War, as the great wealth that had accumulated in the hands of the few demanded that the few find imaginative means to spend it. And while the rich favored steam power for their waterborne socializing and commuting needs, sailing enthusiasts were periodically whipped into a frenzy of patriotic money-spending by recurring challenges from across the Atlantic for the America's Cup, which had become the international symbol of sailing excellence since the first challenge in 1870. Cup competition pushed designers toward the extremes of technology, resulting in such floating astonishments as Nathanael Herreshoff's 1903 *Reliance*, from whose single mast spread over a

William H. Hand Jr. and the Vee-Bottom Motorboat

George Kettenburg's success as a motorboat builder was based on the work of William H. Hand (1875-1946). The son of a navy and revenue service officer, Hand was born in 1875 at Portland, Maine, and grew up in the East Coast ports where his father was stationed. Hand attended Brown University but left before graduating to settle in New Bedford, Massachusetts, and design small boats.

About 1901 he began to adapt the vee-bottom design of small Chesapeake Bay and Buzzards Bay sailboats to motorboat hulls. In 1912 Hand commented: "My first boats of this type were planned to compete with the then popular dory and then quickly demonstrated that they had more speed, were fully as seaworthy and were sturdier. In fact, they possess none of the 'cranky' tendencies of the average small power boat, capable of any speed." Those "cranky" speedboats were long and narrow, making them very wet and difficult to steer. By contrast, Hand's flaring vee-bottom hull reduced the wetted surface for speed while increasing stability and shedding water. Soon, even the fastest step hydroplanes of the period were simply modified vee-bottom hulls.

Hand's vee-bottom design attracted widening attention in 1912 when George Bonnell drove his 24-footer *Old Glory* from Greenwich, Connecticut, to Nova Scotia and back. *Old Glory* could race along at 21 miles per hour with just a 30-horsepower engine. Leo Barker of Catalina Island introduced the Hand vee-bottom powerboat to California that year with his 22-footer, *Snap Shot*. Her 12-horsepower engine drove her at 15 miles per hour.

When the Kettenburgs ordered a set of plans in 1917, Hand's designs were widely publicized in *Motorboat*, *Motorboating*, and other boating magazines. His annual catalog advertised plans for a range of boat sizes and configurations for a reasonable price.

By the time George Kettenburg began to establish his reputation as a designer and builder of vee-bottom powerboats in the early 1920s, William Hand had turned his attention to schooners. In the 1920s he developed the characteristic "Hand Motorsailer," and in the 1930s he designed boats inspired by his passion for swordfishing. Evolving—as would the young California builder—he remained an influential American designer for forty years.

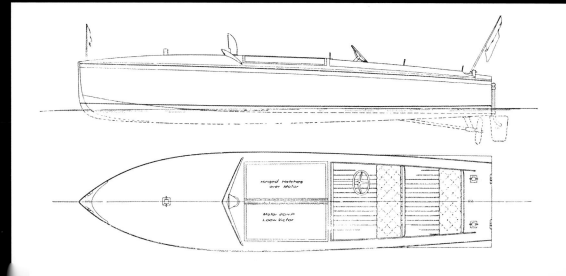

Above: William H. Hand Jr. at the wheel of his schooner, 1923. Left: Hand's 20-foot runabout *Skilligalee*, offered in his catalog as Design No. 337, was similar in model to the slightly larger design ordered by the Kettenburgs in 1917.

third of an acre of canvas.

While the wealthiest "sailors" relied on professional captains and crews to operate their vessels, an avid and growing wave of "Corinthian" sailors—amateurs who sailed for the love of it—wished to sail their own smaller boats and even compete in identical boats as a true test of sailing skill. In the 1890s, their yacht clubs began to sponsor "one-design" classes of sloops suitable for local conditions. Ranging between 20 and 40 feet overall and designed to be raced or day-sailed by a small crew of family or friends, such boats encouraged children to sail and fostered the strong growth of recreational sailing in the early 1900s. The first truly national class boat was the 22-foot *Star*, introduced in 1911 and united in an association to promote competition in 1922. The decade following the First World War also saw more ordinary "stock" sail- and motorboat designs multiply, enabling prosperous Americans to buy their boats, like their cars, straight off the lot.

Since gasoline engines were first successfully placed in boats in the 1890s, a tremendous growth had taken place in engine and hull designs, just as in automobiles. This was becoming an era devoted to speed, as crowds who thronged grandstands at auto racetracks like the Indianapolis "brickyard" also filled waterside bleachers where they thrilled to the equally dangerous new sport of powerboat racing. The elder Mr. Kettenburg was one of those who eagerly turned to *MotorBoat* as it celebrated the harnessing of ever-more-powerful automobile engines to boats. The *Disturber IV* of 1915, he read, was equipped with twin Duesenbergs that churned out nearly seven hundred horsepower *apiece*, propelling her to victory at astonishing speeds of over a mile a minute. And while the War to End Wars proved inconclusive in most respects, it certainly brought change to the powerboating world as governments flooded the market with war-surplus aircraft engines, whose power-to-weight ratios outstripped those of automobiles. Given Mr. Kettenburg's enthusiasm for fast boats, it is

likewise hard *not* to imagine him leaning toward his radio a decade later as a record half-million fans cheered *Miss America* as she roared down the Detroit River to victory, thrust along by a pair of these monstrous aircraft engines. Even on the shores of a backwater like San Diego Bay, such power plants could soon be had for bargain prices.

George Kettenburg Sr., now comfortably settled on Point Loma, apparently concluded that his otherwise satisfactory life would be even better if he had a boat. Mr. Kettenburg was an early member of that species derided as "Monkey Wrench Sailors" by those who preferred the elegance of canvas to any speed attained by internal combustion and the whiff of gasoline. Paul recalled his father as "a powerboat man. He was an old car buff and he liked engines, so he wasn't interested in sailing." Half of the new two-car garage was filled with his lathe and machine shop. A neighbor sold him the 24-foot *Joiselle*, into which he and son George Jr. squeezed the Daimler engine that had come by rail from Pittsburgh. Its four big cylinders did not generate much in the way of excitement. "It wasn't much of a boat," shrugged Paul. Instead, his father "decided that maybe it would be fun to build a better boat."

He turned to William H. Hand Jr., a self-taught designer in Fairhaven, Massachusetts, who had adapted the vee-bottom shape of Chesapeake Bay boats to powerboat designs. Hand's popular and influential designs for fast, seaworthy powerboats were often featured in *MotorBoat,* and he sold full sets of plans for as little as $12.50 by mail order. The Kettenburgs ordered plans for a 22-foot high-speed runabout. But as Paul remembered it, after the plans arrived "George took over and laid the plans out on the floor of the basement of the old house—for lofting it—and he told my dad, 'You know, this would be a better boat if it was 24 feet.'"

This assertion, made by 14-year-old George Kettenburg Jr. as he laid out Hand's plans at full scale on that floor, must have startled his father.

"Dad wrote to the architect and said 'What do *you* think of increasing the length of the boat?'" remembered Paul. Although the designer's written response was reportedly a conclusive "It will ruin it," the senior Kettenburg instead elected to let his son try to prove his point.

As sometimes happens with backyard projects, construction dragged on for two years. The Great War was making parts hard to find, and influenza swept away more lives than bullets did, killing between 40 and 50 million worldwide. In San Diego, 4,392 residents of the little city got sick—and 324 died—in two months of 1918 alone. (To escape the pandemic, at its most lethal among the soldiers in their barracks a few hundred feet from the Kettenburgs' house, the family retreated to a cabin among the pines in the nearby Laguna Mountains.) Young George ultimately took over construction duties on the lengthened boat and launched *Poggy*, named in honor of pug-nosed sister Ella, in 1919 or 1920. Mr. Kettenburg was impressed, despite the underwhelming junkyard engine, and may have wondered "Who *is* this fourteen-year-old, who challenges the expertise of one of America's leading powerboat designers?"

When they launched *Poggy*, however, neither father nor son was satisfied with her performance. As Paul recalled, "the engine didn't do too well for the boat, and they . . . changed engines a couple of times and tried to get more powerful engines for it. Finally, after World War I, the Government started selling the surplus aircraft engines. Dad went over there—and I remember I went over—to look at these engines they had in crates." North Island, across the bay from the Kettenburg house, was then shared by the army's Rockwell Field and the navy's air station, both of which had grown during the war. Mr. Kettenburg and his very young son Paul walked around contemplating crates of aircraft engines, both new ($100) and used ($50).

When his father and brother installed one in *Poggy*, the 90-horsepower V8 Curtiss OX5 "made all the difference in the world. It just came to life,

and started to really go," roaring over the bay at 35 miles per hour. Excited by this success, in 1922 George launched a 26-foot Hand design with a still more powerful aircraft engine: a French-built "Hisso"—a Hispano-Suiza V8 with cast-aluminum block—which Paul remembered "going pretty good!" at around 45 miles per hour. The engines proved such irresistible bargains to their father that 75 crates were soon piled behind the family home.

Hobbies can lead families in unexpected directions. For the Kettenburgs, a father's hobby of tinkering led to a small municipal utility, and, after he moved his family to San Diego, to the inspiration to build a motorboat with the help of his son. As one enthusiast for Kettenburg boats later put it, "his father's hobby was the starting point of George Jr.'s life work." According to Paul, after George Jr. sold his first two homebuilt speedboats, his father told him, "Hell—if you want to build boats, I'll set you up in business." Kettenburg Boat & Engine Co. officially began in 1918, despite the fact that its chief designer and builder was still in high school and could not yet legally drive.

About this time, George met Eulalie Farrow, best known as the namesake of one of his most famous racing sailboats—although she herself was never very enthusiastic about racing. Her father was a U.S. Army surgeon at Fort Rosecrans, an installation built about the time of the Spanish-American War to defend Point Loma from seaborne attack by Spain, Germany, or other comers. The line that divided the military reservation from the Kettenburgs' neighborhood was only a few hundred feet from their house, so it was natural for the kids to associate with their army neighbors. To a girl looking for a ride to high school, George stood out. As his son Bill heard it, George "built a speedboat to go to San Diego High, which was Russ High in those days, and he would take his speedboat and tie up at Broadway Pier . . . rather than go on the streetcar, which took *forever*. . . . And so he went over and picked up my mom," providing a free and

✛ George and Eulalie at the beach, ca. 1925.

George "built a speedboat to go to San Diego High, which was Russ High in those days, and he would take his speedboat and tie up at Broadway Pier. . . . rather than go on the streetcar, which took *forever*. . . . to a girl looking for a ride to high school, George stood out.

evidently friendly water taxi for Eulalie and her friends. It's easy to imagine that George liked the musical sound of her name: *You*-la-lee.

The pretty Eulalie was not the only beneficiary of the rides on the bay in young George's home-built speedboats. U.S. Navy sailors happily hitched rides back to their ships with George when he was on his way home from school. According to Bill, "the Competition"—the navy's own launch drivers—didn't like his father much: "The shore-boat guys said, 'If we can ever catch you, we're gonna ram you and sink you!' Because everybody wanted to go on these 40-mile-an-hour boats— these speedboats."

Time spent together on the water turned into time spent on land, and in 1925 George and Eulalie married. The only child of a doctor father and a mother who managed the medical records library downtown, Eulalie spent her girlhood at army posts in China and the Philippines, but she would become, said Bill, "a stay-at-home mom," focused on her family. George evidently loved her all his life, and she enthusiastically supported their increasingly athletic children, Bill and Jean, giving support that their father, struggling to establish a business, could not offer as fully as he wanted to. Bill remembered her as "the team mom"; she would pick up "half the team—our baseball team, our basketball team" and bring them to games, which work frequently prevented his father from attending.

The Kettenburg Boat Works remained a part-time backyard concern for the first few years. After graduating from high school in 1924, George built a few powerboats on commission for family and friends, and to test his theories. Following his marriage, and as his reputation grew, he expanded the operation. In 1926, 12-year-old Paul started helping in the family business, after his father took his mother and sisters on another steamship voyage, this time around the world. They left him with George and Eulalie, who were then caring for their own newborn son at his parents' house. Paul caught the boatbuilding bug from his brother, ten years his

senior. "I just hated to go to school 'cause I had to be away all day—my only thoughts were boat-building. . . . I always called myself the 'gofer,' because I had to go for anything they wanted or needed. When my brother and the workers would need something downtown, they would call the McCaffrey Co., which was on Broadway." Their underage "gofer" then caught the little streetcar, nicknamed the "Dinky," nearby. If the backyard construction crew needed anything that Paul couldn't carry in his lap, they had to drive. Paul watched, helped, and picked up after carpenters Chet Allenthorp, Jim Crum, and Dick Hershey, who joined in 1926. That year, Paul was given his own boat, designed by George. *Baby Poggy* looked fast despite her little eight-horse-power motor and length of less than 14 feet.

From the beginning, George hired craftsmen of exceptional talent and enthusiasm whose qualities helped build the company's reputation. Dick Hershey, a small, natty-looking man with a Clark Gable moustache, was "one of the finest boat-builders on the coast," according to his assistant, Jim Underwood Jr. The day after he graduated from Escondido High in 1926, Dick drove down to San Diego. There, he asked the senior Mr. Kettenburg for a job: "Be here Monday and go to work," he was told. Dick Hershey built boats for the Kettenburgs for the next 23 years; other employees stayed even longer.

Dick had already built model boats, helped teach high school drafting classes, and had even worked with another student to build a man-carrying biplane glider. Having survived that, he came to the Kettenburg backyard "familiar with drafting problems and adept with carpenter tools." There, Dick remembered, he learned his new trade from the "Grand Old Man" himself, George Sr., then in his mid-50s. "Lathe work would occasionally arrive. Mr. Kettenburg would let me do some of it" while "coaching me on the proper way." Many decades later, Hershey could still enthuse about his mentor: "I think he liked me!"

The backyard boatyard was uphill from the

Eulalie poses on one of George's larger vee-bottom speedboats named *Poggy*, ca. 1926.

bay, which demanded ingenious solutions on launching day. George and crew modified a car's frame into a rolling cradle for the smaller boats; even Mr. Kettenburg's elegant Marmon, with its big cast-aluminum fenders, was occasionally dragooned into service on the end of a tow rope. Other days, Dick recalled, the Marmon "pinch-hitted for the ways hoist motor when it decided not to run."

They launched and hauled out boats from a little marine railway by a fisherman's shed at the foot of McCall Street, where they had to wait for high tide to lift their larger creations out of the mud. Timing was everything, and not only because of the tides. The wakes of the coastal steamers *Yale* and *Harvard*—then still San Diego's most efficient link with cities to the north—sent what Dick remembered as "swells, and they were huge" rolling toward the ways; the ships were up to full speed by the time they tore past Point Loma.

Curious Portuguese neighbors strolled down to watch the goings-on. Dick Hershey recalled that the searingly bright electrical arc emitted while he learned to weld down at McCall Street got unwanted attention: "One of the small Portuguese boys was fascinated by the arc and would not leave. We chased him away time and again, but he would get around the arc shield and just would not leave. As a result he badly burnt his eyes, thankfully not permanently. Next day his mom came down and we caught 'Holy Ned'—and so had he!"

Along with hiring Dick, the most important development for George's future also occurred in the spring of 1926, when Arthur E. "Bob" Childs, a real-estate broker brought George plans for a 22-foot sloop and an order for four boats to be built from them. The plans were drawn by John Alden, a very popular Boston designer of schooner yachts as well as class boats, who was

well regarded on the West Coast for the 1922 San Francisco Bay Bird Class. For Southern California sailing, Alden had lengthened his Marblehead, Massachusetts, O-Boat design of 1921 to produce the Sun Class plans that George received. It was a simple open-cockpit "knock-

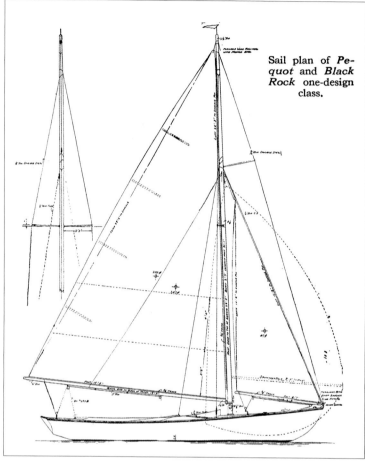

Sail plan of Pequot and Black Rock one-design class.

⊹ The Sun boat's rig was similar to that of the Alden-designed Pequot and Black Rock one-design class.

about" sloop—a colloquial term for a boat without a bowsprit, a style that had been made popular among Massachusetts yacht clubs around the turn of the century. Like the O boat, the Sun boat was equipped with a centerboard, making it suitable for shallow-water use. George built the boats for $1,200 apiece.

"This was my brother's first experience with sailboats," recalled Paul. "These boats were successful, but they weren't what my brother felt they *should* be for San Diego." In the dawn of

published publicity for the company, a newspaperman explained that "Sunboats are comfortable, non-capsizable sailboats suitable for San Diego bay." The publication of this little blurb seemed significant enough to Dick Hershey that he mounted the clipping in his scrapbook—despite the fact that he felt compelled to scrawl "Should be *Kettenburg*" alongside the article, which appeared to be about a "Kennedy Boat Firm." After listing the company's successful powerboats, the reporter concluded by prophetically focusing on sail, and George's "boats for every taste and every pocketbook for those who enjoy the thrills of salt water sailing." By 1926, this newspaperman concluded, recreational opportunities on the bay had grown "from a few obscure boats" into a haven that was "one of the finest on the coast." George & Co. were "one of the factors" behind this growth.

Demand increased for bigger and pricier Kettenburg-built boats. Of the 16 they built in the backyard, two 47-foot power cruisers demanded the services of house-movers on launching day in 1927. Clearly, the Kettenburgs' days as backyard boatbuilders were numbered.

Competitors, too, had begun to notice the upstart company, despite the fact that unlike them, Kettenburg Boat Works was already devoted to constructing boats whose only purpose seemed to be to delight buyers. The patriarch of local shipbuilders, San Diego Marine Construction's "Clem" Stose, recalled that "Mr. Kettenburg, Sr., was a very smart man" and, perhaps more importantly to Clem, "a money-maker all his life. . . . The boys didn't work or anything, but their father had this idea about building boats, that they built in the backyard. They built some very successful boats—naturally, like *anybody* who builds a lot of boats." One doesn't have to be a cynic to catch a whiff of envy in his words.

The backyard boatyard was uphill from the bay, which demanded ingenious solutions on launching day. George and crew modified a car's frame into a rolling cradle for the smaller boats; even Mr. Kettenburg's elegant Marmon, with its big cast-aluminum fenders, was occasionally dragooned into service on the end of a tow rope.

Top: As George supervises, one of the crew fits the sheer plank on a Sun boat in the backyard boatyard, 1926. Below: The improvised boatyard, with bandsaw at right, a mold at center, a planked Sun boat at left, and a finished hull on the rolling cradle at center.

23

They launched and hauled out boats from a little marine railway by a fisherman's shed at the foot of McCall Street, where they had to wait for high tide to lift their larger creations out of the mud.

Launching a Sun boat, 1926.

George Kettenburg Jr.

Photos taken then show a good-looking high-schooler with a winning grin, who was growing up to be "tall, wire-haired, and bronzed about the same tint as russet leather," in the words of a contemporary. His daughter Jean recalled him as "blond, blue-eyed, and very fair-skinned. From all the sailing he started to have trouble—as we all do—from too much sun." Eventually, despite the dearth of effective sun-blocking products, George shielded his sensitive lips sufficiently with a heavy white smear of zinc oxide to allow him to compete, under the shelter of his characteristic floppy broad-brimmed hat. Jean remembered her father as "so enthusiastic, it was just fun to be around—it was fun for everyone involved." Like one longtime employee who maintained that his mentor's character was "good—good to the marrow," Jean's brother Bill recalled him as "always a very personable person, and honest" with customers—not to mention modest: "My dad was a real talker, but he was never talkin' about himself."

Unfortunately, George was highly allergic to toxins like secondhand smoke, and he would suffer from the effects of the cloud of chemical dust that, in the days before pollution controls, floated around every boatyard. Its effects ultimately cut his life short.

George Kettenburg Jr. was never given to pontificating publicly about his business practices, or about anything else. But, occasionally, his words offer a glimpse at what he thought underpinned his success. After the Second World War, one reporter's question elicited a simple response: "Find out what the people want; then figure out how to give it to them in the least time, at the least cost, with the best workmanship." Those four principles succinctly capture how he tried to run his company. (After George died, his partners continued to run the firm in the same way, and one can arguably pin its eventual demise on the impossibility of continually balancing those goals.) George's sense of duty, his son Bill recalled, shaped a work ethic in which "the customer was *king.*" Bill remembered a

⊹ **George at the wheel, a favorite family photograph.**

plainspoken saying that neatly sums up his dad's relationship with boat owners and buyers: "You always give a dollar-ten for a dollar, and you'll always have business." The phrase has the ring of cliché, but its truthfulness is implicit in the loyalty and trust of Kettenburg customers, who either considered him an equal or looked up to him. Although never educated past high school, and always of moderate if comfortable means, George seems to have been considered (and regarded himself) as an exceptionally skilled craftsman, whose love of boats connected him with every educated and rich boater who shared that love. At the tiller in a race, on the floor of his shop, or when surrounded by the San Diego Yacht Club's wealthy weekend sailors, George benefited from the masculine cult of expertise. They all bought and sailed boats; he knew how to build boats and make them go fast.

As a sailor he quickly grew to be regarded as one of the top ten skippers in a yacht club that boasted national champions. He had a gift for squeezing performance out of his boats, as Bill recalled: "My dad could be down in the bunk, half-asleep, and say, 'You guys are screwin' up, up there! Let's get this boat goin' again!' And sure enough, we were—we were maybe talkin' when we should have been racin'."

In the light breezes that frequently characterize southernmost California, George became celebrated for an "uncanny" sense of where to find the puff that would tip the balance from losing to winning. A noted competitor confessed to a reporter that he always followed George's nose for wind in a race. "But what if you passed him?" the reporter asked. "I'd drop anchor and wait," he replied, not wholly facetiously.

His crew would always find George Jr. "very loyal to his employees" as Jim Underwood Jr. remembered, and intimately engaged with them—helping counsel at least one through a rocky passage in his marriage. "Of course, he expected people who worked for him to be the same way" in loyalty, and they would keep Kettenburg a staunchly anti-union shop. But however

big his team grew, George was always in charge. "He was a perfectionist, really," admitted Underwood. "I used to enjoy watching him. When a boat was just about finished, carpenters would say, 'It's done.' You would see him up on the scaffold, and he'd be looking down the lines of the boat—looking at the deck line." "He'd call Dick Hershey over," Jim continued. As he talked, Jim imitated George, pointing to an invisible spot and whispering "a little bit off *right there*." George trusted Hershey's skill with a carpenter's plane to make the adjustment, but, as Jim remembered, "there was a point where he wanted to make sure everything worked just exactly the way he wanted it."

George's primary gifts lay in the design and construction of powerboats and sailing yachts. "My brother George, was a *natural* boat designer,"

explained Paul, himself a high school graduate. "He was not a graduate architect—he never went to college. He went right to work after high school. George could hold his own in any discussions with any college-graduate naval architects." Those designers, all Easterners, were beginning to improve racing performance by combining sailing expertise with science, but at least initially Paul's brother was guided solely by his formidable powers of observation. "He could look at a boat and know if it was right. And if it was wrong, he knew what to do to make it right," remembered Gordon Frost, who watched George at work. George's sense of line, balance, and proportion, and grasp of how a hull would move through water, meant that eventually "he knew what a boat would do by looking at it," Bill remembered. Bill's brother-in-law, Morgan Miller, was

impressed by George's "fantastic eye. Every boat I ever remember, he did the sheer-line on, because he'd get up there and sight that thing—and it'd be *true* when he got done with it." Longtime foreman "Bud" Caldwell agreed; right up to the end of his life, George "always made the final cut on the sheers of the boats. You know—when they turned 'em right side up before they put the deck on, why, he'd come out and crawl up there and take a little cut here, and a little cut there, and get it just the way he wanted." The son of one of the first women racing champions watched him exhibit a related skill: "George could walk around a new wooden hull, chalking a freehand inscription of where the waterline should be. The painters would do their job; the boat would then be launched, and would sit in the water just as intended!"

Chapter Two

Rumrunners, Archers, And Starlets

How a Small Company

Tackled The Great Depression

87:—San Diego Yacht Club, Coronado, Calif.

Cɑ. 1924

With brother Paul sitting aft, George drives his vee-bottom *Poggy III* at speed in 1924. Note the vertical exhaust pipes of the boat's twin "Hissos." Inset: Postcard view of the San Diego Yacht Club with *Poggy* at the float, ca. 1924.

The dark-haired young sailor was accustomed to every unpleasant sensation of motion that the sea could dish out, but nothing had prepared him for *this* moment. Twelve-year-old Paul Kettenburg clung to his seat in the cabin as the big biplane swung over swampy Dutch Flats, high above San Diego's dirt airstrip. Mr. Ryan, piloting the plane from the open cockpit above Paul, dipped the wings to give his lone passenger a clearer view. Just forward of his seat, and roaring so loudly as to render conversation impossible, was a powerful army-surplus aircraft engine. It was the engine that had enabled Paul to wangle this thrill ride in the first place, for his father had sold three such powerplants to Mr. Ryan, selecting them from among the crates piled behind the

Kettenburg house. "When they were test-flying these planes, I used to go down and ride with Claude Ryan," said Paul. "I remember they had a closed cabin for four people and the pilot sat in an open cockpit aft. But I used to really love to go down and ride them when they were test-flying these planes—you'd get a nice ride around San Diego." T. Claude Ryan was then struggling to link San Diego and Los Angeles with one of the world's first regularly scheduled year-round airlines. Paul would ultimately decide that he enjoyed this experience so much that, 35 years later, he took to the skies himself as a private pilot.

But on this wild ride in 1925, as the lone passenger clutched the arms of his seat, he watched his own neighborhood's still sparsely settled shore unroll beneath him. Down there, his father was searching for a waterfront lot to replace the family's makeshift launching site. Their pleasant-looking little city of around 147,000 souls was stretching at the seams; it had tripled in size since his family had moved in only a decade before. This burst of growth sprang primarily from wartime expansion by the naval and air branches of the American military, drawn by San Diego's benign weather and its big bay, although the bay was rendered much smaller by a ring of shallow mudflats.

The view out the airplane window took in the naval hospital in Balboa Park, the air base on North Island, a new naval training center, and a new destroyer base. The navy would loom large in the future of San Diego, as it would in the naval contracts that eventually helped sustain Paul's company. Paul, however, was probably straining harder to catch a glimpse of a center of vice further south. A few miles below the bay's southern rim lay a little border village known locally as Tia Juana. The fact that a foreign country populated by more-or-less-exotic Latins—complete with readily available vice—lay within

20 miles of home was a fact of life for a native San Diegan like Paul. The cultural life of his own stridently American hometown, however, might just as well have existed in a vacuum, for—with the exception of some tile roofs, romantic references to Father Serra, and an imaginary Spanish past on display at "Ramona's Marriage Place" in Old Town—San Diego had so little connection with Mexico that it could just as easily have been Pittsburgh. Until, that is, a few years before this plane ride when Prohibition became law. Certain ideas of the evils of intemperance became national public policy, and smuggling, by land and sea, was giving the border a new reputation.

It was not the exoticism or the porous border, however, that brought refugees like Ryan and the Kettenburgs; they were lured by the sunny weather and the nearly endless days of flying and sailing it promised, and the opportunities to escape Eastern and Midwestern winters. Paul's biplane ride soared over Ryan's own workshop in "Little Italy," a former tuna cannery surrounded by modest houses kept tidy by the wives of

immigrant Italian fishermen. Like Paul's 22-year-old brother George, T. Claude Ryan, aged 27, was becoming known for building his own imaginatively designed, high-quality craft. His customers soon included Charles Lindbergh, another young pilot with the admirable (if crazy) goal of flying a Ryan airplane solo across the Atlantic.

The power of those war-surplus aircraft engines, mounted in George Jr.'s speedboats, was beginning to bring region-wide acclaim to the Kettenburg name. He and Dick Hershey found racing to be very good advertising for the new boat designs—not to mention a lot of fun. After local banker Albert Jones paid around $1,500 for *Poggy II*, Jones began to let George race it, presumably on the belief that whatever glory his skipper might win would spill over onto his own name as well.

George was still a little-known boatbuilder when he entered *Poggy* in a ten-mile race down the bay in the summer of 1924. Local speedboat races were a recent brainchild of San Diego Yacht Club members who sensed their fellow San Diegans' enthusiasm for high-speed compe-

POGGIE II WINS SPEED BOAT RACE

Poggie II, after Poggie I had been forced out of competition by motor trouble, won the speed boat races off the municipal pier at 3 o'clock yesterday. The Poggie II is owned by R. T. Robinson, jr., and was piloted by George Kettenburg, over a three-mile course. Miss San Diego owned and piloted by H. F. Oria, was second, and Poggie III, owned and piloted by Richard Hershey of Point Loma, third.

In the stunt race, wherein the boats started rapidly, went ahead a few feet, then turned abruptly, the Poggie II again won. Several hairraising turns were made in this event, among several aquaplanes.

W. H. Perry acted as starter. Julian Zapp and Miss San Diego acted as judges.

The San Diego newspaper recorded *Poggy II*'s 1924 speedboat race victory, with handwritten corrections by Dick Hershey. On the next spread: Eulalie at the wheel, showing off the size of the later *Poggys*.

A small cabin version of *Poggy*, identified as X40, tows an aquaplane, precursor to waterskiis. Inset: Kettenburg Boat Works timeclock tag.

tition. The Kettenburgs, however, were not the only Southern Californians who had hit on the idea of utilizing surplus airplane engines. George's 24-foot *Poggy* was the underdog that day against three powerful Southern speedboats arrayed against her. One was *Miss San Diego*, whose name echoed that of the *Miss America* racing boats then sweeping international competitions. *Miss San Diego* was longer and heavier than *Poggy*, as were the other two competitors *Selrahc* and *Zig Zag*, but each was about equally powerful.

What the elder George Kettenburg was doing that day is not recorded, but it is hard to imagine that the business manager of Kettenburg Boat Works had anything more pressing to do than to watch his son race a speedboat that he himself had helped build. Presumably he jostled other San Diegans as they climbed to reach the best seats, atop bleachers erected on a pair of coal barges. The difference was that the rest of the crowd, shielding themselves under hat brims from the August sun, expected the bigger boats to prove faster. But as the speedboats roared down the bay, engine trouble forced the sputtering *Miss San Diego* to drop out, and Herbert Graves's *Zig Zag* and Charley Johnson's *Selrahc* both fell astern of *Poggy*. Perhaps the dignified Mr. Kettenburg smiled inwardly, or perhaps he stood up, flung dignity to the winds, and cheered himself hoarse. A pattern of sorts was set for future races: his son's comparatively small craft had taken maximum advantage of the same conditions—engine horsepower, in this case—as her competitors, and beaten them, thanks to better design, which used unusually light displacement to advantage. George's triumph was, as a newspaper reporter wrote, "something of a surprise to the onlook-

ers"—with the possible exceptions of Mr. Kettenburg and neighbors who chatted amongst themselves in Portuguese. "Miss Peggy," wrote a reporter, mangling the boat's name into something more recognizable, "showed her heels to the class contesting against her, much to the amusement of the La Playa Portuguese, who had a while back watched the neat little motor speeder constructed over Point Loma way."

Racing success drew many pairs of eyes to the "neat little motor speeder" and her successors, for reasons having more to do with profit than amusement. A competitor, the shipbuilder Clem Stose, slyly noted of the Kettenburgs that "a lot of the boats they built 'for their own amusement'—let's say—were successful and fast, and the rumrunners bought them and paid a price that Mr. Kettenburg couldn't refuse." Thanks to the Volstead Act, all Americans who drank alcohol now did so on the sly, keeping one eye out for the police. The reformers who had extended the wartime ban on alcohol had hoped to dry out America, but Prohibition instead watered American organized crime into frenzied, bloody growth, and taught Americans a new level of disrespect for the law. During the 15-year duration of this dry spell, San Diego's location on the border made offshore waters ideal for smugglers, who hovered outside the 12-mile limit of federal jurisdiction, waiting for the opportunities that a storm or a well-placed bribe might offer. Even a boy could unwittingly become a criminal. Five decades later, Paul admitted that he had once "run a little booze"—although he remained quick to insist "but I didn't get paid for it!"

> One Sunday afternoon, these guys came up to the house and I was out in the yard, and one said, "Hey—our boat was supposed to have been in this morning and he didn't show up. If he doesn't show by tomorrow morning, we'd like to have you take us out there to look for him." So, I thought—"Okay, if the guy's drifting around out there, he needs somebody to look for him." So around daylight Monday morning, I heard somebody down under my window, and they were calling, "Paul! Paul! We need you!"

The boatyard's handsome work speedboat *Husky* (apparently built for a client who never took delivery) sputtered to life, and Paul and his new acquaintances "went off in the direction they figured their guy should be." It is hard to imagine that this intelligent boy didn't know how his passengers made their living, but if he didn't, he figured it out quickly:

> We went all the way down to where they normally landed, and didn't see him. One of the men went ashore and came back with a handful of tacos—we were getting pretty hungry by this point—so we had tacos for breakfast. We were on our way back up, and one of the men spotted some shiny five-gallon cans floating just under the surface of the water. The man we were looking for had

The *Goose*'s Libertys, Dick was startled to discover, had been made "so quiet I could hardly believe it. Like a pair of sewing machines. One had only to speak loudly to be heard in the engine room."

> apparently tied their handles together and thrown them overboard. There were at least ten of them. One of the guys said, "Oh boy—look! There's the load. Take us back in—we'll give you fifty bucks if you'll pick that up and take it in." So, I thought, "fifty bucks is fifty bucks." We took the cans aboard, and put as many as we could down below the deck level so they wouldn't show. We got back in and there was a big old tuna boat that had been virtually abandoned, laying at anchor off the plant. . . . We pulled up alongside the tuna boat and loaded all this booze onto its deck. That's the last I ever saw of it—and I never did get my fifty bucks. When I went over and tied up to our dock, I found that someone had talked to George, and George had gone out in someone's boat and found the guy we were looking for originally.

"Maybe George wouldn't bring him in with the booze aboard, and made him throw it overboard," Paul speculated—testifying either to his big brother's honesty or his prudence.

If alcohol is a drug, then the Kettenburgs played active (but quite legal) supporting roles in

the illicit drug trade, selling fast transportation to participants in American organized crime. Commissions for "express freighters," like the 47-foot *Galloping Goose*, helped keep the fledgling company afloat. Like all of George's designs in this era, the *Goose* was a completely custom boat, "really just an overgrown speedboat" according to Dick Hershey, who helped build her in 1927. "Everybody that saw it knew it for what it was"—a *very* fast rumrunner. Like the Kettenburgs' other rumrunners, she was "a gray ghost," painted for concealment, with a large open cockpit aft and a pair of V-12 Liberty aircraft engines, each rated at 400 horsepower or better. The Liberty's development had been America's greatest contribution to the war effort, second only to the waves of enthusiastic "doughboys" fed into the sausage-grinder of trench warfare. After the Armistice, the Liberty became America's greatest contribution to the smuggling effort, for a Liberty-powered boat easily outran the U.S. Coast Guard's 75-foot patrol craft that struggled to exceed 18 miles per hour.

The *Goose*'s Libertys, Dick was startled to discover, had been made "so quiet I could hardly believe it. Like a pair of sewing machines. One had only to speak loudly to be heard in the engine room." The otherwise upright engineer, George Kettenburg Sr., had apparently thrown himself into meeting this new technical challenge: "George and his dad really did a job on those mufflers" since, noted Dick, "they had to be quiet for night running, didn't they?"

"One time," recalled Paul about a day spent hanging around the boat shop and its denizens, "the government guys are kiddin' the bootleggers: 'Boy, if we ever catch you . . . we'll catch one of these boats, and you'll *never* be able to get away.'" Startled by the friendliness he observed between these purported enemies, Paul remembered the rumrunner's retort: "You'll *never* get one of those boats."

And he was right. The Coast Guard suspected the galloping potential of this *Goose* and

Jim Underwood hand-rubs the varnish on *Johnnie*'s shapely transom, 1929. Inset: George's hand-drawn profile and layout for *Johnnie*. Opposite, the newspaper recorded *Johnnie*'s salvage after her mysterious middle-of-the-night escape from her mooring in March 1930.

stationed a cutter nearby during her fitting out and final testing. But according to Dick:

> The cutter needed supplies, so while away the Goose just sort of disappeared! She went south of the border to pick up a load of "hooch." Unable to deliver it to San Diego—as the Coast Guard were waiting—she went up the coast to Oceanside, and again the Coast Guard. Up the coast to Balboa, but again more Coast Guard. Under a heavy fog, she slipped into San Pedro, and had most of the load unloaded when the Coast Guard showed up. Hurriedly casting off she—as the Coast Guard wanted the boat more than the "hooch"—was chased out of the harbor. Being able to do about 55 miles per hour she quickly outran the cutter. Then, not being able to complete the unloading, she went south of the border onto the beach with the drain cocks of the gas tanks open. And with a match, the Goose galloped no more.

The government men were disappointed, for Dick agreed that their possession of one of the coast's fastest boats would have brought the "Rum Fleet" to a speedy end. But he also testified to the economic power of this underground economy: "I later learned that the load delivered in San Pedro paid for the boat and the crew's wages."

The last boat built in the backyard apparently ventured into booze smuggling as well, although under stranger circumstances. The Johnnie, launched in 1928 with a pair of 220-horsepower "Hissos" (and clocked by Dick Hershey at over 43 miles per hour) "decided to take a cruise all by itself" in 1930. During a storm it broke from its mooring at the yacht club and somehow drifted northward through the night to the wealthy village of La Jolla. After "threading its way between several dangerous rocks and beaching itself" (at the foot of the street where her owner, a Chicago amusement-park owner named Mr. Schmidt, amused himself at his second home), Johnnie was discovered the next morning.

Although he couldn't resist noting that "why nobody saw it or reported it is still a mystery," a good boatbuilder like Hershey knew enough to avoid speculating; his task was simply to extract boat from beach. Whether Johnnie sleepwalked to La Jolla on her own or with the aid of smugglers, the Kettenburg boatyard endured the Depression's harsh early years in part through a policy of asking buyers no questions.

The long-term significance of the wandering Johnnie, however, lay in the introduction of another outstanding craftsman (and outsized personality) to the Kettenburg crew. In 1929, the volatile but talented Jimmy Underwood became the boatyard's celebrated chief painter, and much more. "My dad was a little man," recalled his son Jim Jr., "but he had kind of an 'Irish' temper. He was a nice guy, but he could blow up." (Jim Jr. speculated that his father's grandiose profanity may have compensated somewhat for that short stature.) Jimmy started behind the Kettenburg house, hand-rubbing multiple coats of varnish onto what Hershey described as Johnnie's "fancy mahogany carpentry."

"My dad noticed an ad in the paper for a painter: someone was building boats for the movies on Point Loma," Jim Jr. remembered. "Boats for the movies" was an odd euphemism: these were rumrunners, intended to neither be seen nor heard. ("I remember my dad saying,

SAN DIEGO, CALIFORNIA, TUESDAY, MARCH 18, 1930

This Boat Slipped Away Alone, High, Dry It Has Been Thrown

This little cruiser, the $20,000 express cruiser Johnny, went to sea Friday night during a heavy wind, which tore it from its moorings at La Playa, and after the blow was found beached at La Jolla. Pictured here are the cruiser and a crew working to get it up a skidway, so that the craft may be loaded on a truck and taken back to Roseville.

The banker who owned *Poggy*, apparently not content with whatever glory had settled on him from George's victories, ordered himself another boat, naming her *Aljo*, perhaps in an attempt to restore his own name—Al Jones—to center stage.

'building boats for the *movies*—but I have to camouflage 'em so they can't be seen too easily against Point Loma!'") Jimmy had remarried several years after the tragic death of his wife—struck by a car while towing toddler Jim Jr. to church in a wagon—and decided, as many did, that Southern California offered good prospects for starting over. Leaving Springfield, Massachusetts, the family arrived in town at the end of a three-month camping trip, where Jimmy went into partnership with his brother Art in painting elaborate building interiors. After Art's death by drowning near their Pacific Beach home, Jimmy answered the ad for one-time work—and stayed for more than a decade and a half, till severe angina forced him to retire.

Charlie Underwood agreed that his father, a skilled interior decorator with a few inventions to his credit—which must have endeared him to the senior Mr. Kettenburg—was "overqualified," but "since the Crash on the Stock Market occurred around this time, my father was more in an 'acceptable' mode to take George's offer, because of the fact that business slowed down." Charlie explained:

> My father was George's senior by about fifteen years or so, and had a great deal of business experience, and George was short on experience at that time; his long point was the design and production of boats. So therefore he leaned on my father to help him develop company policy, both in handling

employees, and services that would help build the company. One of the things that my father was able to do, was to bid—or figure—the prices for which various services should be sold. And George, as a craftsman, knew what he could do, but had little experience in actual bidding on jobs. So this took a big load off of George's mind.

Another special skill that this painter of murals brought to the boatyard was the formulation of new marine paints. According to Charlie, "he developed a complete line of paints and had them manufactured by a paint company with the Kettenburg label—which gave George a complete line of materials that were unavailable anywhere else."

Despite his fiery temper, Jimmy Underwood could be a patient teacher. "The head painter at Kettenburg's was a chap by the name of Jim Underwood," recalled Gerry Driscoll, whose own yard eventually took over Kettenburg's repair business, "and because I was there working on the boat a good deal, he taught me how to paint." Gerry told Jim Jr. that "your dad taught me all I know about painting. He taught all of us kids"—or at least those willing to listen in properly respectful silence—how to care for boats. Future racer Wally Springstead remembered that, "if you were willing to work, and you'd listen *really* carefully, and not say a word, he would really help you. And he became like a fatherly figure, y'know?" Onetime Kettenburg employee

Loch Crane, to whom he taught the exacting boat-painter's trade, noted that "Jimmy Underwood was like the grandfather there—everybody worshiped the ground he walked on."

Underwood's reputation spread far beyond the boatyard. Jim Underwood Jr. can hardly be counted impartial, but his impression is accurate: "He was an excellent painter, and he could make a boat just shine like a mirror. And people would bring their boats from all up and down the coast to be painted by him."

Racers and rumrunners built the Kettenburgs' reputation, but in the late 1920s their business was built on "putt-putts"—little hundred-dollar outboard motorboats of good quality, designed with a hydroplane step to increase their speed. More refined and well-heeled customers seeking a cruising motorboat of 26 feet or longer could expect to write a check for about $2,500. For daredevils who wished to hurtle over the bay at a reputed 50 miles per hour, $1,500 to $3,000 would harness the power of one of the backyard "Hissos."

The banker who owned *Poggy*, apparently not content with whatever glory had settled on him from George's victories, ordered himself another boat, naming her *Aljo*, perhaps in an attempt to restore his own name—Al Jones—to center stage.

By this time, George's speedboats were developing distinctive lines. Charlie Underwood remembered that these boats, powered by aircraft engines, offered a "soft, fast, dry, com-

The jaunty *Aljo*, with Al Jones
at the wheel and Dick Hershey
in the after cockpit, 1928.

fortable ride," protecting passengers from spray with their concave flare forward. George's designs featured "a tumblehome aft to make that good-lookin', racy, special 'Kettenburg' look. . . . The high-powered cruisers were set apart slightly from the sport fishers and speedboats, because they were using high-powered aircraft engines, and his theory was that the flat planing surface aft had to be the shortest possible area that could be put up onto the correct planing position," and hold it firmly once the throttle was wide open. "This," said Charlie, "was his own special genius."

Not long before *Johnnie*, George's second speedboat had been bought by a prototype for the extravagant, optimistic developers of the 1920s, who sold communities like San Diego on their enticing visions of civic growth. Dick Robinson was about to begin work on his towering El Cortez Hotel, an emblem of the city's 1920s-era expansion, and San Diego's tallest building for decades. The developer was so impressed by his first Kettenburg boat that in 1926 he ordered a 47-foot high-speed power cruiser for about $25,000. An awed Paul watched, as "Dick Robinson drove into the backyard there in his fancy Cadillac roadster, got out of the car, and came up and saw my brother, and said, 'George, I want you to build me the fastest God-damn power cruiser on the West Coast, and I want to put *three* of those Hispano engines in it.'"

Robinson named this new boat *Agilis* in praise of the agility provided by those 220-horsepower engines; the men down at the yard preferred to call her "Agile-Ass." All were awed by the boat's speed and power. When, in 1929, Robinson raced her between Los Angeles and San Diego, her competition was the celebrated Los Angeles-area boatbuilder Joe Fellows and his *Fellowship*. In all but name *Fellowship* was a rumrunner: an oversized speedboat with twin engines, two low cabins, and a stripped-down interior—quite unlike the luxurious *Agilis*. At the starting line in San Pedro Bay, *Fellowship* was the

The 47-foot cruiser *Agilis* shows her speed off Avalon, Santa Catalina Island, 1928.

George (right) and the crew pose in front of the speedboat *Knotty* in the new boatyard, 1936. The yard built the 21-foot speedboat for Paul Kettenburg and shipped it to him in Chicago.

equivalent of a Chevy NASCAR racer jockeying for position against a very powerful Jaguar. As Joe Fellows recounted it, "we both powered slowly out to the race course, the *Agilis* sort of lagging, so we thought we had the race in the bag. But—all of a sudden with a big double 'Whoosh,'" three roostertails of spray shot out from beneath *Agilis*'s transom, "and we never saw her bow again until it was all over." *Agilis* covered the 125 miles in just three hours and ten minutes, averaging nearly 40 miles per hour in the open sea. The first advertisement for Kettenburg boats, in the September 1930 *Pacific Coast Yachting*, happily trumpeted the firm as creators of "the undefeated cruiser" *Agilis*.

Increased demand for Kettenburg boats meant that their neighbors had to plug their ears during hours of unmuffled airplane engine testing in the backyard, which was increasingly hemmed in by the growing city. The time had come to split the functions of home and business. According to Paul, "one of the reasons why my father had my brother move down there was

because we were making a mess here—and the neighbors were starting to complain, and they didn't like it. We moved down there, and there was a cannery on one side of us and a cannery on the other side of us. We figured that nobody would ever bother about us making the noise and mess."

In 1929, between the Hovden and High Seas canneries at the foot of Dickens Street, the Trepte Co. (owned by Point Loma neighbors) built them a big wood-framed building, with roof and sides of galvanized steel. The tuna plants on either side certainly made the economic power of San Diego's commercial fishing industry inescapable—although the wind usually blew the smell out into the bay. The business prospects for the new boatyard also looked good. After all, in 1929 the United States boasted 434 yacht clubs besides the local one, and 4,750 yachts longer than 24 feet navigated the nation's waters. Orders for more boats were sure to come to the Kettenburgs, given their growing reputation for fast and well-built boats. Local newspapers, too,

reflected the happy hubris of investors—but the nation's economy was dangerously overextended.

When the Stock Market crashed in October, the results in the recreational boating world were immediate. *Agilis*'s owner, speculator Dick Robinson, found himself spectacularly broke and sold her. He found work driving an oil truck.

Paul Kettenburg recalled that his family fared better than many: "Fortunately, my father, when he retired, had bought property here in San Diego, and so he was never dependent upon the yard for any income. The only one at the time who was really dependent on the yard for money was my brother George." The men who worked for his brother, it apparently went without saying, did too. They were lucky, however, or as lucky as laborers could be during the hard times that rolled over San Diego's economy like a smothering blanket in the early 1930s.

When Prohibition was repealed in 1933, Charlie remembered, George's most reliable customers vanished "and the other shoe dropped. *Now* George became desperate." Dick Hershey recalled that, "during the Depression, we all would show up for work 'just in case.' Maybe there would be an hour or two and then, again—nothing." Dick felt fortunate to have a family friend who wanted shelves installed and needed enough garage remodeling to enable him to make ends meet. Since George felt that his little crew were so much like family—and because their skills would be so hard to replace—he made every effort to keep them busy. When work was lacking, George kept the crew strung together with what a reporter called the "big archery contest that takes place every noon in George Kettenburg's boat yard." Charlie Underwood recalled that

it was real boring standing around all day long when we didn't have any work, yet we didn't dare go home in case there was some work. And at some time George got a bright idea, and thought: in order to keep busy, it'd be a good idea if we each bought some lemon wood, and made a bow, and then bought some arrows, and practiced archery. And we put some bales of hay against one side of the shop, and stood the right distance away from the target, and had archery tour- naments. That kept us a little more happy— but it didn't put any more bread on the table.

Charlie and the rest of the seven highly pro- fessional boatbuilders and novice archers passed time this way when work was slowest in the grim year that began in November 1935. At least launching arrows inside the big metal building offered Loch Crane time with his "pretty quiet, but very friendly" boss. "I got to know George well, because he was an archer. He had a bow that was too heavy, so I bought it off him." George paid particular attention to the wiry kid who was strong enough to pull an adult bow. Between shooting arrows and sweating at his

Champion archer George Kettenburg shows off his technique in 1940.

work, Loch observed that George Jr. permitted his employees "no corner-cutting—their reputation was worth more than anything else." Loch once mentioned to Paul that George Jr. had paid him 25 cents an hour. Paul replied, "what are you bitchin' about? *I* only made 15 cents an hour!"

George's loyalty to his workforce came back to him. "Things were *tight*," remembered Jim Underwood Jr. "In order to sell boats George had to have the price cut—to the bone. And more than once, we've gone back at night—without charging for our time—and worked like beavers trying to get a boat . . . up to a point where it wasn't going 'in the hole.'"

Although its membership dwindled in the years after the "Crash," the San Diego Yacht Club had a core of affluent and determined sailors who remained active despite financial pressures. By the mid-1930s, according to Loch Crane, Kettenburg had become "not just a boatyard, but really a part of the Yacht Club" thanks to the yard service it offered. A newspaperwoman agreed that it was becoming "a social rendezvous where a great deal of painting and building is being done by yachtsmen." With the lack of new construction, servicing boats had rapidly grown into the financial mainstay for a yard that had been designed with only the production of new boats in mind. Since in that day every boat's hull had to be repainted several times a year, someone realized the yard could charge a fixed annual maintenance fee. Customers who subscribed would be put on a regular calendar, and maintenance work was scheduled when it was convenient for the boatyard. "The price that we were able to give," remembered Charlie, "was a great deal cheaper than when they managed the upkeep themselves, and some of 'em just could not believe that we were gonna do . . . the things that we had agreed to do for the price, because it seemed completely too low—and of course, *that's* what made it the greatest success." During

George (third from left) and his crew pose in front of one of their remarkably fast Star-Class hulls. Inset: A builder's plate from one of the Kettenburg boats.

those tight years of the 1930s, "We were actually using the yard for the prime source of income, either by hauling boats out for people to work on their own boat, or to keep our own people working," summarized Charlie.

Loyal customers saved the day for George's underemployed boatbuilders. By profession, Charles Springstead was an importer of Mexican-grown peas, but by avocation "he was a hell of a fishermen," his son Wally recalled. "For five or six years my father had all the records on the coast for marlin fishing." George and his crew had already built the cabin cruiser *Grace Marie* for Springstead's fishing trips, powering her with a pair of Chrysler engines. "The Catalina Marlin Club used to . . . follow the *Grace Marie*, hoping to find his 'secrets' of marlin fishing. We would lead the Catalina fleet towards La Jolla waters, reel in our lines, and take off for Coronado Islands at 20 knots—leaving them far behind!"

As George scrambled to find enough work to keep his crew together, Charles Springstead made a significant contribution to the Kettenburgs' welfare in 1931 when he brought in plans by Los Angeles designer Daniel M. Callis for an 86-foot boat, the largest the yard would ever build. "The dual purpose of this yacht was to take cruises and go south and fish around Cabo"—Cabo San Lucas at the tip of Baja California, about 800 miles south of San Diego—"and later to go into Guaymas"—400 miles further in the Gulf of California—"and bring back pea seed and different vegetable seed that my father was growing," Wally explained. "He wanted a yacht *and* he wanted a commercial boat that could haul loads. And George said 'We'll build it.'—and he needed the business, y'know." Springstead could probably have ordered *Joanne* more quickly and conveniently from San Diego Marine Construction or Campbell Shipyard, both of which specialized in commercial fishing boats. But, as Wally recalled, the great care that went into *Joanne* made it "a great boat. The motor merely 'played with it' at eleven knots," thanks to a 250-horsepower Atlas

Imperial diesel. "George gave him credit for saving the boatyard." The *Joanne* was a godsend for George's workmen. "This freighter really gave them something to do during the Depression," recalled George's son Bill. "My Dad wanted to make sure everybody got enough to live on. A job would come along, and they survived." Times were indeed hard for boatbuilders; *Joanne* was the only large vessel of any kind built in San Diego County in 1932.

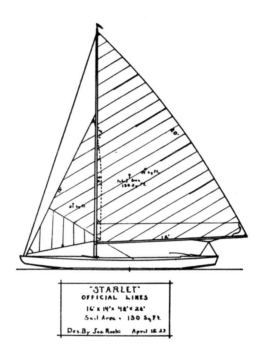

Joe Ruski's 1927 sail plan for the Starlet.

As the Depression settled in to stay, George Kettenburg Jr. had a much bigger reputation for speedboats than sail, except for the four Alden-designed Sun boats of 1926, and a pair of Star boats launched the following year. Bob Childs, the customer from the yacht club who had commissioned one of the Sun boats, had ordered a Star boat because, Paul thought, he "wanted to get in and race with the big shots at the Yacht Club." George studied the standardized specifications for the 22-foot Star closely, and he took maximum advantage of the few inches of leeway they offered to build a faster boat. He sold one for about $900 and built another without a cus-

tomer in mind. When no buyer came forward, Mr. Kettenburg bought George a set of sails. With his kid brother as crew, George happily resigned himself to "demonstration racing" to attract potential buyers, in his *Miss II*. In 1928, Star racing on the West Coast was dominated by Joe Jessop, who had risen to state champion after four years sailing in the class. Joe was the most passionate skipper among the sailboat-happy Jessop family of jewelers; he was influential in the community, and particularly so at the San Diego Yacht Club. But suddenly, the papers reported, he had a new local rival: "Kettenburg, sailing his craft in its third race, and a new man at the Star boat game, made a surprising showing" against Joe's Star *Windward*. Not only was George Jr. new to Star-class racing, but "he hadn't sailed *any*, and neither had I," remembered Paul. Joe held onto first place without difficulty against the neophyte sailors, but that summer he grew intrigued by his young rival's craftsmanship.

"Joe came up to George one day and he said, 'Hey—let's trade boats!'" Paul continued. "So, 'Sure, well, it's okay—we got nothin' to lose.' So we traded boats. Joe got into that boat of ours, and he was so far ahead of everybody else that you couldn't even see him—and we were clear back in the back of the fleet!" Thanks to George's fine-tuning of the basic Star design, "the boat was just hotter." Paul recalled, too, that Joe's interest aroused interest among the rest of the sailboat-racing set, since it was obvious that "the two of them were damn good boats. Everybody began to think, 'Well—maybe he's got something, there!'"

In 1929, influenced by the sailing qualities of his Star, George Kettenburg Jr. introduced his first original class of racing sailboats. The essential plan and name for the Starlet—a junior-sized racing boat for junior skippers—had come from a young builder named Joe Ruski, one of the original "lucky thirteen" disaffected San Diego Yacht Club members who had founded the Southwestern Yacht Club two years before. Star Class racing boats were 22 feet six inches long overall, and the Starlets Joe Ruski began building in 1928 were about 16 feet long, or two-thirds of a "grown up" Star. If the San Diego Yacht Club could establish a fleet of the little boats too, it would sharpen competition between beginning sailors.

Gordon Frost, a 13-year-old whose father was a San Diego Yacht Club stalwart, had a set of the plans that Joe Ruski had been selling for $5.00 to support the junior program he was starting at Southwestern. Gordon brought them to "an old guy"—George Kettenburg Jr. who was then all of 24. "He said he would study them and I should come back in three days, and

he would tell me what he thought. George was Paul's older brother and a very innovative guy. When I came back three days later, as he bid me to do, George said he would build a Starlet."

But, "he said he thought the boat would be much better with certain design changes," including "using a heavier boilerplate slab for a keel, with no bulb at the bottom. He also narrowed up the cockpit to avoid shipping water," and raised the freeboard to keep it drier inside. "His price was $250 with sails—and Dad said we could order it"—despite the fact that George's proposed Starlet cost about a hundred dollars more than Joe Ruski's homebuilt versions. Ruski

had built five Starlets for juniors at Southwestern, and "George said he would build three boats rather than just one, which would make the price of each one a little less."

Frost continued: "The crowning glory for the Kettenburg Starlets occurred when the first three boats were raced against the Ruski Starlets in a bay race, that started off the municipal pier, went down to the South Bay, and then returned. It was a choppy day and the Ruski Starlets started shipping water and sinking. The Kettenburg Starlets were shipping water too, but had no bulb on the keel and a narrower cockpit, so we were able to bail fast enough to stay afloat and finish the race."

"That was the beginning of the Kettenburg Starlets—and the end of the Ruski Starlets. Joe Ruski teamed up with the Kettenburgs a short time later," where he worked at the boatyard alongside other teenagers. San Diego's young sailors would buy nearly every subsequent Starlet from Kettenburg Boat Works.

To a boy, the Starlet had endearing virtues: you could buy one cheaply, tow it to races on a tiny trailer behind parents' or friends' cars, and you could scrub marine growth off the bottom without paying anyone to haul your boat out. Bob Sharp remembered that his own Saturday morning ritual was to sail from his mooring to the float just off the clubhouse in Coronado. "We would tip them over at the float, and tie the mast to the mooring rail on one side of the float, and then stand on the keel" while they scrubbed growth off the bottom.

What attracted boys like Gordon Frost to the Starlet was simple: it was quick. "It was a very, very good design. Actually, after these first three boats I think he perfected it a little bit. He gave it a little bit more freeboard—probably an inch or two—because they were a little better that way."

And, Gordon continued, thanks to several inches of deck between the boat's rail and the cockpit coaming, "if you had the rail in the water you still had some freeboard—basically on the deck" even as your boat flew along. When a

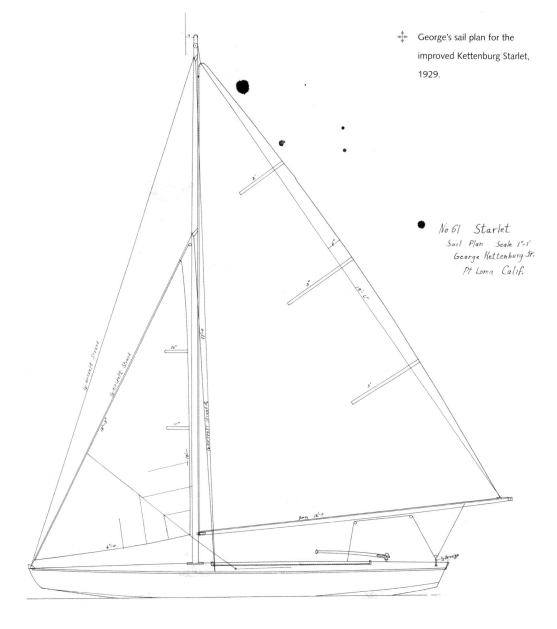

George's sail plan for the improved Kettenburg Starlet, 1929.

More than thirty years after its introduction, the Kettenburg Starlet remained popular among young San Diego sailors. Here, Bruce Wright hoists his boat in 1960.

Starlet sailor over-reached in competition and capsized, there was still "enough deck that when you were lying on your side, the cockpit was above water," remembered Doug Giddings. "So all you do is go over and climb on the keel and straighten it out. That was for Juniors so they wouldn't get into trouble." While Ruski's original design was sound, Gordon said "it was the *difference* in the Kettenburg Starlet that made it such a good racing boat." The other attraction, of course, was the fun of sailing against one's peers; rituals of competition included homemade pies contributed as prizes by moms, and mandatory dunks in the bay for winners. Once they were back ashore, their horizons for getting into trouble expanded significantly, as Gordon Frost's carefully chosen words suggest: "Although the

lads were sometimes a little rowdy, they never *really* disgraced the club."

While the Starlet fleets never spread outside San Diego Bay and largely faded from competition during World War II, they fulfilled their main purpose: young sailors graduated from them to compete in bigger boats. Starlets introduced some skippers who became stars in their own right; in Gordon Frost's words, "that fleet produced some of the finest sailors in the nation," like national Star-Class champions Ash Bown and Milt Wegeforth and Star-Class and America's Cup victor Dennis Conner. Looking back on his Starlet days, PC Class champion Doug Giddings said, "I kind of wish they still had that Starlet" to train racers.

But the Great Depression rendered George Kettenburg's boat business more popular than

profitable. No number of celebrated speedboats, rumrunners, archery tournaments, or $300 Starlets could keep such a labor-intensive business afloat without extraordinary measures. As a high school kid working for George in the 1930s, Jim Underwood Jr. saw that even a first-rate builder could seldom be "in the money" in the best of times. In general, "you don't make a good income as a boatbuilder" since "it takes so many hours to do so little," thanks to the mass of detail work. "It doesn't *show*. It takes a lot of hours to build a boat"—as anyone knows who's tried. By the beginning of the Depression, however, long-term salvation for George's struggling company was at hand, in a design for a dramatic new class of racing sailboats.

Chapter Three

The Birth of The PC

DESIGNERS *and* BUILDERS

of the new

Pacific Coast One Design Class

Priced at $2100 Complete with Sails

═══

The Starlet Class

which we designed and built at $300

═══

The undefeated cruiser "Agilis" and the Pacific Coast champion runabouts, "Aljo" and "Cigarette," were also designed and built by us.

Kettenburg Boat Works

POINT LOMA, CALIFORNIA

One of the new Pacific Coast One-Designs

With her crew riding the rail, the Springsteads' *Imp* drives to windward in a good blow, ca. 1934. Inset: A Kettenburg Boat Works ad from the early 1930s celebrates the company's PC, Starlet, and powerboat designs.

"In the office Mr. Jones is Jones, but the moment he climbs aboard his thirty-foot sloop he becomes Capt. Jones, and the business world fades into a distant shadow." A sizeable handful of San Diegans had enough money in the 1920s to leave this shadow behind, at least on Sundays.

By most measures, George Kettenburg Jr.'s introduction of a new racing sailboat class in 1930 should *not* have succeeded. As a business rule of thumb, it is seldom considered smart to leap headfirst into a bold new venture from the brink of global economic catastrophe. By any standard, March 1930 was such a brink: Americans were pitching headlong into their worst-ever economic depression. Like everyone else in the recreational boat business, George's prosperity depended on the spending habits of men with disposable income. His market was small, too, for there were fewer than 150,000 San Diegans, whereas the oft-resented city of Los Angeles, 100 miles to the north, already boasted two million residents in 1930. Further north, logic dictated that the natural center of gravity for sailing in California lay on windy San Francisco Bay, among the comparatively cultured and sophisticated "old money" that populated its yacht clubs. San Diego, notwithstanding its pleasant climate, was an unimportant corner of Herbert Hoover's America, worlds away from the patrician sparring-grounds of American yachtsmen off New York, Newport, Rhode Island, and Marblehead, Massachusetts.

Twenty-five-year-old George Kettenburg Jr. was himself an inauspicious choice, for until the previous year he had been a backyard boatbuilder equipped only with a high school diploma. He was best known for speedboats and had never created an original sailboat design. But he did come up with exactly the right design for the cultural moment—if not exactly at the right time for his own prosperity.

Two reasons seem to have made 1930 the right moment for George Jr. to step into the limelight, as perhaps the last "amateur"—as opposed to university-trained professional—among his peers. First, the twenties roared somewhat louder in San Diego than they did in most of America; the city witnessed fantastic growth, and its booming economy left some with a little

extra spending money. And secondly, sailboat racing had reached an impasse in which "one-off" designs were increasingly toys affordable only to the richest Americans.

The effects of newfound prosperity showed in the strained smiles of San Diego's young men as they chased their fortunes up elevators into offices in downtown's handful of new tall buildings. Some glanced enviously down at the sparkling bay, already dotted with a handful of sails flown by luckier souls. More than one rising young businessman—riding a crowded trolley to an office where he would spend another sunny day perched precariously on the Ladder of Success—must have caught this glimpse. And more than one daydreamed of himself, tiller in hand, achieving victory under billowing canvas, in properly triumphant, manly fashion, with the tan skin and athletic build of a man who did *not* spend his days behind a desk. As a local newspaperman put it, "in the office Mr. Jones is Jones, but the moment he climbs aboard his thirty-foot sloop he becomes Capt. Jones, and the business world fades into a distant shadow." A sizeable handful of San Diegans had enough money in the 1920s to leave this shadow behind, at least on Sundays.

To reach these businessmen, however, George Jr. needed a mentor who already had their respect. Thirty-one-year-old Joe Jessop was George's senior by six years. Outside a boat's cockpit, the newspaper's society pages depicted him as a smiling, stylish dresser—but inside the cockpit he traded that demeanor for an air of pure competitive menace. Joe had won California's championship in the Star Class in 1924, and he was voted one of the top ten West Coast sailors a decade later. Endlessly voluble about the joys of racing, he competed in Eastern regattas, and in 1929 he was the new annual commodore of the San Diego Yacht Club. Joe was "the outstanding sailor in the San Diego area for quite a few years—I mean, nobody could touch him," recalled Paul Kettenburg. "Whatever Joe Jessop was sailing, boy, that was *it*." This

KETTENBURG BOAT WORKS
SAN DIEGO, CALIFORNIA

educated and widely experienced sailor was impressed by the high-school educated trades- man. Joe and the San Diego Yacht Club would play key roles in the Kettenburg family's future.

Joe was the ablest sailor in a yacht-loving family that ran the city's best-known jewelry business. Racing trophies occasionally popped up amongst watches and jewelry in the display windows of Jessop's Jewelers (sometimes known as "Yachtsman's Headquarters"), and assorted Jessops owned a small squadron of boats. In 1929, Joe's greatest desire was to work with other enthusiastic club members to select an official "one design." In a racing world charac- terized by out-of-control spending, the new class would be a type that members could buy and sail against each other without the headache of handicaps—those strange and always disputable computations that enable yachtsmen in mis- matched boats to race one another. Any one- design must be built within very specific rules—length, beam, weight, keel shape and size, type of wood, length of mast and boom, and size and material of sails. Fairer and fiercer competition was guaranteed if enough sailors could be convinced to buy identical sailboats, since a one-design is always fairly matched against any other in its class. Victory would rest on the skipper's merits alone; Joe liked that.

The problem for Joe Jessop lay in selecting an official design for San Diego Bay. What would be competitive with classes at other yacht clubs north up the coast, and could be sailed overnight there to compete? What could be affordable enough to bring dynamic young men into the sport? What could take advantage of every puff of the light airs that often characterize the California's southernmost seas, be comfortable enough to day-sail with a family and—most of all—be fast enough in any conditions to be

⊹ A stylish dresser and champion sailor, Joe Jessop led
   the search for a new San Diego Yacht Club one-
   design sailboat and was a principal supporter of
   George Kettenburg's PC design.

exciting, whether in harbor or on the open sea?

Joe himself was a champion sailor in a one-design class, but in his mind, the Star was definitely not in the running for his club's proposed design. "A lot of us did a lot of racing—we were all in the Star class—and we decided that we needed larger boats that we could sleep on when we went to Los Angeles and Santa Barbara to attend regattas." Star boats were then as they remain today: competitive open boats without cabins—challenging to sail, far from comfortable, frequently wet, and nobody's idea of a "family" boat.

During the summer and fall of 1928, Joe debated potential designs with fellow Yacht Club members Bob Childs, Emil Schmidt, Bob Mann, Ed Peterson, and his brother George Jessop. The racing sailboats owned by these leading local yachtsmen were classed as R boats, under the intricate Universal Rule of yacht measurement devised by Nathanael Herreshoff for the New York Yacht Club, and adopted in 1902. They were all aware that their expensive boats were falling out of favor in competition thanks to the arrival in America in the early 1920s of the Six-Meter yacht—so called for its classification under the International Rule of yacht construction, first established in Europe in 1907, which took into account a boat's girth and freeboard as well as its length and sail area. As the writer of a regional yachting magazine explained, "The six meter class has never found favor in San Diego because it is so near the R in size and because it is felt to be a little too expensive." Like the Universal Rule classes, the Six-Meter Class was not a one-design class, meaning a buyer could open his wallet to America's finest naval architects and builders to ensure that his own craft would be a winning design. With its open cockpit and length of about 36 feet, the Six Meter was the most competitive "Meter" boat, but, despite being one of the smallest, its cost was indeed galling, given the club's goal of bringing young blood into the sport.

The bar for one-designs in the size range that

Jessop's cohort thought best had been set by Rhode Island's brilliant old "Captain Nat" Herreshoff, the father of modern recreational boat design as well as the mightiest America's Cup racing machines. Herreshoff had introduced his fast, 27-foot one-design sloop of the S-Class in 1919. Distinguished by its stubby bow and stern and a swept-back curve at the top of the mast, the Herreshoff S-boat had spread west as far as Hawai'i. S-boats had partisans in San Diego, and Jessop and his debating partners seem to have agreed that any design they selected should fall within the "rules" of the S-Class, to permit the two classes to race against each other.

The yacht club men looked most intently at a design newly introduced in the East in the summer of 1928, when Joe was competing there in regattas. Yachting magazines were full of news of new German-built Atlantic Coast Class racing yachts, the first of which was being campaigned around Long Island Sound that summer by her distinguished American designers, W. Starling Burgess and Jasper Morgan. The MIT-educated Burgess was as interested in aeronautical engineering as in naval architecture. Twice Kettenburg's age, Burgess would soon design the elegant America's Cup champion, the J-Class *Ranger*. His new Atlantic Coast one-design class boats, at 30 feet long overall, were a bit longer and more graceful than Herreshoff's S-boats.

Starling Burgess was developing his designs in an increasingly scientific direction, applying research on the behavior of wind and water to shape his hulls—quite the opposite of the San Diego High School-educated George, who based his designs primarily on his "feel" for how a fast hull *should* look. Burgess received 90 orders almost immediately, and his Atlantics seemed to fulfill all Joe's hopes. Burgess replied to Joe by mail that four of the first group of his boats, then under construction in Germany, could be diverted to San Diego in April. "We had tentatively ordered four of the Atlantic type boats which were then in great demand, being the

The bar for one-designs in the size range that Jessop's cohort thought best had been set by Rhode Island's brilliant old "Captain Nat" Herreshoff, the father of modern recreational boat design as well as the mightiest America's Cup racing machines.

✛ Designed by Nathanael Herreshoff in 1919, the fast, responsive, 27-foot S-Class sloop performed well in both light airs and strong blows. With fleets established from New England to Hawai'i, the S-boat was a contender for the San Diego Yacht Club one-design class.

The S-Boat and Atlantic Coast Class

Back around the year of George Kettenburg's birth, Nathanael Herreshoff wrote a new yacht measurement rule for the New York Yacht Club to reverse the trend toward very long-ended, shallow, over-rigged racing sloops. The new rule favored hulls with shorter, fuller ends and penalized craft with very light displacement and big rigs. Called the Universal Rule, it divided racing craft into 19 length-based classes, the smallest being the S-Class.

In 1919 Herreshoff designed an S-Class sloop that was quickly adopted by discerning small-boat racers. Herreshoff's S-boat may have been the first one-design class to do away with the gaff mainsail in favor of the new Marconi rig. Herreshoff added a distinctive feature in the form of a gentle aft curve to the top of the mast. The 27-1/2-foot boat's short keel and 425 square feet of sail made it fast and very maneuverable, while the deep cockpit and small cuddy cabin made it a comfortable boat to sail. Though a very good light-air sailer, the S-boat could take strong winds and heavy seas, rolling its rail down to a point of great stability. About

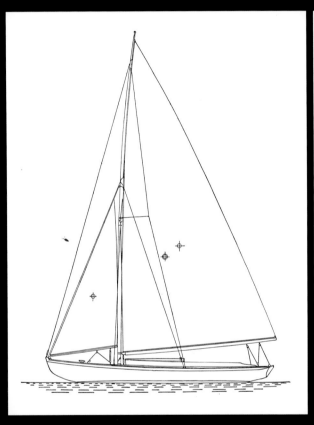

The S-boat was one of the earliest Marconi-rigged one-design sloops. The sail plan shows the gentle curve in the upper portion of the mast.

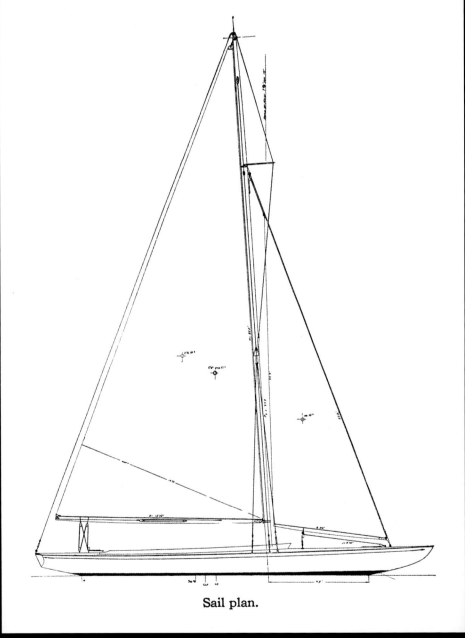

Sail plan.

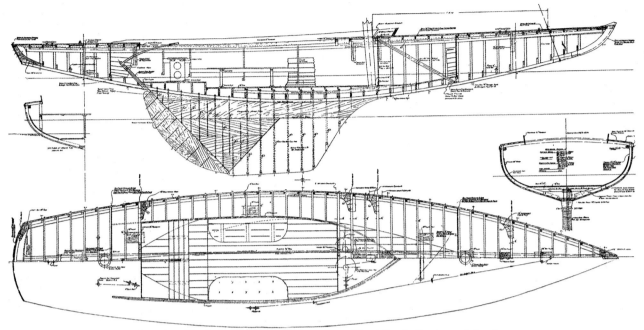

Inboard profile, deck plan and midship section of the Atlantic Coast one-design boat.

The Atlantic Coast One-Design Class

85 S-boats were built with typical cedar planking on oak frames at the Herreshoff Manufacturing Company in Bristol, Rhode Island, during the 20 years of their production. Five S-boats were built for Hawai'ian owners in 1928.

W. Starling Burgess had recently reestablished his design business in New York, with financial backing from the Morgan family, when he drew up plans for an economical new 30-foot one-design racer that he hoped would be adopted by many centers of competitive sailing to encourage broad competition. He had been working with the yacht builders Abeking and Rasmussen of Lemwerder, Germany, so he sent them the plans for the new Atlantic Coast Class and the first boats arrived back in the U.S. in 1928. Yacht clubs at the western end of Long Island Sound took up the new design, purchasing the first 35 Atlantics that year.

Abeking & Rasmussen built 101 Atlantics between 1928 and 1930. Though planked of cedar on oak frames

like them, the Atlantic was a clear departure from the heavy displacement boats of its size, such as the S-boat of the Universal Rule or the Six Meter of the similar International Rule. The new design was considered competitive with a number of one-design classes, including S-boats, Triangles, and the popular Sound Interclubs of western Long Island Sound.

With its short keel, long waterline, and rounded sections, the boat was fast and maneuverable despite its conservative 378-square-foot sail area. The rig featured a three-quarter forestay anchored well aft of the stem head and a jumper strut to counter the permanent backstay. The high-aspect mainsail, with short foot, made an efficient wing while allowing a fixed backstay instead of a pair of running backstays. The Atlantic's open cockpit, low freeboard, and short ends made the design most suitable for sailing in protected sounds and bays.

The Atlantic Class sail and construction plans show the boat's low freeboard, light construction, short keel, and conservative rig (left), with three-quarter headstay, jumper struts, and no running backstays.

only ones of their design," Jessop explained—but the San Diegans abruptly cancelled. Joe later clarified that he felt Burgess's boats would not be quite right for Southern California conditions, since these open sloops with little freeboard were "too flat forward" and not seaworthy enough to make the long ocean passages between regattas along the West Coast. There may also have been a vaguely distasteful feeling that ordering an Atlantic sloop was somehow unpatriotic for an inhabitant of a city on the Pacific shore.

They also considered jettisoning the "one-design" concept entirely and specifying instead a class in which design restrictions were loose, but in which the quantity of sail area was tightly regulated. This was a common approach in Scandinavia, where elegant Nordic "square-metre boats"—refinements of that region's traditional skerry cutters—plied the waves. The Nordic approach would allow San Diegans the freedom to order boats from any builder they wanted in a variety of sizes, materials, and costs, provided they precisely restricted their sail area. In late summer 1929, at the peak of the Roaring 'Twenties, a 22-square-metre yacht was shipped from Norway for their consideration. *Lyn* was impressive, and club members learned that Norwegian naval architect Bjarne Aas was working to design a 25-square-metre boat specifically for San Diego wind conditions. Joe Jessop and his compatriots, however, ultimately rejected *Lyn*'s design as "badly undercanvassed" and too pricey. But at least one of the features of this boat, with her elegantly overhanging bow and stern, was carefully noted by club member George Kettenburg Jr., who looked her over with great interest. Practically alone among classic yachts, *Lyn*'s slender hull displaced very little water.

Despite looking eastward, Joe Jessop had kept in mind that Southern Californians should,

at least in principle, be the best suited to tailor a design to local conditions. Los Angeles now boasted several first-rate yacht designers. These were Easterners who had followed the new stream of money to its source in Hollywood, where it flowed from the pockets of movie people—most of whom seemed to be landlubbers dazzled by the rich-sounding word "yacht." Among the best emigrant designers in L.A. was Edson Burr Shock, now nearing 60, who had been design editor at *The Rudder*. Shock was then designing the big ketch *Vileehi* for a San Diego Yacht Club member, and he knew of the club's interest in selecting or creating a one-design racing boat. Agreeing that a few changes to the Atlantic Class would suit it better to Southern California, Shock sketched a similar boat flying about 400 square feet of canvas, equipped with a pair of bunks. Most of Joe's group leaned toward adopting a design based on Shock's sketches, but the architect faced scheduling problems.

And then there was George.

Joe Jessop knew George Kettenburg Jr., having frequently beaten him as they raced their Stars. Commodore Jessop, who dealt in elegantly reshaped precious metals and stones, clearly found himself drawn to the likeable younger man who dealt in elegantly reshaped wood. As Paul Kettenburg recalled, Joe discussed their one-design problems with George, telling him that, although he truly loved sailing in the Star class, "You know, we're looking at bigger boats so our girlfriends or wives could be able to sail with us."

In the fall of 1929, George made Joe a startling proposal. According to Joe, "about the same time the orders were in the mail" to Starling Burgess in New York for four yachts, Kettenburg "declared he could build us a boat that in every way would meet our specifications. Convinced, we canceled the Atlantic order and told him to go ahead." The idea captivated Joe. "How well this sounded—an individual Pacific Class," liberated even from echoes of that other ocean, and tailored to Southern California's fre-

quently light airs. George also promised he could build it for a very low cost compared to competitors. The group agreed to wait long enough to sail Kettenburg's proposed boat before settling on any other design. George Jr. went to his father for money. Once again, Mr. Kettenburg came through with money for a prototype, since his son lacked the funds to purchase even a basic suit of sails from a sailmaker back East. Father and son agreed that, should the boat prove unsatisfactory on trial to these prospective buyers, the "Old Man" would keep it himself—despite his well-known lack of enthusiasm for anything that could not send up a roostertail of spray under its own power.

As with most creation myths, there are several conflicting accounts of the birth of the design that remains the cornerstone of the Kettenburgs' national reputation. According to a friend and client of George's, it took recognizable form as a sketch of a very light-displacement boat scrawled on a cocktail napkin on the front porch of the San Diego Yacht Club, in Coronado. Another told a more refined tale of Joe Jessop "leaning back against the comfortable cushions" aboard Hiram Horton's *Vileehi* and debating designs with Bob Childs, with George quietly looking on. George dramatically breaks his silence: "I have it!" he interjects. "I've listened to your requirements and think I know exactly what you want. Suppose I design a boat—build the first one at my own expense. Then you try her out, and if she *doesn't* suit, you're not under any obligations."

Perhaps the most satisfying account of the PC's birth comes from Paul, who was 15 when his brother went to work on it in earnest. "One day we were down there at the yard," when Joe Jessop dropped in.

George and Joe were just chatting and I was standing there—maybe I had been talking to George about something else—and Joe . . . started telling George about the fact that the Star boats were not comfortable for what

Altantic 1 cuts through a light chop during a race, ca. 1934. Despite the extended cockpit coaming, the low freeboard and open cockpit make the Atlantic best suited for sheltered waters.

57

THE BIRTH OF THE PC

they wanted to do, so they were looking at these other boats. George, out of the blue, said, "Well, you know, it seems to me I could build a better boat for San Diego than those." Joe's comment was, "Well—if you want to build one, why don't you build one, and we'll wait. And we won't do anything until you get that built, and see how it goes."

The actual PC, of course, did not spring forth fully formed, but came about through a time-honored process. In an age when designers had come to draw their plans in three dimensions on linen, George reverted to the old shipbuilder's method of carving an exact-scale half-hull model. As Paul explained, "what he did was carve out a model, an inch to the foot, with layers of wood that could come apart. He carved this model out, and that was the design. When he got the model built the way he wanted it, he took the layers apart, laid them out on the loft floor, and made the measurements for the PC hull design."

As Paul implied, they used the wide second floor of the new tin building to expand the lines

of the half model to full scale. With help from foreman Dick Hershey, George "laid it all out, and all I did was tack down the battens wherever he said to tack." Once the lines were fair, the lofting crew made wooden patterns called molds that represented the shape of the hull at specific stations along its length. These molds were then set up square and precisely spaced on the building floor as a template around which to bend the frames and planks.

In January 1930 George was showing prospective buyers a finished drawing of a yet-unnamed "One Design Class" for San Diego Bay. After five months of construction, a newspaper-man snapped a photo of George silhouetted atop the cabin as the slender boat sat in the cradle on launching day. Just as the financing, designing, and building of it had been a family affair, so was her name. They christened her *Scamp*, their father's nickname for Paul. It's a name that also suggests an upstart's quickness and youthful spark—qualities George worked into his design.

Apparently borrowing the "Pacific Coast

One-Design" name from Edson Shock, a hopeful George chose a name that intentionally echoed W. Starling Burgess's widely publicized Atlantic Coast boats. Within a few years, not long after the Atlantic Coast Class became the Atlantic Class, George's "PC" came to stand for Pacific Class, as his design spread up Southern California's coast.

The "interested parties" who watched George take *Scamp*'s tiller on her shakedown cruise on March 4, 1930, agreed that the boat, 31 feet 10 inches overall and unusually light in displacement, was strikingly handsome. They waited for her first race, however, to judge how well she fulfilled George's promises. She was indeed close in size to the Atlantics and S-boats, but would she prove faster than a Star or a Nordic square-metre yacht, and be as comfortable for day-sailing as a Six or an R? In the early spring of 1930 the club staged an impromptu race, on whose outcome rode the hopes of one small-time local designer. With George at the tiller, *Scamp* tore down San Diego Bay alongside the Nordic 22-square-metre boat *Lyn* and two

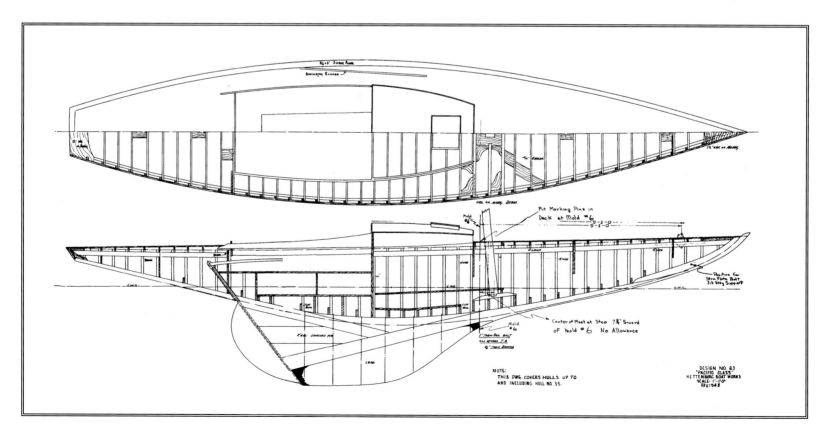

The PC construction plan, left, shows the boat's large cockpit, small cabin, and light construction, with plenty of diagonal bracing around the mast partners. The PC's keel is longer and shallower than the Atlantic's. The sail plan, right, is dated January 1930. It shows a conservative rig, with two-thirds jibstay counterbalanced by running backstays, and both a stemhead forestay and a fixed backstay. The forestay was later replaced by jumper stays.

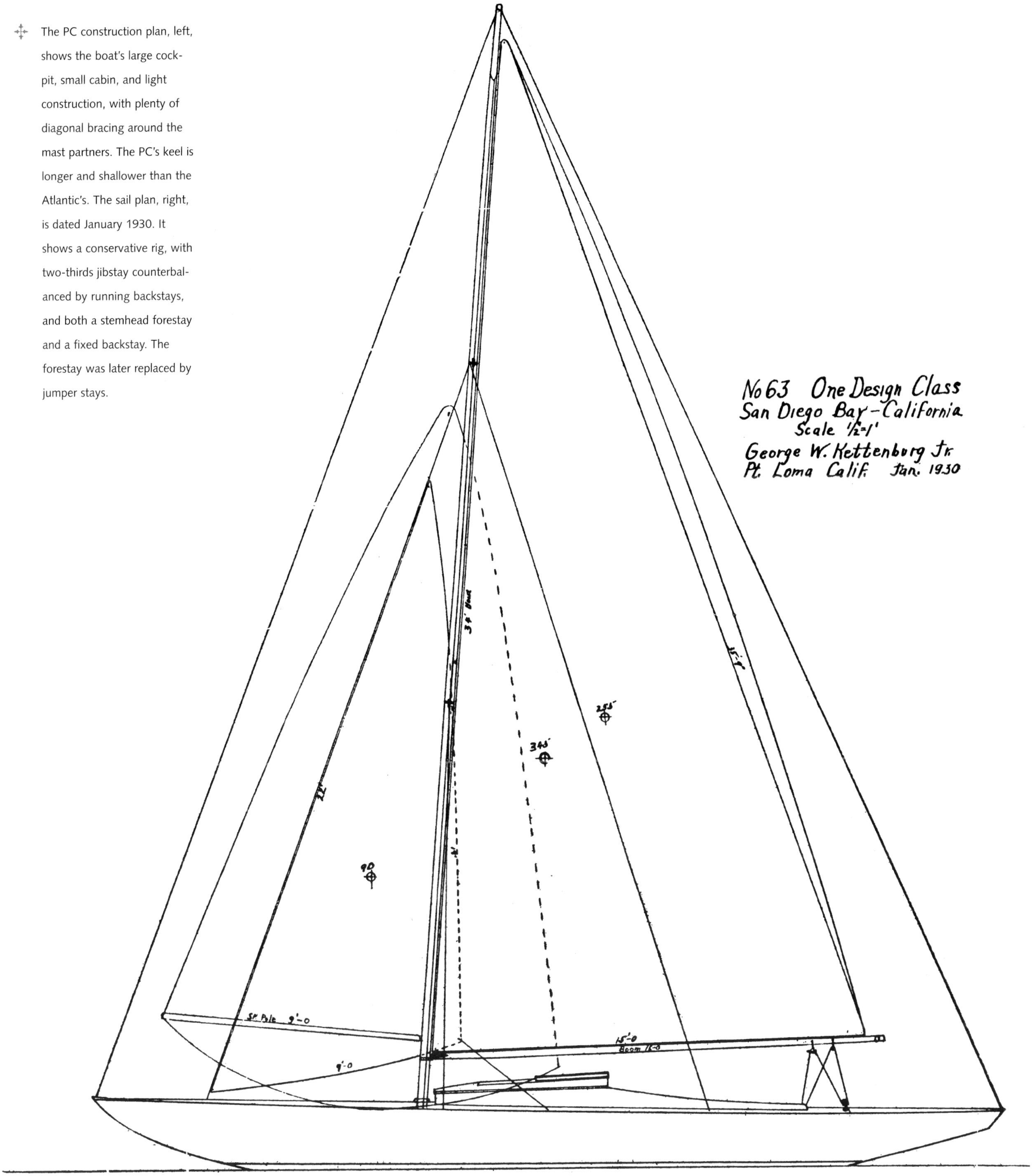

No 63 One Design Class
San Diego Bay – California
Scale ½"=1'
George W. Kettenburg Jr
Pt. Loma Calif. Jan. 1930
Sp Pole 9'-0
9'-0
15'-0
Boom 15'-0

Above: *Scamp*, the first PC, under construction in the Kettenburg shop. At this stage Kettenburg boats were built right-side-up. Planking has progressed down from the sheer plank. The garboards along the keel are in, and soon the plankers will reach the shutter plank to complete the operation. Right: *Scamp* awaits her launch in 1930.

R-boats—both of which flew considerably more canvas than *Scamp*. "Joe Jessop, and George, and my dad and I went out and raced on our boat"— Paul grinned at the memory—"and we beat the hell out of 'em!" The winner was clear, and although the pleased—if chagrined—competition insisted *their* boats would have won had the bottoms been cleaner, everyone agreed that they had witnessed "a very gratifying demonstration of the boat's ability." The Pacific Coast now had its first native, race-winning, one-design sloop.

A few months later, George proudly ran

Kettenburg Boat Works' first magazine ad, trumpeting "The new Pacific Coast One Design Class, priced at $2100 Complete with Sails." The price was about two-thirds what one would expect to pay for an S-Class yacht, a little more than a Star boat, and vastly less than a Six-Meter or an R. It was, however, twice the price of a new Ford car, and in 1930 almost no-one was buying new Fords. In October 1929, as George, Dick Hershey, rigger Dick Leonard, Roy Stowe, and George's brother Paul labored inside their building on the first PC, the world's economy collapsed and the

U.S. stock market dropped vertiginously. "Old Man" Kettenburg, like most Americans of means, had watched the value of his assets wither. What was waterfront land worth, if no one was buying? Instead of a 1920s-style rush to buy this handsome new yacht, the flow of cash slowed to a trickle. To sell one of the first PCs, George had to barter it with the owner of an empty house lot on Point Loma. Only seven PCs were built in the first two years of the new yard's operation, far below capacity.

The best advertisement for the new sail-boat—and all the struggling firm could really afford—was the existence of the prototype itself. The new boat left quite an impression on young Wally Springstead:

As we sailed by Kettenburg's, in the water on a mooring was a beautiful sloop-rigged sail-boat named Scamp. *We fell in love with that beautiful vessel. At the time, Yachting maga-zine was about the only publication on boat-ing that we could find. They featured many Six- and Eight-Meter sloops—sleek vessels—*

all designed in Europe. So we figured Scamp *had to be a European design. The conversa-tion at the Springstead dinner table was always about that beautiful European-designed sloop that we passed every day when we were sailing.*

Luckily for the Springsteads, about this time Wally and his brother took their grandfather sailing out to the kelp beds off Point Loma in the boys' leaky old centerboard sailboat. The old onetime sailor of square-riggers, apparently shaken, demanded that his son-in-law beach that boat and buy his grandsons something seaworthy.

"As a result, my father went to George Kettenburg and tried to buy what turned out to be PC number two. To help stimulate sales, Joe Jessop—for whom number two was being built—agreed to let the Springstead brothers have the boat." The only condition George placed on the boys was that they use a sail emblazoned with the number five, a higher hull number than he had yet built—and free advertising that the new class was apparently booming, despite the Depression. San Diegans looking out at their bay in 1930 had the pleasure of watching the Springstead brothers' new *Imp*—her name inspired by George's original boat—leap nimbly to life.

It was customers like the Springsteads who made the success of the PC possible in a season of economic disaster. The motives of those who bought the PC were less than altruistic, but this was the great gift of Joe's idea of a one-design class: each PC buyer had invested in what was announced as a highly competitive class. Without more competitors there would be very little point to buying in, so each new owner was, in effect, a missionary beating the bushes for converts to his new religion. The most passionate missionary of all was Joe Jessop, the PC's seemingly tireless unofficial spokesman and chief booster. While in later years he perhaps claimed responsibility for a bit more of the PC's design than was strictly truthful, Joe's ingenious efforts at promotion helped generate widespread enthusiasm for the PC. "I am not a salesman, only an owner," Joe insisted unconvincingly in an article titled "A Successful One-Design Class," one of several that he wrote for Western yachting magazines. Late in life, he remarked that "the boat was so successfully designed and beautiful that we had no trouble getting it out and getting the class

going" (certainly an overstatement!), as was his assertion that "we had seven people ready to sign ten minutes after we had the boat all set up." But given the gifts of hindsight, these state-

ments sound less like exaggerations than like the boasts of a proud father.

Since consistency among the boats was one of the chief advantages a one-design offered, an association was quickly formed to limit the amount of money and care that could be lavished on a boat. How often, for instance, could an owner pay to haul his pride and joy out of the water, and scour her bottom to its speediest slickness? There were rules: Joe stated that "the manly art of sandpapering is not permitted in this class." The purpose of these restrictions, in the words of the rulebook Joe and George helped write, was "to keep the PACIFIC CLASS within the financial reach of the man of moderate means." Or, as a Kettenburg Boat Works sales brochure put it, rules enabled "the skipper on a budget to keep his boat in just as fine sailing trim as the skipper with a bulky pocketbook." After buying a PC, owners were allowed to spend no more than $250 on niceties like stainless steel rigging, a restriction that no doubt flabbergasted owners of Six Meters, accustomed to almost any extravagance they could afford.

While one of Joe's goals was to raise the level

of competition by bringing fresh blood like the young Springsteads into local racing, these rules were also intended to preserve something of the lingering air of gentility that hung about the sport. Owners possessed of "undue youthful energy," as the author of one magazine article termed it, should be inhibited in their efforts to make their boats' hulls slipperier, since part of the point of yachting remained sailing "without making recreation too much work."

"PC's are Fast! PC's are Comfortable! PC's are Easy to Handle! PC's are Safe! PC's are Durable! PC's are Economical! PC's are a Good Investment! PC's are an Active Class!" the boldface in George's company's first brochure hurrahed breathlessly. The copywriter continued in more measured tones that "scientific design, the best materials and rigid specifications are vitally important in the construction of good boats." This was certainly true of the PC, though how "scientific" George's essentially intuitive design methods were is debatable. "The final result still is dependent on the skill and integrity of the builder. Kettenburg says: 'ask the man who sails a PC…'" In the world of advertising, not usually known for truthfulness, this echo of the Packard auto company's "Ask the Man Who Owns One" slogan hews unusually close to the truth.

Advertisements could not ensure success, but customers' praises—and victories on race day—could. Thanks in large part to Joe Jessop's enthusiastic help in creating and selling a new one-design racing boat, in the teeth of the Depression George Jr. successfully bucked sailing's trend toward ever-more-expensive custom yachts. All his life, Joe remained PC Promoter Number One. "They're still a wonderful boat," he bragged to an interviewer, 60 years after he and George Kettenburg Jr. gave birth to San Diego's iconic sailboat.

In a good Pacific breeze,
Scamp races another PC in the
Los Angeles area, ca. 1935.

Chapter Four

"Pacific Class Takes all the Firsts!"

The First PC Racers

PACIFIC CLASS

PC *Takes All the Firsts!*

RACING OR CRUISING

THE LEADING CLASS OF THE WEST

With spinnakers barely inflated, a fleet of PCs races in San Diego Bay, ca. 1935. The Jessop family's *Wings* (PC 8) is at left while *Scamp* is in the middle of the fleet, just to the right of the Springsteads' *Imp* (PC 5).

The Kettenburg Perpetual Ocean Racing Trophy for the San Diego area yacht clubs annual regatta.

To sell a racing boat, George and Joe both knew, they needed first to win races. The growth of Kettenburg Boat Works before the Second World War is primarily a tale of how these two men's racing victories sparked the racing adventures of others.

"Out of the blue," marveled George's younger brother as he gazed back across 70 years, Paul had watched the 25-year-old George create a classic. The first Pacific Class racing boat, *Scamp*, was indisputably "good looking, inexpensive to buy and economical to keep up," as Kettenburg Boat Works advertised, but establishing any new one-design racing class at the Depression's outset was a tough sell at best.

When George launched *Scamp*, he was a little-known young boatbuilder in an out-of-the-way corner of the U.S., at a moment when opportunities for even the best-schooled designers of the East to sell racing yachts were dwindling. George visualized that competitive young men of relatively modest means would become the core group of PC owners, but persuading them (or their fathers) to part with the purchase price demanded more than the natural friendliness that he brought to sales, or the unrelenting charms of the PC's chief booster, Joe Jessop. It certainly demanded more than the few advertisements that George could afford to run in trade magazines.

To sell a racing boat, George and Joe both knew, they needed first to win races. The growth of Kettenburg Boat Works before the Second World War is primarily a tale of how these two men's racing victories sparked the racing adventures of others. While even the relentlessly optimistic Joe was forced to admit that "the Depression retarded activity somewhat," their hopes were realized to a remarkable degree: the fleet spread as victories established "Kettenburg" in the minds of West Coast yachtsmen as a synonym for quality and speed under sail.

The well-connected Joe Jessop continued to pull every string he could to bring the PC into the public eye. Unlike George, Joe's livelihood was not at stake, but his reputation was: Joe's persuasiveness had pushed the San Diego Yacht Club to choose a virtually untried local design for its new racing class. Winning over out-of-towners to buy PCs would be crucial, for if no other fleets sprang up outside San Diego, his club's purpose of creating economical (and fast) competition would founder. His most important success in establishing San Diego's homegrown racer as a nationally competitive class came in 1931 in the vividly blue waters off Diamond Head, Hawai'i.

It seems to have been Joe's idea to catch the interest of as many potential PC buyers as possible by challenging the nationally known S-boat class to a publicized team match race. The PC had purposely been built close to S-boat specifications in order for the two to race together, and by 1931 Kettenburg Boat Works had completed six PCs, whose skippers were convinced that they could not only compete with the S-boats, but win. Acting for the San Diego Yacht Club, Joe challenged the S-Class fleet headquartered at the New York Yacht Club to a race series, with the winning design to be determined on total points.

The parties agreed to stage a four-boat match race in Hawai'i, where the Pearl Harbor Yacht Club had an S-boat fleet. *Pacific Coast Yachting* magazine promised coverage, but if the San Diegans failed to make a good showing, bad publicity could only harm the fledgling sailboat builder's prospects. There was no certainty of victory; Joe Jessop explained that despite their considerable differences, "the two classes were just like a total one-design fleet, they were so equal in racing." The new design would face skilled competitors in familiar S-boats, racing in their home waters.

First, however, San Diego's PC enthusiasts had to figure out how to transport their little boats across 2,500 miles of open ocean to Honolulu, and how to arrive there fresh and ready to race. With their "roomy cockpit, plenty of deck space and bunks that a man can SLEEP on," as a Kettenburg ad insisted a few years later, a PC *did* offer better accommodations than other boats in their size range, but nowhere near enough for a cruise to Hawai'i. Jessop's charm and Navy League connections came through,

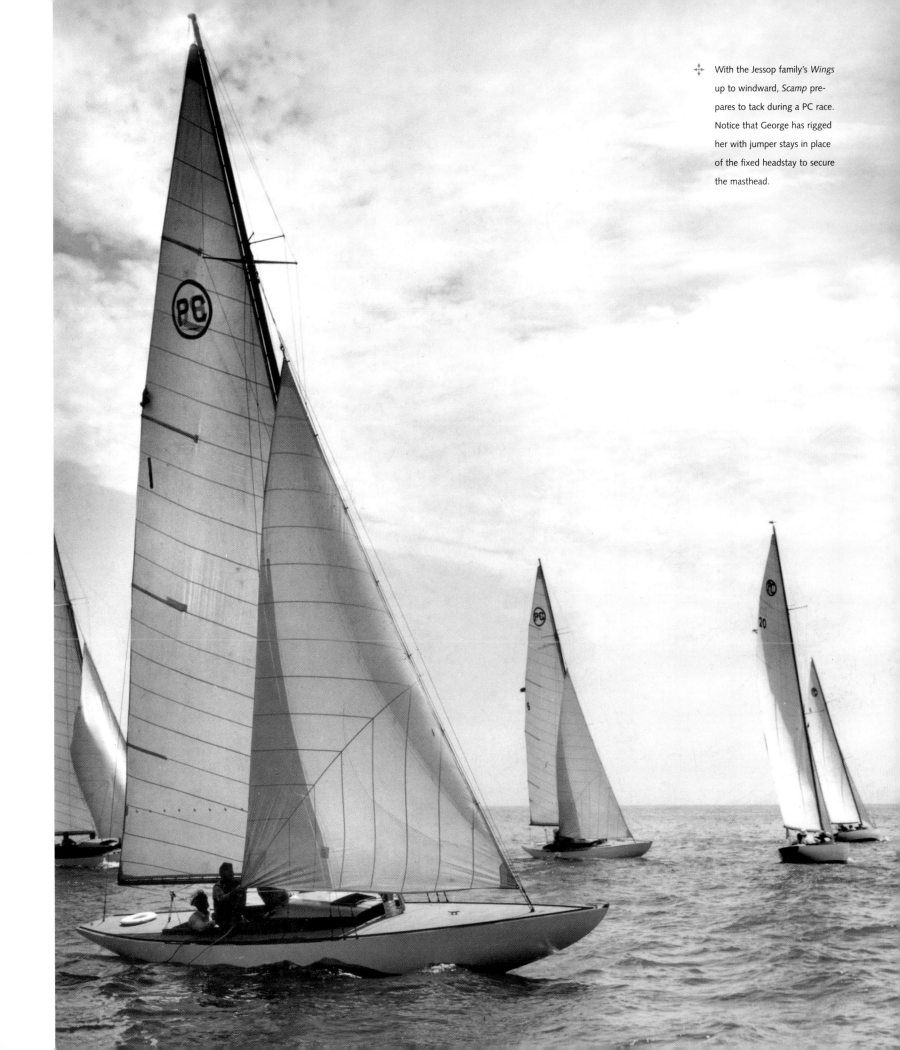

With the Jessop family's *Wings* up to windward, *Scamp* prepares to tack during a PC race. Notice that George has rigged her with jumper stays in place of the fixed headstay to secure the masthead.

Jean (PC 4) was one of the four PCs taken to Hawai'i in 1931, where they established their reputation against the Honolulu S-boats and then remained. She is shown sailing off Oahu. Right: *Yachting* magazine covered the May 1931 showdown between the PCs and S-boats.

however, and with a panache that is hard to imagine today, Joe persuaded the navy to transport four PCs and their crews to Honolulu, free of charge. Cradles aboard the minesweeper *Lark* and minelayer *Ogalala* bore *Blue Jacket*, *Jade*, *Tiana*, and *Jean* to Pearl Harbor. En route, several otherwise-jaded navy sailors grew so interested in the upcoming contest that they spent hours polishing the bottom of the sloop each favored. Joe Jessop and his older brother George, Bob Childs, and Bob Mann watched from the navy ships' decks as Point Loma slipped behind them. George Kettenburg stayed behind, building up the business in San Diego and, one can assume, anxiously awaiting word of the outcome.

Safely in Hawai'i and floating in Pearl Harbor, the much lighter-displacement PCs offered onlookers a noteworthy contrast to the S-boats. *Pacific Coast Yachting*'s correspondent pointed out that "it will be noted at once that the Pacific Coast One-Designs follow in the line of modern development, being longer, leaner and with a good deal less sail area." Since no one knew which type of boat would perform best in what conditions, six races had been scheduled, both inside Pearl Harbor and at sea off Diamond Head.

On May 2, 1931, the eight boats squared off inside the harbor for the first race, on the reputedly difficult inside course. The lead was quickly taken by the S-boat *Huapala*, skippered by Harold Dillingham, whose family's corporation owned an enormous slice of Hawai'ian real estate. Dillingham dealt "a crushing defeat for the men from the mainland, demonstrating that S-boats are the faster in light breezes and smooth water," according to a local journalist.

The shaken San Diegans again met their adversaries at sea off Diamond Head. There, shortly after the first turn, "the breeze freshened, whereupon the San Diego boats began to show

some real speed." San Diego real estate speculator Bob Childs in *Tiana* soon overhauled and passed the land baron Dillingham to win, but the outcome still left the Hawai'ians ahead by a dozen overall points. In the third race, back inside the harbor in heavy wind, the PCs led the field until the spinnaker run, when the 425

Rounding the windward mark in the recent team match between the Pearl Harbor Yacht Club, Hawaii, and the San Diego Yacht Club. The races were sailed in Herreshoff Class S yachts and the new Pacific Coast One-Designs. The latter won by a point score of 109 to 103

The Month in Yachting

square feet of canvas of the S-boats overwhelmed the 353 feet flown by the PCs. Pearl won by a single point, leaving Kettenburg's 13 points behind overall.

Returning to the sea for the fourth race, however, the mainlanders wiped out the Hawai'ians, with the first Pearl Harbor boat trailing over three minutes behind the slowest PC for most of the race. But the overall point lead still stood firmly with the Hawai'ians, at 77 to 65, "thought by many to be an unbeatable advantage with only two races left to be sailed."

The fifth race was the most hotly contested. When the water was smooth, as inside the harbor, the S-boats proved themselves superior. "The San Diego boats had the better of it for a time, but the positions soon began to shift continually, until it was anybody's race." On the final beat to windward, Harold Dillingham, "sailing like a demon" in *Huapala*, passed *Jean*, *Jade*, and Joe Jessop's *Blue Jacket*, which had been holding the lead. But as he rounded the spar

buoy after narrowly squeezing past George Jessop's *Jean*, Dillingham's mainsail struck the buoy, forcing him to drop out. San Diego now held the lead—by a single point.

But light winds turned the sixth race, out at sea, into a "luffing match." Conditions deteriorated to the point that, before the race was called off, the S-boat *Panini*'s memorably named skipper Everadus W. Bogardus and "his famous quartet, while pressing the *Jade* very closely for fifth position, crooned a few Hawai'ian lullabies" to their bored Southern Californian competitors looking forward to the last race.

On May 22, the day of the final contest, the breezes outside the harbor were again extremely light. George, however, had intended his boats to harness even the slightest puff, and the race gave the Kettenburgs another narrow win, clinching the series. The overall point score stood at 109 to 103, which, as *Pacific Coast Yachting* reminded its readers, "cannot be considered as indicating either that the Pacific Coast boats are faster than the S-boats or that they were better handled," but nonetheless handed Kettenburg a clear and much-needed public-relations win. The sweetest victory for George was perhaps a line in the magazine that directed readers to one salient point: the new racer "cost only about half as much as the S-boats."

Lasting benefits came to Kettenburg Boat Works after the victors had finished hoisting the silver trophy bowl—donated, not surprisingly, by Jessop & Sons, Jewelers—smiling, and shaking hands. Of first importance was the publicity splashed across four magazine pages. Readers could compare George's drawing of the PC's sleek modern lines to the S-boat on the facing page, and cluck along with the article's author at the Herreshoff boat's unflatteringly "snubby ends." Then there was the arrangement the

⊹ Far removed from the helm of a PC, Doug Giddings practices with a sextant during his World War II service, ca. 1942.

four skippers had made to proselytize the new design by leaving their boats behind; as Joe gloated, "the Honolulu helmsmen liked the PCs so well, they bought the entire quartet." Their vanquished hosts promised that other Hawai'ian buyers would soon begin building up a larger PC class, and George was cheered by confidence that the San Diegans would quickly order new PCs to replace those they had sold, once they returned aboard the cruiser USS *Chicago*—guests again of an obliging navy.

The excited returning racers suggested elaborate plans to follow up the Hawai'i series with a return engagement at San Diego in 1932, and for further matchups to be held on the East Coast to pit their exciting new class against Atlantic-Class boats and other comparable designs. But even Joe Jessop could not stop the rapid drying-up of America's money supply; almost no one was ordering boats. According to another influential early booster of the PC, retired Chicago businessman and yachtsman Samuel Dauchy, even the four PCs that George expected the returning champions to order failed to materialize, for "along came the Depression and the paralyzing fear of further collapse made them hesitate to order new boats." Only the irrepressible Joe ordered a new PC. The promise of a growing Hawai'ian fleet, too, went unfulfilled, another casualty of the Great Depression.

After the Hawai'ian victory, however, the Jessop family continued to keep PCs in the news in Southern California. A few months later in 1931, George Jessop borrowed a new, still-unsold boat from its designer, and sailed to Santa Barbara to contend for Southern California's most distinguished yachting trophy. The Lipton Cup had been donated to the San Diego Yacht Club in 1906 by the British tea magnate—and perpetual *America*'s Cup also-ran—Sir Thomas Lipton. It had spent eight years decorating trophy shelves in other California yacht clubs, the last two of them far from San Diego. When George Jessop's borrowed PC surged ahead to win, skippers of the larger Eight-Meter boats and other

competitors were left struggling vainly to make up the handicap time—and closely studying their new rival.

The Lipton Cup win also demonstrated how slow local newspapers were to catch wind of the fact that they had an extraordinary new boat on their bay. Perhaps the sportswriter who ventured that George Jessop won "because the *Scamp II* seemed to know that the Lipton trophy really belonged to their city" was being facetious, but other reporters sounded genuinely puzzled at the PC's repeated success. "By an odd coincidence," one wrote, "the first three boats all were of the P.C. design, although the handicap method gave all classes of craft an equal chance."

Joe Jessop kept up his own charm offensive on the PC's behalf, persuading Doug Giddings's father to buy his 15-year-old son a PC in 1932. "My father said, 'He doesn't know *anything* about racing a boat.'" Joe replied, "No problem"—and offered, as a bonus, to throw in the expertise of his nephew Arthur Jessop as a tutor in racing's finer points. "So, for one whole year Art crewed for me and coached me on the sailing of a PC"—a sort of human rebate offer that Joe and Art also extended to the Springstead brothers.

George Kettenburg Jr. proved highly skilled in both sailing and sales. Doug Giddings recalls him as "the world's best salesman. He had a way of being friendly, and he had a way of convincing you that he was talking sense—he helped Joe talk my father into buying me a PC." George needed every available ounce of his natural charm to sell yachts in the depths of the Depression, even as membership in the Yacht Club itself steadily slipped. He regularly took potential clients sailing, to wow them with his boat's characteristics. Racing "was all a part of the business," George's younger brother explained. "If we could prove that the boats could do what we thought they should do, why, people would be interested."

As his crew, George frequently brought along a high school student named Jim Underwood Jr.,

whose older brother Charlie already worked alongside their father at Kettenburg Boat Works. "During the summers of my high school years I would hitch-hike from Pacific Beach to Point Loma almost every Sunday to sail as George's regular crew," recalled Underwood. "We'd take out prospective buyers so that they could crew along with us and get firsthand experience of sailing on a PC." The experience was an eye-opener for young Underwood. "I felt awkward—I was a poor kid from Pacific Beach, and our circumstances were pretty meager, and here I was over there with people of means, you know?" But, "George was a wonderful skipper, and a terrific person," commented Underwood, who would spend years working for Kettenburg.

Honing his sailing skills as a form of inexpensive advertising, George Jr. became a strong competitor at the tiller of *Scamp*. Soon he was recognized as one of the yacht club's top ten skippers. He never seems, however, to have let his competitive urges overmaster his naturally pleasant disposition, even toward high schoolers who worked for him. "Before we ever started in the race, he would say, 'Now, I'm gonna get

excited and say some things I don't mean,'" Underwood remembered. "If you've ever done any sailboat racing, you know what *I* mean. George wasn't one to use profanity—but he'd get the idea across!"

"My memory of George was that you couldn't race against a nicer fellow," agreed Doug Giddings, "he'd never get mad and yell." The volatile team of Doug and his older brother Don—who, according to Doug, deserved the sobriquet "the Nasty Giddings Brothers"—put this quality to the test. In August 1935, as they dueled with *Scamp* down to a marker off the B Street pier, "George Kettenburg was racing, and just before we reached the mark he happened to swing over right in front of us. My brother got mad because he thought he cut us off, so he ran to the bow of the PC, and those were the days when they had a fixed backstay." Reaching across the water to *Scamp*, "he grabs the backstay and *pulls* it—and cracks George's mast!"

"He didn't blow up," Giddings recalled, with something like awe.

Win or lose, after races George Kettenburg joined his competitors on the yacht club's float to

talk over details of the race, often sipping a Coke alongside underaged competitors who clearly idolized him. In 1934, the float moved much closer to the boatyard, as Dick Hershey and others volunteered to tow the San Diego Yacht Club's clubhouse across the bay from Coronado to the club's new location, conveniently close to Kettenburg's.

PC racing took place in a far more relaxed atmosphere than the intense competitiveness that has come to characterize yacht racing since the Second World War. "You didn't really have to win—you'd have fun if you came in last," says Giddings, who found the atmosphere truly "Corinthian," in the best tradition of yachting.

The PC class did something quite unusual: we were up to about, maybe, eighteen boats racing at a time on Sunday, and the same boats were coming near the tail end all the

Right: *Scamp* leads *Wings* on a spinnaker run past the navy base. Opposite: A fleet of PCs races down the bay, mostly under spinnakers, ca. 1941. Out front is *Skylark* (PC 31), one of the new "DeLuxe" PCs with elongated cabin.

time. So one of the fellas … came up with the idea; he said "Let's start a Saturday series, so that if you were in the group of the last eight boats, you may race on a Saturday—but those were the only people who could race, and there will always be a winner of that group." And it was very popular, because those fellas who didn't have the experience or expertise now were able to go out and know that they were going to do well in a race.

In this comparatively casual atmosphere, pranks were commonplace. When Art Jessop and Bob Hemming challenged another PC to race home from the Coronado Islands after a day spent diving for abalones, they won handily, although it was pointed out "what a coincidence it was that six of the shellfish should have been found growing on the hull of the losing boat!"

The most competitive young racers, of course, were not exactly nodding off over their tillers. Doug, who won San Diego's PC fleet championships four times before the war, bent the class rules by having *Windy* hauled out at the yard while he was away at college to enable him to sail her "dry" when he returned—always a slight advantage with a wooden boat. Competitive sailors like the Giddings brothers took advantage of every conceivable opportunity—and occasionally some misconceived ones. Doug recalled one race in front of the Yacht Club, in which competitors included *Varya*, skippered by retired businessman Samuel Dauchy, lately commodore of Chicago's yacht club:

> There was a south wind blowing, and I told my brother (who was always my crew), I said, "You know, we're going to have to put the spinnaker up as soon as the starting gun goes off, so let's wrap the spinnaker—this

time, to get a real quick break, we'll wrap it in toilet paper." Which we did; we got some toilet paper out of the yacht club head. . . . The starting gun went off. We broke that spinnaker out, and the toilet paper flew all over Samuel Dauchy's PC. Well, Samuel Dauchy was about in his seventies at the time—he almost fell off. A couple minutes later the red flag went up. And he filed a protest: "unsportsmanlike conduct." I got thrown out of the race.

Don Giddings, who later became a comparatively dignified high school principal, was at least as competitive as his younger brother Doug, who recalled that Don "thoroughly enjoyed it, but the trouble is that he got a little uptight when somebody did something that he thought shouldn't be done—and he *did* tee off on them." The six-foot-four-inch crewman could be a little intimidating:

We're racing out in the ocean, and a fellow by the name of Kelly owned a PC, and we were coming up to the windward mark—and remember, both of us were on port tack—but I was leeward of Kelly and he was even with the buoy, which meant that if he gained a little bit, we'd lose our wind—and we were barely making the mark. Well, my brother saw this and, all of a sudden—to my horror—he leans over almost with his head in Kelly's cockpit: "GET OUT OF HERE!" Kelly pulls his tiller and shoots to windward and, of course, we went around the mark first—so the next day he put up his boat for sale!

Don Giddings also once took on the U.S. government, thanks to the Coast Guard's tradition of officiating at sailboat races; "We were racing and it was a light air, and therefore every breath of air counted." When an unwary cutter off Newport took *Windy*'s wind, "suddenly my brother stood up and challenged every sailor *and* the Coast Guard to meet him on the beach that night—and called them a few names." Doug

Giddings was later ordered to apologize by his club's commodore, for officialdom had been miffed enough to insist that "unless there was some apology made that evening they would no longer patrol any yacht race in Southern California. That was the only time I can recall ever calling the Coast Guard to tell them I was sorry for what had happened!" Capturing this same competitive spirit in a few words is Doug's 1939 telegram to Joe Jessop: "Best of luck until we meet—then watch out."

Joe Jessop and his brother George were another pair of fiercely competitive siblings—but toward each other, as a magazine reported: "Their favorite pastime is sailing their Pacific Coast one design sloops and the brotherly rivalry is continuous. Not long ago Joe quit pricing Christmas jewelry long enough to inform his brother, George, that he (Joe) could collect a team of sailors that could and would lick the sox off a similar team headed by his brother." Joe's boast proved on target, but barely; his team narrowly took the impromptu series.

As the new design was putting San Diego on

the sailboat-building map, the map of the bay itself was being gradually transformed as dredging and filling reshaped its shoreline and bottom. Dredging was principally intended to encourage a reluctant navy to expand its presence there. In 1936, when Joe Jessop's *Ni-Ni-Nie* beat George Kettenburg's *Scamp* and "romped home" as winner of a local newspaper's handicap trophy, Jessop won despite the fact that "mud flats, and winds cut off by battleships proved to be hazards as the race progressed." Dredges would scour away the mud flats, but the big haze-gray wind barriers would steadily increase in number. As the first PC was being lofted, a major round of dredging was completed to permit the navy to ease its biggest ship, the aircraft carrier *Saratoga*, up to San Diego's front door.

The view from the boat works itself was changing, too. Dredging had begun in late 1934 to deepen the yacht basin, and under navy auspices they continued to pile spoil atop a shallow sandbar near the club. In an informal contest to give their growing sandbar a name, yacht club members debated suggestions like the mundane

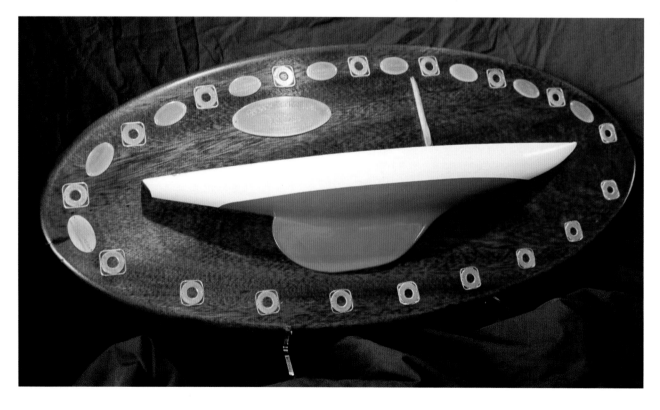

Left: The George Kettenburg PC Class trophy. Right: DeLuxe PC 31, *Skylark*, built in 1941, races in San Diego Bay with a U.S. Navy aircraft carrier in the background.

Right: Having survived the worst of the Great Depression, George Kettenburg (standing center, with sweater vest) and his crew smile for the camera as they prepare to launch a new PC in October 1937. Below: Sitting in a cradle on the ways at low tide, the new PC has her rigging set up in October 1937.

"Channel Island" and the more descriptive "San-D," before settling on "Shelter Island"—reflecting hopes that it would protect their club's new home from the waves. When Joe Jessop and Paul Kettenburg were boys, Joe recalled, "all of us kids thought it was great stuff to go out on Shelter Island and tramp around," an experience like "going to the South Sea Islands." Paul remembered that "when I was a kid I went out there and got clams, and sold 'em to the fishermen on the beach." More dredging would follow World War II, as Shelter Island would grow into a palm-fringed peninsula of hotels, restaurants, and marinas by the mid-1950s.

The muddy shallows could provide advan-

OCT. 1937

tages to those skippers who knew how to use them. The canny George Kettenburg, recalled Jim Underwood, knew

where the shallow water was, and he'd cut it—depending on the tide; he'd always take advantage of the tide, one way or the other. If the tide was going in and we were going out, he'd go over to the shallow as close as he could. And once in awhile he'd miscalculate, and we'd feel the boat just sort of— UGGGH!—dig in, and then really quickly grab the spinnaker pole and start pushing in the mud, and then somebody else'd grab hold of the shrouds on the leeward side, and try to heel the boat over a little bit more—so it wouldn't have quite as much draft.

At least one PC owner used these shallows to more personal advantage. Scofield Bonnet, heir to a wealthy local grocer, "would invite a girl-friend out on his PC at a time when high tide was about three o'clock in the afternoon," according to Doug Giddings. "He would sail around the bay, then at the exact high tide he'd run aground. So they were there and they couldn't get off and so he would tell her, 'I'm sorry—we're stuck here for at least eight hours.'" Giddings recalled, "I thought *that* was very clever."

Leisure boating in Southern California continued to grow despite the Depression. In 1934 Southern California's expanding marinas boasted 4,200 yachts, and a few years later San Diego alone claimed about 600 yachtsmen. Dredging was also transforming a smaller muddy estuary 70 miles up the coast in Orange County into another yachtsman's haven—and a crucial new market for the PC. As Newport Harbor's dredging neared completion in 1936, its fleet of PCs had already been threading through their evolving harbor for three years. By the end of the decade, San Diego's dozen PCs were regularly challenged by 11 Newport boats, the first and largest fleet outside San Diego Bay. "So we had a Newport PC fleet and a San Diego PC fleet.

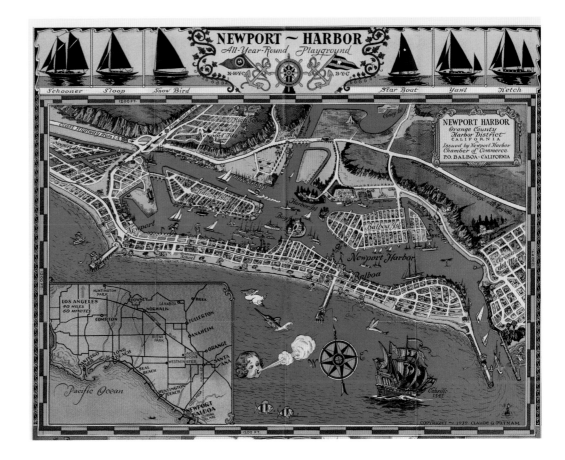

Well, that made an excellent competition," remembered Giddings.

After this success, George began making contacts still further north. As L. G. Swales began selling PCs for him in Newport Harbor, the Willis Hunt Company set up to do the same in Los Angeles. And, Giddings recalled, "George went to San Francisco to see whether he could start a fleet in San Francisco, which never really took off . . . he was hoping that he could get PC fleets all up and down the Pacific Coast." San Francisco Bay, with its heavy wind and weather, did not get its first PCs until winter 1939, when two left the Kettenburg yard on trucks. One was headed for Kettenburg's newest representative, Ernest "Bud" Coxhead of Richmond, and the other for former Olympian and international Star Class champion Glenn Waterhouse.

Perhaps at the invitation of fellow Star Class champion Joe Jessop, Glenn Waterhouse had sailed a PC during a lull in the 1935 Star national championships, held on San Diego Bay to coin-

"The vast resources of Nature coupled with the genius of man have transformed Newport Harbor into the finest all-year-round play-ground on the Pacific Coast" proclaimed the chamber of commerce on this 1939 promotional map. San Diegans might disagree, but they happily took their PCs up there to race.

cide with the California Pacific International Exposition up the hill in Balboa Park. "Having decided after mature consideration that the PC would do well on San Francisco bay," journalist Jerry MacMullen reported, Waterhouse "began discussing matters with George Kettenburg, and lo and behold, soon there was a bit of signing on the dotted line." Waterhouse raced this PC vigorously on San Francisco Bay before the war, and afterwards became Kettenburg's San Francisco Bay area representative. He even undertook, for "fun" and publicity, to sail a PC the 500 miles from San Diego to Berkeley, against winds and currents. What with the PCs spreading to San

ness." Hubbard also had a reputation as a "tough guy," a heavy drinker who didn't get along with a lot of people.

His South Coast Boat Building Company quickly grew to dwarf Kettenburg after he founded it in Newport Harbor, just to the north in Orange County, in 1933. Gerry Driscoll, who worked at Kettenburgs' before starting his own boatyard, was astonished by its scale: "I remember going up to South Coast, and my eyes just bugged out—here's a whole *paved* yard; everything was so different!" Driscoll thought it was "by far the best. If you wanted a yard, that one you'd better take a look at." Like Kettenburg,

sory George wouldn't acquire until 1939.

"George Kettenburg was so successful selling PCs to Newport, that Walton Hubbard of South Coast couldn't stand it," and—Gene also remembered—"he couldn't stand George. He said, 'Give me some rights and I'll pay a royalty to build PCs up here.' So George gave him the lines." After seeing the PCs race in the 1933 Santa Barbara regatta, several members of Newport Harbor Yacht Club had ordered PCs of their own from South Coast. "Here's a class at last," Hubbard himself enthused, "comfortable, dry, and evenly matched where winning is in no way dependent upon the amount of money the

After seeing the PCs race in the 1933 Santa Barbara regatta, several members of Newport Harbor Yacht Club had ordered PCs of their own from South Coast. "Here's a class at last," Hubbard himself enthused, "comfortable, dry, and evenly matched where winning is in no way dependent upon the amount of money the owner spends."

Francisco and the four boats already in Hawai'i, a magazine article's title could legitimately trumpet that these "Fast, Scrappy Little Racers Interest Yachtsmen in Many Pacific Ports."

As PC competition blossomed at Newport, however, a formidable commercial adversary also appeared there. Fifty years after the fact, at least a few Kettenburg veterans still harbored a grudge toward Walton Hubbard Jr. and his boatyard. "The rip off by South Coast Boat and the PC's struggle for survival" was the tart phrase chosen by George's master carpenter Charlie Underwood, painter Jimmy's son.

Walt Hubbard was a few years younger than George, and likewise a well-respected yachtsman and fierce competitor; as a 19-year-old he had captured the world Star class title in 1927. Giddings remembered him as "a very businesslike person—he wasn't the type of George, who was very friendly; Walt was strictly busi-

but on a grander scale, Hubbard pursued a dream of a fully integrated boatyard that would design, build, repair, and sell yachts.

"Kettenburg's was kind of built on a shoestring," agrees Gene Trepte, whose father's company had constructed the yard's buildings. As a boy, he too had been impressed when he visited Newport Harbor: "South Coast was in a very populated area—a very nice commercial area near the end of the peninsula, and it had a beautiful showroom where they sold all kinds of little boats. It was a beautiful yard, and he had all the big fancy Six Meters and Eight Meters in a row there."

It was indeed a revelation compared to its mostly unpaved and certainly unglamorous San Diego rival, where George himself frequently ran the Ford Model A engine that pulled boats up the single-track marine railway. South Coast boasted space to store yachts dry, plucking them out of the water with a large crane—an acces-

owner spends." By 1934, his South Coast crew had built three PCs, launching a fourth in 1937, but they proved slower than the boats George's shop was building. PC sailor Milt Wegeforth recalled that "George Kettenburg didn't particularly like the way that they had built them, so he stopped them from building any more." Gene Trepte, too, noticed that "those boats were never very fast. I said, 'George, did you really give him the *real* lines?' I used to kid him."

Speaking as the designer he became, Charlie Underwood explained that any naval architect's "hull 'lines drawing' is a treasure—you don't let *anybody* have that; they have your innermost secret when they have your lines drawing, and they can duplicate your work. Well, George being a good honest man, wasn't suspecting anything, and he also gave them all of the templates, and assisted them in any way he could to get the boat into production."

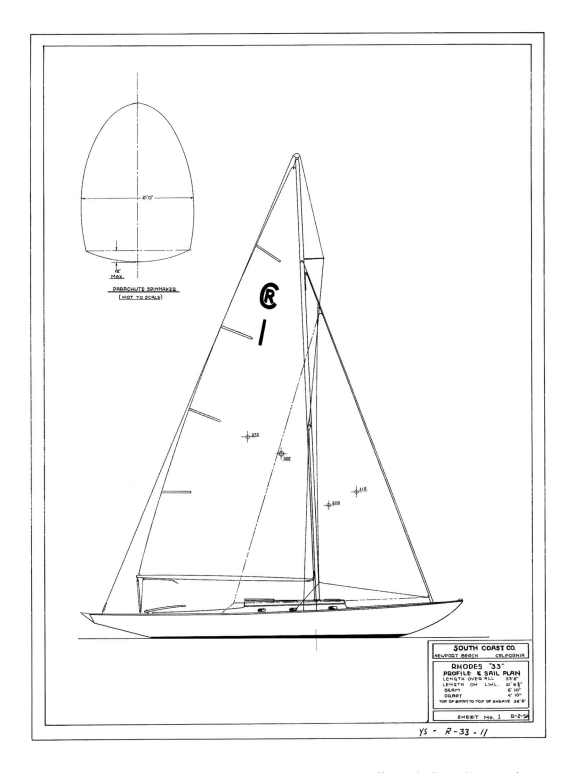

PARACHUTE SPINNAKER
(NOT TO SCALE)

SOUTH COAST CO.
NEWPORT BEACH   CALIFORNIA

RHODES "33"
PROFILE & SAIL PLAN
LENGTH OVER ALL   33'6"
LENGTH ON L.W.L.   21' 6¾"
BEAM   6' 10"
DRAFT   4' 10"
TOP OF BOOM TO TOP OF SHEAVE 36'2"

SHEET No. 1   R-2-5A

YS - R-33 - 11

⊹ To compete with the PC, South Coast intro-
duced the Rhodes 33 in 1938. Although it
was based on a Rhodes design for the
Great Lakes and had a larger cabin than the
PC, the 33's hull was rather similar to the
PC's; however, the rig was more like an
Atlantic's, with three-quarter headstay,
jumper struts, and no running backstays.

"The rip off," as Charlie put it, occurred once
George pulled the plug on Hubbard. Perhaps
feeling stung, the Newport yacht builder decided
to try beating Kettenburg at his own game. He
turned east, asking New Yorker Phil Rhodes to
create a design to compete precisely in the PC's
market niche. Philip L. Rhodes, nine years
George's senior, was an MIT-educated naval

architect who designed boats for Cox & Stevens.
Hubbard was building several of his small
designs. While George was untutored, with
design methods rooted primarily in intuition and
observation, Phil embodied naval architecture's
future, relying increasingly on science to guide
the lines he drew.

In 1938, South Coast introduced the Rhodes
33, one of several narrow racing boats with deep
cockpits that Phil Rhodes was then designing.
Heavier and just slightly longer than a PC, the
33's sail area was greater by only a single square
foot. Significantly, however, the 33's interior fittings far outshone the more primitive PC, with
amenities that the Kettenburg boat noticeably
lacked, and, at $2,950, was identically priced.
The "airy cabin" advertised for the 33 was far
pleasanter than the PC's cramped wooden dun-
geon, and it featured an inboard well into which
one could drop a small outboard motor whenever needed. The Rhodes' two-burner stove and
head were luxuries about which PC owners had
fantasized for years. As Giddings recalled of the
PC, "it didn't have any toilet facilities aboard, so
we would carry a bucket on which our . . . round
life ring would fit. So, you *could* sit on the life
ring"—a less than ideal setup for what was
intended as a "family" racing-cruising boat.

"The Rhodes 33 smashed the Kettenburg PC,
because of its added facilities," Charlie
Underwood ruefully admitted. From a sales perspective, the 33 was a triumph, and a considerable setback for George. "Before you buy any
boat," Hubbard gloated in an advertisement,
"check it for cruising comfort with the Rhodes
33'. If you'll do that, we're sure to be seeing
you—in a Rhodes Class Cruiser." Hubbard sold
20 of his 33s before the war to people who
might otherwise have bought PCs, and South
Coast launched 22 more after Hubbard's
untimely death in 1944. As Charlie recalled,
"when George found out, he also found out
there was nothing he could do about it. Because
of the increased headroom in the cabin, and the
added facilities of the head and galley cabinets,

The "DeLuxe" PC *Lady Jene* ready for launch in 1946. She was one of nearly 50 of the improved PCs built between 1945 and 1952.

The introduction of this "DeLuxe" PC was something of a local news event, drawing 20 skippers south from L.A. to test-sail it. Visitors admired the expanded cabin's much-improved cruising accommodations, praised as "an entirely new feature in this hitherto strictly racing class of boats."

this stopped George's sale on the PCs dead in their tracks. And there wasn't anything that he could do to revive the PC"—short of radically revamping its interior. Kettenburg scrambled to catch up.

Duels between the classes began immediately, for Don Giddings persuaded George that "the way to beat Hubbard is to set up a race with the Rhodes and the PCs, because we're all sure the PCs will win." Off Newport in 1939, the Giddings brothers in *Windy*, George Kettenburg in *Scamp*, Joe Jessop in *Misty,* and his brother George in *Wings* met their Rhodes 33 rivals in a race on points. They had the satisfaction of taking the novice 33-racers 59 to 48. Doug Giddings said of the Rhodes that "those who raced it felt it was a better racing boat, but I never perceived that—I think a PC could outsail it." Skippers who have raced both agree that the Rhodes was faster in heavy going, but, says Doug, "we were able to outmaneuver them with the PC. It was relatively a friendly battle, but there was no question about it—Hubbard was fighting Kettenburg."

The shop introduced several improvements to the PC to counter Phil Rhodes' better-appointed design. The San Diego Yacht Club's newsletter reported in 1940 that "the P.C. skippers, voting to have wells built in their boats, will soon be 'outboarding' around the bay between races. No longer will they be thumbing rides when the winds fail." The first Rhodes-inspired well was installed in the cockpit floor of the much-publicized new "DeLuxe" PC in late 1940, permitting an outboard engine to be dropped into place when needed. Those who could endure the gasoline fumes wafting up from the floor no longer had to suffer adventures like the 23-hour sail (not including the three-hour tow) that *Ni-Ni-Nie* required to return from Newport in 1937—a distance of around 70 miles—or that of the sailors who drifted home from a Catalina regatta "in a wind that failed to waft cigarette smoke from the cockpit."

The introduction of this "DeLuxe" PC was

something of a local news event, drawing 20 skippers south from L.A. to test-sail it. Visitors admired the expanded cabin's much-improved cruising accommodations, praised as "an entirely new feature in this hitherto strictly racing class of boats" by local yachting columnist Josephine Israel White. A relative of hers had designed the raised dog house over the cabin entrance that minimized head-banging by tall owners. An appreciative magazine writer noted that "the new cabin is furnished with plenty of portholes, thus affording ample light, which is a great relief and improvement over the present PC cabins." ("Room like the civic auditorium," wrote another, in simulated awe.) Forward of the mast was a new hatch affording easy access to the jib, a feature also found on the Rhodes 33. As another writer noted dryly, the new boat "will have a galley, bunks, and even running water. It is asserted that some PC skippers drink water."

"Needless to say," Charlie Underwood put it, "everyone at our plant was furious with Rhodes and South Coast for doing that to George's PC design. Somehow we wanted to recapture the market, and put Rhodes and South Coast back in their place. I personally wanted revenge." After the war, Charlie supervised the PC's comeback, and "really caught the South Coast Company off guard" as George's company slashed a quarter off the PC's price and outproduced the Rhodes 33. Thanks in part to these changes, Kettenburg's sales regained their competitive footing.

The first of very few performance-enhancing alterations permitted to the PC class had come about in December 1935, in order to improve the boats' already impressively close finishes against far more expensive boats of the Six-Meter Class. The PC Association's members sat down with Hubbard and Kettenburg at the Newport Harbor Yacht Club and agreed to alter the PC's rig and increase its sail area, replacing the conventional jib with a larger Genoa sail that overlapped the mast. Some racers remained skeptical of these unwieldy Jennies. George explained to Doug Giddings that, "'we've got to

✧ The airy, enlarged cabin and roomy cockpit of a new DeLuxe PC gleam with varnish.

go to the bigger sail, in order to get faster," but decades later Giddings still groused that "I didn't like 'em worth a bean. It took the pleasure out of racing—racing became just a job, then."

With more pressure on the forward side of the mast, a pair of running backstays was added aft to offset the stresses on the mast. The new Genoa (which had to be let go and sheeted in again each time the boat tacked) and the running backstays on either side of the mast (which had to be alternately eased and set up as the boat tacked) made for some awkward racing. "What Bill and I used to do was run the backstays back and forth when we were little kids," recalls Trepte. Gene and young Bill Kettenburg began their sailing lives by rapidly sliding the "cars" attached to the port and starboard backstays along their tracks as the boat tacked, hauling the windward one taut and sliding the leeward one forward, out of the way of the boom. Forgetting to adjust backstays could have disastrous—not to mention expensive—consequences. Wally Springstead, a postwar PC champion, remembered the much-cursed backstays as "an encumbrance."

George—who designed everything—figured that they were not fitting for the kind of

boat that he wanted to be the author of. It was supposed to be a convenient boat, that was easy to sail, and that your families could sail, and that we could race. Oh God—if you were a little bit late, sometimes they'd hook around the spreader, y'know, goin' downwind, and you couldn't get 'em back—it just wasn't a smooth deal.

George Kettenburg had established a trophy, and the PC Association itself, to encourage class racing. By the late 1930s, the PCs burgeoned into California's largest racing class, helped a great deal by racing's free publicity. In 1934, for example, newspapers covered a match on San Diego Bay between officers from the visiting German cruiser *Karlsruhe* and American naval

officers in PCs borrowed from Joe Jessop and George Kettenburg. The Nazi Navy won this round, but soon officers from His Majesty's Navy (which would send the *Karlsruhe* to the bottom when she was supporting the invasion of Norway in 1940) praised their borrowed PCs with characteristically British aplomb as "extraordinarily trim" after their own race a few months later. Joe and George likewise succeeded in placing the skippers in the first intercollegiate sailing competition held among West Coast universities at the tillers of loaned PCs. In an odd twist, the victor in this 1936 event hailed from a college many miles from salt water. Journalist Jerry MacMullen rubbed that salt into the wounds of other schools: "Jokes about the Swiss Navy and the yacht clubs of the Rocky Mountains are in bad

taste these days, and their telling, especially around the campuses of seaboard universities, may be risky. For the first Pacific Coast intercollegiate regatta has been held—and it was won by the University of Arizona." The student sailor at the helm was Doug Giddings.

The finest publicity coup for Joe Jessop was recruiting "Jimmy," son of the avid sailor President Franklin Roosevelt, into the PC fleet. Bob Wise's photo of George with the younger Roosevelt, aboard *Half Moon* at her 1938 launching, was picked up by the wire services and brought the class wide publicity.

Travel to distant regattas along the West Coast was routine for "The P.C. Boys" on their way to race. "We'd go up to the regattas in Santa Barbara and live on the boats, and

Left: At the 1938 launch of James Roosevelt's *Half Moon*, PC 29, Joe Jessop presented Roosevelt with the life preserver carrying the boat's name, then George Kettenburg joined Roosevelt on board. Right: George Kettenburg and Ken Bojens with a PC trophy, Memorial Day 1940.

Catalina and all," remembered Joe Jessop, "so we had lots of fun racing. It was a great class." Getting there was another matter. Samuel Dauchy told *Yachting* readers that "four hardy sailors can—and do—pass fairly comfortable nights on the long passage (two hundred miles) to Santa Barbara," but almost no-one made those passages for fun, given the challenges that winds and currents pose to boats sailing north.

The young racers usually tried to hitch a tow. After Newport Harbor Yacht Club hosted its first annual Race Week in 1937, Oakley Hall, who owned San Diego's Star & Crescent ferryboats, was one of those who helped out. As Doug Giddings remembered:

the PCs in groups always went to the

Newport Race Week, and also the Pacific Coast Regatta when it was held up the coast. So a deal was made with old Captain Oakley Hall, and in those days Oakley Hall had an oil barge that came down from San Pedro full of oil, filled up his tanks here, and then went back empty. He said, "OK—I'll tow your PCs to where you want to go, behind the barge when we are going north." So, when we would go to Newport Race Week, we'd all tie up at each corner of the barge. The barge would swing in off Newport, always whistle, we'd toss the line off, and we'd go on in.

The positive effects of a quick tow to the next race could sometimes be undercut by ill effects, mostly digestive. Jim Underwood Jr.

remembered a nighttime arrival at Newport, when he was crew for George Kettenburg on *Scamp*:

I remember one time, there were a string of us—I guess there might've been six PCs in a row behind a navy tug. And that navy tug was putting out black smoke and we were first in line, and it was coming back. . . . I got really, really sick that time. We were just off Newport Harbor . . . and we were cut loose, and George hollered to me, "Get the sails out!" And I'm down in the bunk . . . and I put my hand over on the sail [bag], and I couldn't move, and he looked down there and said, "Omigosh! Jimmy's sick!"

"George got us into the Newport Harbor

Yacht Club safely," despite his crew's queasiness.
"You know how it is," continued Jim: "you feel
as though you're going to die but you're afraid
that you won't."

When another Kettenburg boat, the handsome big motor cruiser *Joanne*, served as a tow-
boat, it had similar effects on Doug Giddings:

*the Pacific Coast Regatta was scheduled for
Santa Barbara, and we were trying to figure
out how in the holy heck would we get to*

*Santa Barbara. So, Wally Springstead said, "I
got an idea." The next thing we knew, his
father volunteered. . . . He said, "I'll tow you
to Santa Barbara." Well, we arrived down
here for the day of the tow and learned it
was a single line. He was just going to have a
big hawser. I was "coming up"—I got fourth
or fifth place in line . . . put the hawser over
the deck, tied our bow line to it, with a stern
line just to keep us from swaying. Off we
went. One of the things that I didn't like was
that the meal that my mother put up in a
sack for all of us was all fried chicken. And I
was very susceptible.*

The state of Doug's stomach had improved
by the time he woke up the next morning—until
he discovered that "the hawser had sawed a
complete groove in the cabin top of the PC,
because it was resting on the cabin top and
going back and forth. We had a groove about
three inches wide, clear through the cabin!"
"Well," remembered Doug, "*that* was pure stu-
pidity."

Doug also was among those who found
another "interesting way to use the PC": as a
surfboard to ride Ralph's, a break near the tip of
Point Loma. "The PC was a great large surfboard, and you could get in a long swell in the

"When you are working to windward—toward L.A.—as you are going up to the weather mark you have to stay in close to the surf, so we all tacked back and forth along the surf line. Well, sometimes you could judge it wrong, and you go up on a big wave as *Scamp* did and you come down—*Boom!* You hit the bottom."

westerly breeze, because you were in a reach. Then by balancing the boat, you could actually ride the swell into Ralph's. The trick was, of course, to get out of the swell before you got into shallow water." Doug remembered that on one occasion his PC "happened to land us with its mast stuck up in the bottom." With some embarrassment they refloated their boat, but the next PC to go ashore was not so lucky.

In 1939, near the end of a decade that began with George Kettenburg designing the first PC, and during which the class had spread up along the West Coast, disaster struck. In a handicap race at Newport in August, Gene Trepte was sailing in an Eight Meter when he saw trouble suddenly overtake George. Gene explained of the Newport course that, "when you are working to windward—toward L.A.—as you are going up to the weather mark you have to stay in close to the surf, so we all tacked back and forth along the surf line. Well, sometimes you could judge it wrong, and you go up on a big wave as *Scamp* did and you come down—*Boom!* You hit the bottom."

Newport sailor Bob Allan was crewing for Harlan Beardslee, a world champion in the Star class who would become the first Rhodes 33 champion. Bob watched too, transfixed with horror:

I was crewing with "Hook" Beardslee on his Rhodes 33 in a team race against the PCs. We were covering George Kettenburg, and George got in a bit too close. A wave caught him and threw him up on the beach, and one of his crew members . . . went to jump out, and just then another wave threw the boat

right on top of him. I watched all this with horror as a crew member, and "Hook" Beardslee, in his best sailing competition manner, said: "Well, that's one boat. Don't watch him anymore. Watch your jib." So you see—I learned you have to concentrate in racing.

The culprit? Beyond George Kettenburg's own competitive instincts, the Giddings Brothers in *Windy* were nearby. "I ran George Kettenburg aground at Newport," admited Doug.

We were racing—George and I having a head-to-head, and you had to tack as close as you could to the breaker line in order to get out of the current and get the most wind. And I'll have to admit it was my aggressiveness that caused George to wait too long to come about on starboard tack, and a wave caught him, and he ended up on the beach. By the time the workmen had got there, the PC had filled completely with sand. Therefore, when they went to move it, it just broke in half. That was the end of PC number one. But Mabel Jessop will never forgive me, because she was on the beach.

Joe Jessop's wife "really bawled me out," remembered Doug, with a shudder.

The original PC was lost. "Well, George was philosophical," Gene Trepte recalled. "I think he was sort of embarrassed, but he was a kind of quiet guy, you know, and I don't think he made a hell of a lot of fuss over it—it was just one of those things that happened."

Not long after that unexpected wave cap-

sized the first PC and left her builder drenched on the beach, history overtook Kettenburg Boat Works just as the PC was catching on in the brightening wartime American economy. A 1941 ad proclaimed "The Pacific Class Takes All the Firsts!," a statement that was beginning to be perceived as more than just advertising hyperbole. Racing success had carried the company through the nation's hard times, with one result evident in another ad's more-or-less truthful headline: "The Pacific Class Sloop is in Every Port in California and Honolulu." In April 1941, Honolulu buyers ordered three more PCs, augmenting the four that Hawai'ians had bought from the victorious San Diegans a decade before. Until December 7, that is, when Japanese torpedo bombers and fighters roared over the harbor where Joe Jessop had raced PCs into the national spotlight. Before the smoke cleared, Pearl Harbor was choked with the broken pride of America's Pacific Fleet, including the battleships *Arizona*, *Oklahoma*, *California*, and *Nevada*. Unnoticed amidst the catastrophe and carnage that Sunday morning was a damaged sloop, formerly named *Blue Jacket*, in which Joe Jessop had once beaten Hawai'i's S-boats.

Virtually overnight, pleasure boat construction, leisure sailing, and offshore racing halted in America. Shortly after the "DeLuxe" 31st PC was afloat, Doug Giddings and the other young racers joined the navy or were drafted. George did not stay stunned and stranded for long; he sought government contracts to keep his boatyard afloat. In the process he would discover talent among his crew that would radically change the way every future Kettenburg boat was built.

Chapter Five

Learning to Compete in Wartime

From the Ugliest Boat in the World to the Cadillac of Fish Boats

A group of Kettenburg-built navy plane-rearming boats plows across San Diego Bay. Inset: George (left) and Paul Kettenburg pose with Ken Baker (right) outside the main shop, ca. 1944.

George Kettenburg (second from left) and the expanded yard crew pose in front of one of the 33-foot plane-rearming boats. During the war the crew included women and most of San Diego's ethnic and racial groups.

Dick Hershey and Lucretia
drift placidly in a Rhodes-
designed, Kettenburg-built
Penguin, an 11-foot frostbite
dinghy built in 1942.

G ravel sprayed from beneath the tires
as a late-model Ford coupe swung
into a dirt parking lot on Point
Loma. The man behind the wheel
may have grinned to himself with
a touch of family pride to see the
welcoming black-on-white letters
spelling "Kettenburg Boat Works"
on the side of the big metal building. His car's
Illinois plates, windshield adorned with 1943's
most coveted priority gas ration stickers, and
ticking engine—shedding heat built up on a long
haul across mountains and desert—were dead
giveaways; he had driven far. Twenty-nine-year-
old Paul Kettenburg unbent his six-foot frame,
straightened up, and perhaps winced—his sole

souvenir of the 2,090-mile drive down Route 66
from Chicago was a sore back. Anybody who
made this drive in wartime—when everything
from gas to tire rubber to highway speed was
rationed—would be thankful to have arrived, but
Paul especially so. When he left home in 1933 he
had anticipated that he'd be gone a year, but ten
years had passed. It was November 1943, and in
the months since he and his brother George had
excitedly spoken on the phone, Paul had hacked
through a thicket of red tape to get here.

When Paul had left, "this boatyard was practically dead, because of the Depression," which
dictated that "by ten in the morning we were all
through with everything we had to do." He
remembered, too, that "there really wasn't

The Second World War had begun at the yard with a last flurry of peacetime pleasure-boat building. Just over a month after Pearl Harbor, early 1942 saw a mass launching of almost 20 frostbite dinghies 11-foot open sailboats of a style intended for winter racing in the Northeast.

enough to keep us both busy at the yard—my brother could handle everything that there was to be handled." After graduation in 1933 Paul had followed his high-school sweetheart back to Chicago. Years of responsibility there as a field engineer at General Electric, where his new father-in-law had hired him, had matured the baby of the family. Wartime policies, however, froze him into his job, despite his efforts to join the Seabees or return home. But now the time had come to get back to business, and back to his first love of building boats. During his ten years away, however, another man—a paragon of efficiency named Charlie Underwood—had risen to become his brother's trusted right-hand man. Who would stay at Kettenburg, and who would be shown the door?

The Second World War had begun at the yard with a last flurry of peacetime pleasure-boat building. Just over a month after Pearl Harbor, early 1942 saw a mass launching of almost 20 frostbite dinghies 11-foot open sailboats of a style intended for winter racing in the Northeast. Unlike George's junior-level Starlets, the Phil Rhodes-designed Penguin was a new nationwide class of cheap miniature racing boats for adults. They "sold like hotcakes," recalled Paul, and proved immensely popular on the bay during the war, giving sailors a sense of freedom despite the clampdown on ocean racing, and helping them forget the antisubmarine net that sealed off the harbor itself. They were christened in showers of ice cubes, with many given punning names; the younger Kettenburgs chose SS *Iceburg* for theirs. (War work, however, kept George too busy to sail, and he sold her.) More than 50 sped about the bay by the war's end. Newspaper columnist Josephine White thought "the boats—nineteen

of them at George Kettenburg's, all turned bottoms up—look like a bunch of Easter eggs with their gayest of color schemes." The vivid colors of peacetime pleasure boating, however, would soon turn to wartime grays.

By the time Paul returned in 1943, Kettenburg Boat Works had become a wartime success story, having mastered high-volume production, on budget, without sacrificing quality. But success had come neither quickly nor painlessly. Shortly after the U.S. declared war, George attained every businessman's goal and landed a lucrative government contract: his crew would build plane-rearming boats—a utilitarian navy design intended to ferry munitions to seaplanes. But he miscalculated badly on the time his inexpert crew needed to construct these 33-foot wooden boats. As Charlie Underwood, his master carpenter, recalled, "George was trying so hard to get his prices down, that he underpriced everything. And he figured man-hours at the speed he could produce when he was most productive—and no one else could produce that fast; he just was a whirlwind. And so when he figured labor that way, things came out wrong."

George had based his bid on Charlie's projection that they could complete a new boat every four days. Each boat, however, was demanding over five days of work. Rather than being lucrative, this government contract was rapidly pushing George towards bankruptcy. The consultants who were called in to fix the problem identified a potential savior in his own shop. Charlie, they thought, could staunch the hemorrhage of expensive production time. "He was the smart one," Gene Trepte remembered.

The consultants' visit was a key event for Charlie Underwood. After the war, its repercus-

sions enabled the little shop to transform itself into a builder of sailboats that were both competitive in racing and competitive on the market. These consultants, remembered Charlie, had been in Point Loma

for about three weeks "on the Q.T." without most people knowing they were even there. And they were interviewing all of the crew, individually. And checking on everyone's ability. At the end of this period of time, two people walked up to me, and said, "Charlie, you don't know us, but we know you, and we've watched you for the last three weeks—in fact, we've talked to everyone in this plant about you. . . . What we want you to do, now, is tell us what you're gonna do, because we're going to put you in charge of the plant. And we're gambling our fee against your ability to put this plant on a paying basis."

Charlie continued:

When I went home that night and went to sleep, I couldn't believe what had happened: that I was actually in charge of the plant—and could do anything I wanted to bring it onto a paying basis. At about two o'clock that morning, the phone rang, and it was the business engineers, and one of 'em said, "Charlie, we just been talking about what you want to do, and have checked the progress you've already made, and we decided we want to give you a raise, starting immediately." Now this was quite a shock to get awakened that way, and I was really excited about that—and got really busy on it the next day.

As everyone who knew him knows, the sight of Charlie "really busy" was something to see. He was given responsibility for stepping up production, and George approved the raise recommended by the consulting engineers. Like George and Paul, Charles A. Underwood was a high-school graduate without further formal training, but who admitted to being "a perfectionist," equipped with what his son remembers as "tremendous attention to detail." Charlie began work as a roustabout during summer vacation in 1930, then apprenticed to his father

In his less busy days Charlie Underwood enjoyed marlin fishing.

after graduating from La Jolla High as a football and track star. Young sailors looked up to him with awe; Wally Springstead remembered that "this guy was an *athlete*. He could do so many pushups with one hand that you just couldn't believe it!" In peacetime Charlie's brains and brawn had become valuable to George, particularly after Charlie replaced Dick Hershey as master carpenter in 1938. He was intensely loyal, and, as Bill Kettenburg recalled, "my dad really liked Charlie, and Charlie'd give his right arm for my dad."

Pridefulness in his work was a byproduct of Charlie's unceasing initiative and confessed perfectionism. A telling example appeared early on, when he worked in the shop, while the elder Mr. Kettenburg reluctantly kept the books:

When he found out that I'd taken typing in high school, he gave me the job of makin' out the bills. I decided I'd better go back to night school and learn a little more of typing and machine calculation—which I did. And I became very useful in making out the bills and other office work. The strange part of this arrangement was that I may have been up a mast, varnishing, when a need for typing became necessary, and I had to come down, go in, do the typing, then go back up the mast and finish that job!

Any employee who takes night classes in order to become the man his employers seek is either craven or driven—and Charlie was far from craven. During the Depression, he explained, "there was a lot of competition between the individual employees to see who could be the best, and thereby get the most work." His own deadly serious approach to work occasionally left others scratching their heads. After the war, when he had risen to head the firm's divisions of new boat design and navy work, he suggested to the naval officer in charge of a repair project on which Charlie suspected other contractors were "cheating" that *if he would tighten up the specs, then he would get the work done on the bid price and not some other price. Well, he said, "If you think you can do it, you go ahead and do it, and then I'll use your specs"—and he was only kiddin'. But I thought he was serious, so I spent the next three weeks and developed a fool-proof set of specifications, took 'em down and delivered 'em to him. . . . he didn't even remember the incident! And when I explained it to him, he said, "I can't use those!" And I said, "Well, why don't you just give 'em to your planners, and let them look 'em over, and see what they think. And if they think its good, you have 'em at your disposal—you let 'em use whatever they want to use in it." Well, as a matter of fact, the next set of boats that came out, were word-for-word my specifications!*

Any partner who is so intensely focused that he mistakes a tossed-off remark for a directive to spend three weeks on a project—a byproduct of which happens to be much more work for his company—is somebody too intense to trifle with.

The crisis in building the plane-rearming boats threatened to sink the company because they were essentially building boats as they had in 1918. The machine-shop foreman, Charlie's brother Jim Jr., explained the techniques they shared with nearly every other boatbuilder: "The way we'd always done it was building 'em from the keel up—and you're always working at a disadvantage."

To make your steam-bent frames you would have a man inside the boat. You'd go over to the steam box, where the oak would be steaming. You'd grab one of those hot pieces of oak, hand it to him—he'd press that down with a foot, and hands, into shape—and then the workers outside would clamp [it] to the longitudinal pieces, and then also we would—at the same time—cut the butt end into the keel. That was some fancy chisel work we had to do! And then screw-fasten that, and that frame would be left alone until it cooled.

Engrossed in the tedious job of lofting a plan to full-scale, Charlie Underwood checks the details of the hull lines on the loft floor. Thin wooden patterns will be used to shape the vessel's timbers.

Essentially, Charlie's "secret" was himself. His persistent, patient ability to mentally take apart and reassemble their boatbuilding processes ultimately remade the company after the war.

Charlie remembered being a carpenter squinting up at a new hull, "reaching up over your head and trying to sand, and plug the bottom, and having all of the debris fall in your eyes."

For starters, instead of building boats right-side up in the same logical but awkward fashion, they began building hulls upside down. Inverted boat construction itself was hardly novel; after Captain Nat Herreshoff watched Europeans do it this way in the 1870s, he engineered a similar construction method for small craft built at the Herreshoff Manufacturing Company in Bristol, Rhode Island. The prestigious Henry B. Nevins yacht yard on the East Coast used the process,

and in the 1930s, Herreshoff's protégé Nick Potter introduced the practice to the West Coast when the big Los Angeles builder Fellows & Stewart built his Cal 32s. But Charlie realized that building boats upside down while moving them down a production line was the key to efficiency. He set up three work stations, where separate teams of builders manned a jig, or mold, mounted on casters for easy movement. On that jig, Paul recalled, a hull took shape, was lifted off, then "we'd do the next boat—lay keel timbers, bend the frames, bend the ribs over, and then plank it—and when it was planked, we'd take it off, turn it right-side up, do the

George's crew mushroomed from just a dozen at the war's beginning to over a hundred. During the wartime labor crunch they competed for workers with Southern California's burgeoning aviation industry; Douglas Aircraft, for example, lured their onetime master carpenter Dick Hershey.

interior and the deck." Just after the war, a newspaperman marveled at Kettenburg's "production methods previously unheard of in the boat-building business." As he described: "Huge wooden molds ten feet high were designed and constructed, and upon these, the hull and planking of the plane rearming boats were laid to form an upside-down hull. Moved along by overhead cranes, the individual hulls were in convenient position at other stations for plugging, caulking, painting and inspection."

What Charlie introduced was no magical technique, but a carefully thought out, much-refined, sequence of mass production in a small shop. He planned it out carefully, for

in order to build this inside-out, upside-down creation, you had to understand how to go about it. And, in looking at it, it looked like the right way to do it, but it took me an awful long time after I got the idea to figure out how to do that. Well, I know that various people that saw that [inverted jig] decided the best thing to do would be go home, and, at their boatyard . . . start "doin' it" right away. However, the trick was, just like any secret—just like George's secret on design— that I had a secret here, and you had to know what the concept was—how it was developed—in order to go ahead and copy it.

Essentially, Charlie's "secret" was himself. His persistent, patient ability to mentally take apart and reassemble their boatbuilding processes

ultimately remade the company after the war.

Jim Underwood Jr. remembered his brother pushing the men to squeeze out "a little more speed, a little more production—get 'em out faster!" They slashed the unwanted extra day of work off the five-day building time, and began rolling boats out at the rate of five per month. Jim called the navy's snub-nosed design, complete with its pudding fender on the bow, "the most ugly boat in the world." But the 60 they finished set George's shop on a solid financial footing and taught the crew new ways of inexpensively producing formerly labor-intensive wooden boats.

George's crew mushroomed from just a dozen at the war's beginning to over a hundred. During the wartime labor crunch they competed for workers with Southern California's burgeoning aviation industry; Douglas Aircraft, for example, lured their onetime master carpenter Dick Hershey. As Jim Jr. recalled, "for us to find workers was really a challenge—we had to get a lot of old timers who'd been retired." Memorable among them to Charlie was "a one-eyed butcher, and a retired man from General Electric, who was eighty years old!" Charlie continued that, "George was left with unskilled workers. The balance of the crew was made up nearly of all schoolboys that were sixteen or seventeen

⁜ The 1944 Kettenburg Boat Works family picnic brought together a large crowd. George and Paul Kettenburg are identified in the front row; Dick Hershey is at upper right.

years old, and went to school for half a day, and work for half a day. We had thirty-two of these, with sixteen on each shift. This was almost an unmanageable task—to control those boys and to teach them something of value for the production of the boats."

A generation of women began learning the pros and cons of earning regular paychecks outside the home, for Kettenburg, like big shipyards around the nation, dealt with the wartime labor shortage by recruiting them. They were led by still another Underwood; Jim Jr. recalled that "my mother and a neighbor lady were the screw fasteners. These boats had double-thickness planking, and they put what they called 'quilting screws' in—every four inches, every direction." So, "Mom and 'Rosie the Riveter'" drove screws during the war. After V-J Day, they went home—but a change had begun in the work culture of San Diego and in America as a whole, that would lead to generations of women trading the kitchen for the paycheck.

Jim Underwood Jr. was drafted, but Charlie's bookkeeper wife Ann, who managed the office, completed the Underwood family dynasty—in later years, they were joined by Charlie's namesake son, a designer, and his daughter Susan, a receptionist. Charlie would always insist that "this was not a case of nepotism," for every member of the hard-driving clan apparently felt some of his own need to prove that "we had a higher rate of productivity, and greater ability, that any other employee in the shop."

While working his way up, Charlie spent late nights at the shop or in the relatively modest two-story Kettenburg house on Browning Street in Loma Portal "trading my evenings for research, drawings, and design understudy work with George." By 1943, Gene Trepte remembered, Charlie was George's "right-hand man," and "the horsepower in coming up with ideas on how to build boats on a production line." But Paul, only a few years older than Charlie, was back; his return after ten years away catapulted him into position as George's new right-hand

man. Gene imagined Charlie's thoughts: "Paul leaves General Electric and comes home, and here's this guy who hasn't been around during all these days I've been with George—but he is a Kettenburg—and his name is on the building."

Charlie made room for Paul, and later the two worked closely in designing and building postwar sailing yachts, though not without friction. Charlie's brother Jim Jr. recalled that whatever the job was, "You darned well better do it his way!" By contrast with the hardworking but enthusiastic George, for whom boatbuilding began as a hobby, Charlie and Paul were both serious and headstrong. Paul would become the company's public face, racing their postwar sailboats, whose design and efficiency of production were primarily improved by Charlie. "It was Charlie's job to set up the production," recalled foreman "Bud" Caldwell, "and so sometimes they'd have some—not arguments—but good hot discussions on what they were gonna do." Caldwell continued: "Charlie was very, very talented, but it was hard to—boy, he wanted it his way. So once in a while, why, Paul or George had to put their foot down." Paul himself was a little unfair when he characterized to an interviewer that "Charlie lost all interest when a boat went down the ways." But Paul never forgot of Charlie that "whenever he decided to do something, he really went out and did it."

The U.S. Navy was a daunting client, but the plane rearming boats withstood the severest tests, leaving the new client impressed enough to continue to provide crucial business to Kettenburg in postwar decades. Dick Hershey recalled that "on one of the tests I went along with George, and the Navy testing officer really gave the sample boat the works."

When the boat was moving at top speed with the throttle wide open, the officer yanked . . . the shift lever from FULL AHEAD to FULL ASTERN. No in-between hesitation at neutral . . . You could just about feel every nut, bolt, screw, nail and everything else grab

on for dear life. . . . George and I also grabbed whatever, and looked in amazement at each other, but the officer merely said that "If the 'swabby' skipper suddenly saw a mine dead ahead, he surely would yank everything he could to evade that mine. . . . so the boat has to be able to take illogical abuse." Thankfully, the boat took it well!

Oddly, however, these plane-rearming boats may never have fulfilled their designated purpose. Instead of rearming seaplanes, the boats' size, speed, and capacity seem to have made them popular general utility craft across the Pacific.

More important in developing the boatbuilders' mass production techniques was a project that would bear fruit after Paul returned. Shortly after the outbreak of war, San Diego's world-famous tuna fleet vanished, as 50 Southern California boats dispersed across the South Pacific, where their refrigerated holds suited them for transporting chilled food for the military. Many of the brothers' old schoolmates, now fishermen, found themselves without boats, and in 1943 some approached George to ask for a new small fishing boat. "Here were all these fishermen sitting around with nothing to do, and there was a shortage of meat," Paul explained. With beef scarce, the government urged consumers to switch to protein-rich tuna. "Right after I came back to the business," he remembered, "the National Food Administration wanted fishing boats. They came up with a size of boat they felt would be most efficient, which was about thirty-five or forty feet long, and about ten to twelve feet in the beam. They wanted it to be able to carry—hopefully—about ten tons of fish."

George brought the proposition to Charlie:

"Charlie, why don't you go home early today"—it was a Saturday—and he said, "Over the weekend, I want you to draw up your concept of a . . . fantail fishboat. Now

there are some conditions that the fishermen want included: They figure that if we can put a ten-ton hold in a 38-foot boat, we'll have about twice the hold capacity of any ordinary boat, and probably *the Department of the Interior will give you a priority.* . . ." I asked George what we would use for hull lines on a boat [of] this type; since I had only worked on one fish boat in my life, I didn't have very much in the way of an idea! And he said, "Well, we'll just take the Joanne, and scale it down so it fits the 38-foot length and beam, and we'll go from there—that'll be the starting point. It's a cargo-type hull, and with a few modifications that we can make on the loft floor—why, we'll work it out." So, with that information, I went home, to spend a weekend designing a 38-foot boat. Now this is ridiculous—because it takes a lot of man-hours to design a boat. I had one thing in my favor, however . . . while looking at those old boats, I just could not understand how they "got along" in the little cramped corner there in the bow . . . And that was one of the main points of my concept. Now I started with this design by drawing a ten-ton box. And I drew the boat around that . . . I drew a good-looking deck house, had accommodations in there—good work room, nice table, several bunks, good cook stove, and a little comfort—including a toilet and shower. I made the outside of the house, too, so that it was a good-looking house. . . . when I

This construction drawing for the Kettenburg 38-foot "fan tail fishboat" shows the heavy scantlings of these practical workboats, designed by Charlie Underwood in 1943. The yard built 86 fishboats between 1944 and 1949.

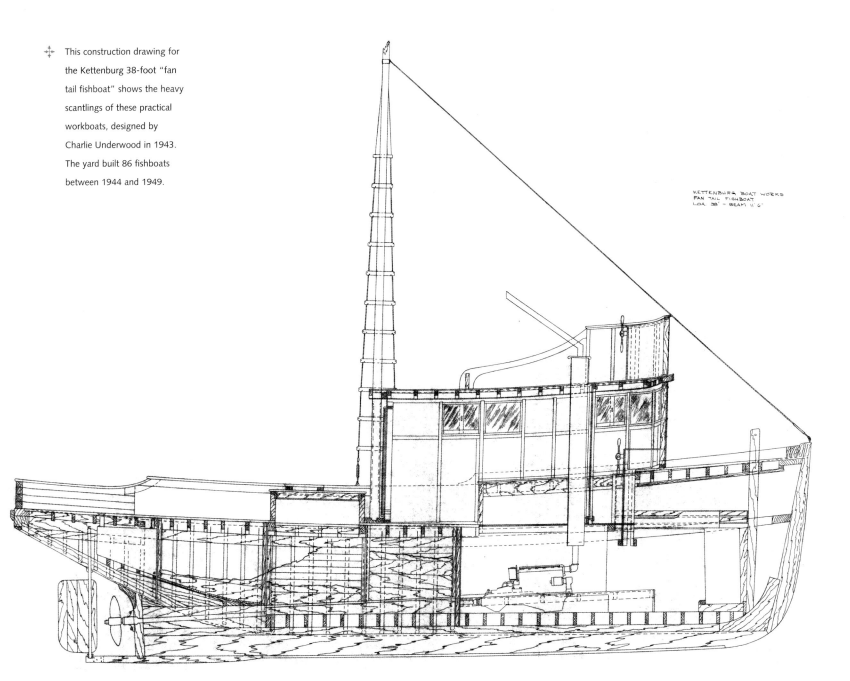

KETTENBURG BOAT WORKS
FAN TAIL FISHBOAT
LOA. 38' - BEAM 11' 6"

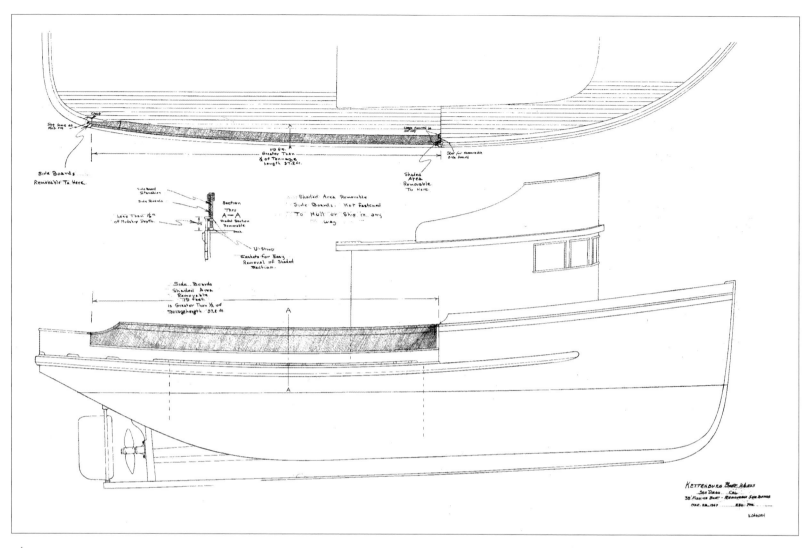

In 1947 the Kettenburg yard modified the fishboat design with removable sideboards aft for more efficient tuna fishing.

came back to work on Monday with my concept, and George called the customers in, they were really pleased and excited. They had never any idea about having the accommodations, and they were just more-or-less thrilled with the fact that we were able to come up with anything that would haul ten tons. Because when you arrive in a school of fish, and you have your five- or six-ton boat full, and you haven't fished out the school, you can throw four, five or six more tons in that boat in a hurry.

George, Charlie, and Kenny Baker, a friend of Paul's, took cleaned-up versions of these drawings to the Interior Department representative in

Los Angeles. They were accepted on the spot on October 6, 1943, as "exactly what they were waiting for," and George took the pair out to celebrate—a memorably rare event.

In "the greatest single production run of any design that ever came from Kettenburg," in Charlie's proud words, the shop rolled out 86 fish boats before production ended late in 1949. According to the now-returned Dick Hershey, "when we started building the fishing boats George was not too sure of his design details, so he sent me out to the various boat yards 'spying,' so to speak. I made a number of sketches of various boats under construction" to help George finalize their production. With food now "a higher priority than bombs," as Bill

Kettenburg recalled, these fish boats actually outranked their own navy craft in priority to receive scarce construction materials under wartime restrictions. Charlie perfected his time-saving production methods, and they launched their first in 1944, priced around $12,000.

Fishermen thought very highly of the little craft launched by these novice fishing boat entrepreneurs. Plywood, for example—a material suspected by men who trusted their lives to the sea's moods—only appeared in deckhouses and bulkheads, and the boats themselves featured the accommodations typical of much larger vessels. "This thirty-eight-foot fish boat was, by far, the 'Cadillac' of the albacore boats," recalled Morgan Miller. Their reputation among the men

who worked aboard—a very different set than had sailed Kettenburg's prewar yachts—mattered most. "We're proud of the fact that we own one," the *Pamela Sue*'s captain told an interviewer in 1949; she was "the most seaworthy small boat I have ever been on." Another skipper disagreed: *his* boat, the *California Maid*, was "absolutely the best sea boat that I have ever been aboard. Loaded or empty. For their size and different kinds of fishing, capacity and cruising range—and, speaking from nineteen years of experience, I say the Kettenburg boats cannot be beaten."

The design's only weak point was stability when unloaded, which was vastly improved once fish began filling the hold, as they rapidly did. One boat brought back 20 tons of sardines, doubling

Above: Kettenburg fishboat number one, *Lococo*, shows off her sturdy lines. Note the high insulated box for additional fish on the deck aft. Right: A Kettenburg ad for the fisboats proclaims the yard's ability to complete a boat in 10 days.

the already extravagant ten-ton hold capacity.

Demand continued well after the big requisitioned tuna boats began returning home, for as Paul marveled, "those boats made *fabulous* incomes" at a time when canneries were paying better than $750 a ton. Some owners actually paid off their boats with a single season's catch; Morgan Miller recalled that "the albacore fishing was just like a gold rush."

Thanks to efficient production, a new fish boat rolled off the line every dozen days. Charlie wedged three more work positions, or stations, each with its own crew, in among the three stations on which the plane rearming boats were already taking shape. The yard was a beehive of efficiency; wherever possible on the line, pre-assembled sections of fish boats were brought in and rapidly set in place. The crew, for example,

lowered completed deckhouses onto the decks from the loft inside the big building. Paul recalled that "We had it set up so one station would lay the keel," while "all the parts were 'made up' separately—we would make up the keel assemblies and planking sets and the floor timbers. They had one gang of people who would set the keel, bend the frames, plank it, and then take it off the mold and turn it over. Another group would do the interior and decking; another group would do the mechanical work."

The last station, where the boats underwent final assembly, was outside. "Every ten days, everything would move, ready or not! After the war, that's how we got started building pleasure boats—the same way." The newspaper reported that Kettenburg now "expects to convert many of the wartime methods into peacetime produc-

Left: The owner's family proudly prepares to launch their new 38-footer, *Little Saint Anthony*, in 1947. Right: *Baby Doll* rigged to troll for tuna, with her removable sideboards and a canopy above the fish box on deck. *Baby Doll* has been modified with an enclosed bridge.

✛ The yard crew was still much larger than in prewar years
when they launched the yard boat *Poggy*, a modification
of the fishboat design, in 1945.

tion;" they emerged from the war, Charlie proudly recalled, "the most productive and competitive yard in the industry," ready to jump into the reborn recreational boat market.

When V-J Day came at last and San Diego's streets exploded in wild celebration, Paul, however, was nowhere to be found. He was out fishing in their new *Poggy*, launched for family use that June with "accommodations worthy of a luxurious cabin cruiser." "I'm not really a fisherman," Paul confessed, "but I tried it so I could understand what the fishermen were talking about when they discussed their problems," and he tested this vessel thoroughly in daily use, just as he would test every postwar sailboat design. "To prevent spying, they didn't allow us to have radios. As a result, I missed V-J Day and didn't know the war was over until I got back to the dock!"

The same day found George and Charlie on a promotional trip north to Puget Sound, having stopped in San Francisco. "We were standing by Glenn Waterhouse's boat, talking to him about the new PC, and right then all the sirens and whistles and everything start blowin', and we said to Glenn, 'Jeez—Does this happen every night at quittin' time?' He says, 'No—I don't know *what's* goin' on.' And shortly after that, we found out it was V-J Day, and it was one great big celebration."

George was showing his Bay Area sales agent the plans for a postwar "cruising" PC and a yet-unbuilt big sailboat he called a PCC. His son Bill remembered pessimists worrying that San Diego, whose population had mushroomed by one-third in the wartime boom to over 330,000, "was gonna blow away when the war was over." But George was hopeful about the future, and, along with other boatbuilders thinking ahead to the postwar era, he hypothesized that demand would run to more comfortable, bigger sailboats. As Gene Trepte, who later won races in the resulting boat, remembered, "after the war, people were getting more attuned to cruising. Before the war we didn't have anything to cruise

on, other than the little dinky PC." George planned to introduce a class of bigger racing sailboats, built economically with the production methods they had perfected. He focused on a likely competitor: the 44-foot Island Clipper class, which Los Angeles architect Merle J. Davis had

⊹ The 44-foot Island Clipper, designed by Merle Davis in 1939 for Fellows and Stewart, had a practical monopoly on the one-design cruising boat market in San Diego at the end of the Second World War.

Right: George (right), Charlie
Underwood (with PCC half
model), Paul (standing), and
Ken Baker review the boat's
full-scale lines revealed by the
battens bent on the mold-loft
floor. Below: Newly launched,
the first PCC, *Eulalie*, rests at
the Kettenburg fitting out
pier, with Eulalie and Jean
Kettenburg on board, 1946.
Opposite: *Eulalie* under sail off
Point Loma, with San Diego
still welcoming the troops
home.

designed in 1939 for Fellows & Stewart. The war
had halted their production, but one of the two
built lay moored near the shop in San Diego.
Paul remembered of his brother that "during the
war he kept seeing this
Island Clipper at the Yacht
Club. He'd walk by it
every day, and every time
he went out . . . he'd say,
'*That's* the kind of boat
I'd like to have.' So during
the war he dreamed up
the PCC, and Charlie and
I lofted it."

The actual lines of the
Pacific Cruising Class one-
design—like its predecessor, known to nearly
everyone only by its initials, "PCC"—emerged at
full scale on the loft floor upstairs, as Paul and
Charlie assisted George in the frequently hot
space under the sun-blasted sheet metal roof.
Given the heat, new designs were sometimes
lofted by George and his crew in their under-
shorts and socks—reportedly to the shock of
occasional, unexpected, women visitors. Gene
Trepte watched a fully clothed George at work:
"I can remember George doing the original lofting of the PCC . . . up there—he did it all by eye.
He had these battens, and he'd push the batten
a little bit this way, or he'd tell Charlie to move it
over a little closer to him."

The wooden battens Charlie helped bend on
the loft floor gradually revealed the hull's precise
shape, taken off George's lines drawing. The war
was over, and neither Charlie nor Paul had
chased the other out of Kettenburg; instead,
George harnessed both of their sets of skills and
set them up for a long—if never trouble-free—
partnership. The hull of the sailboat on which
they worked was an enlargement of the PC,
which had proved to be such a fast boat. Like
the PC—and unlike every other purpose-
designed ocean racer—the new boat would be
constructed unusually scantily, as the PC had

been. Its tally of victories would make it
Kettenburg's most successful racer, and every
future Kettenburg boat would be a variation on
this same hull design.

"I didn't want us to
shrink down into a little
twelve-man yard again,"
explained Charlie
Underwood, who hoped
his new concepts in boat-
building would raise the
company to a new level of
competitiveness. "I wanted
us to be one of the big
guys—or at least as big as
we could be, with our
capabilities. Here we were with over a hundred
people working, and earning money. So I just
didn't want to go backward." He was certain
"that if we could produce more boats more economically than anyone else, and have good
designs . . . we could . . . break into the market
that the Island Clipper and other boats had
'sewed up' and were well established in. And slip
the PCC in there at a more competitive price—
because of the 'new system'—than any other
builder could do."

The war years taught George how to manage that "new system" of high-volume production in a small shop, but left him exhausted. His
only outlet beyond work and family was archery.
Sometimes, his daughter Jean recalled, when
clients stopped by, her father would "have his
bow out, and he'd be practicing—I mean, not
with an arrow, but just *pulling* the thing. He'd be
practicing, right in the middle of somebody coming in to ask him something about boats!" Even
weary, however, her father "had this enthusiasm
that you just can't imagine," according to Jean's
husband Morgan Miller. George's enthusiasm
made his teenaged daughter think of him "like
another kid," and even she and her brother
called him "George." But he was very much a
man in need of a family vacation.

Chapter Six

The Greyhounds
Of the Sea

'EASY SAILING'

Malaspina Straits, B.S.

July 7, 1950

The spirit of the PCC design: Dennie Barr's *Mickey* on a broad reach in
the open sea, in a 1952 painting by Kipp Soldwedel. Inset: PCC *Bolero*
on an easy run in the Malaspina Straits, British Columbia, July 1950.

"I think I was the one who was below, and Charlie Benton was on the helm, and he said *'Watch out!'*" Glimpsing the huge wave out of the corner of his eye, George Kettenburg and Charlie barely had time to brace themselves as a wall of foaming water roared over their 46-foot PCC, which had been struggling south along the Oregon Coast with an out-of-season Aleutian gale from astern. Charlie desperately swung the helm to turn them perpendicular to the onrushing sea, but was too late. He "didn't make it, and it just went *BANG*—right over—and I thought the boat blew up!" As the boat hung on her beam ends and Bill Kettenburg struggled to catch his breath, he dreamily noticed that "God—stuff was floating around down below." Above him, the spacious, comfortable cockpit— recently much admired in Northwestern yacht clubs—had nearly filled to the tops of the seat backs and threatened to flood the cabin. The three sailors were alone on an angry ocean, and Bill's father, George Kettenburg Jr., may have fleetingly wondered: will my design hold together, or will we become new "Lost at Sea" statistics?

Since George had hardly ever taken a vacation, working or otherwise, he *ought* to have been enjoying himself at the end of a glorious 1950 trip to Washington and British Columbia. It had been his third summer sailing Pacific Northwest waters, showing off his big 46-foot Pacific Cruising Class boat, the new ocean racer known to all as the PCC. George and the group of co-workers and family who accompanied him had been warmly received, and they had raced well. He had skippered one PCC to victory in the

PCC 3, *Selene*, heeled down and driving toward the California coast. *Selene* saw her share of wind, finishing 13th in the 1947 Transpac Race and being a top boat in Santa Barbara Yacht Club racing through the 1950s and 1960s.

Pacific International Yachting Association (PIYA) regatta, while another PCC won the regatta title and captured the big Swiftsure Race too—155 miles of straight-line sailing down the Straits of Juan de Fuca and back to Victoria. PCCs had drawn attention and admiration, and they had proved to be a joy to cruise on afterwards. But at that particular instant in the summer of 1950, George was primarily concerned with keeping three people alive. George's college-aged son Bill, a friend of Bill's, and George himself were

Bill Kettenburg remembered:

We went around Cape Flattery, and in those days you didn't have all these weather beacons, and technical was nothin'. And you'd call the Coast Guard to find out what was going to happen in the weather. . . . My dad always wanted to know exactly where we were before we left; and at the bell up there, it was fog—you couldn't see the bow of the boat. . . . So we sort of drifted

the last of the 25 built, "are absolutely terrifying downwind in a blow. The rudder is so close to the center of the boat that it makes a great aileron that accentuates the wild rolling and frequent accidental jibes." George could feel his boat straining to make just such spur-of-the-moment decisions about which direction she wanted to go, but kept her in hand. "It got rougher and rougher," shivered Bill years later, recalling the cold spray: "where the wind was blowing the tops—when it's *really* blowing—is

"The wind died down—that was the dangerous part: we had these big swells, and the wind died down—and one just *curled* on us. Just when we, we had been really watching them, up until that time, and then, all of the sudden, this broke on us." Thankfully, George had insisted on lashing the helmsman into place in the cockpit with safety lines, which saved Bill's friend from being pitchpoled into the darkness to leeward by the huge wave.

huddled in the cockpit of a PCC as it sliced south toward California, thrust down the coast by the full force of an out-of-season Aleutian gale. The hull of the new boat on which they were now surfing down gigantic waves displaced substantially less water than its competitors. Some observers had voiced doubts about how the new class would do in heavy weather. Was this light boat, designed to win races in San Diego conditions, too flimsy to ride out a gale roaring down out of Alaska?

Although Northwesterners shook their heads at the idea of only three men sailing a 46-foot sloop down such a notorious stretch of coast, their voyage had begun uneventfully. At the close of their summer of racing and spreading the Kettenburg banner, George had offered to take the fourth PCC built, *Mickey*, back to her owners in San Diego. In their borrowed boat, they approached the Cape Flattery buoy at the mouth of the Strait of Juan de Fuca, ready to turn for the south.

around, and we found that [buoy], and we called the Coast Guard. And they said, "Light airs: 5-15 knots"—or something like that—coming down. So we, as soon as it sort of cleared up, and we knew . . . where we were, we took off. And as we went further south, we kept getting heavier and heavier winds—and this was in the summertime. And it was sort of a freak storm.*

Those "light airs" lasted for about ten hours until, as Bill recalled, "it was really windy—it was the heaviest winds I've been in, sailing." The winds rose to velocities of 50 knots or more, with gusts surging well above that. To reduce the sloop's tendency to round up when off the wind, they doused the mainsail and ran under only a jib. Even under jib alone, Bill attested, "I *know* we pinned that Kenyon" knot meter to the edge of the dial, as *Mickey* surfed short distances down each swell.

"Stock PCCs," remembered the owner of

like BBs blowing at you. And it was blowing sorta horizontal stuff" in their faces, as walls of green water intermittently crashed over their starboard quarter. He felt thankful that the light-displacement PCC lifted so well in most of the big following seas bearing down on them, "because the waves were gigantic: you'd look up and you'd see a 30- or 40-foot wave behind you."

But that wasn't the worst: "The wind died down—that was the dangerous part: we had these big swells, and the wind died down—and one just *curled* on us. Just when we, we had been really watching them, up until that time, and then, all of the sudden, this broke on us." Thankfully, George had insisted on lashing the helmsman into place in the cockpit with safety lines, which saved Bill's friend from being pitchpoled into the darkness to leeward by the huge wave.

Smacked down momentarily on her beam ends, however, *Mickey*'s cockpit rapidly drained, and everything "held." Once again the PCC was proving her ability to take open-ocean conditions, although her skeleton crew was hard-pressed at that moment to appreciate them: "We *were* going to sail it all the way from Seattle to San Diego. Well, my dad says, 'We're too beat up. We're going to take it into San Francisco.' We went into Saint Francis Yacht Club and sat in the showers for two hours to get warm—because this was before the days of, you know, all the good insulation that you have nowadays." These ocean sailors did not have much protection from the cold Pacific: "we ended up usually with just a swimming suit on, and yellow foul weather—those 'skins—and that was it, because, God, you were dripping wet anyway!"

The three working vacations George spent racing and cruising in the Northwest in the summers of 1948, 1949, and 1950 marked the postwar expansion of his Southern California boatbuilding operation into a major West Coast presence. It also offered him a lot of pleasure. "George was always out on his own, pretty much confined between home, and runnin' this yard—and workin' hard as hell, in the deal—and he was a 'workaholic,'" observed Gene Trepte, who joined George for two of these expeditions to the Northwest. Around the boatyard after the war, agreed Jim Underwood Jr., "George was usually a hard person to find—he was so busy, you know: here, there, and everywhere." Except for his family and archery, George's passions had been confined to the boats he built. But on these trips north, he excitedly experimented with making home movies using 16-millimeter equipment. He had even built a projection booth in a corner of the yard's big metal building for his new hobby. Gene remembered that "somebody encouraged him, 'Well, why don't you take a "spec" boat up to Seattle, and see if we can get something going, and people buying those boats . . . and cruise, and do your picture-takin'—or filming?' And so he did that, that first year that I went up with him, and he *loved* it.

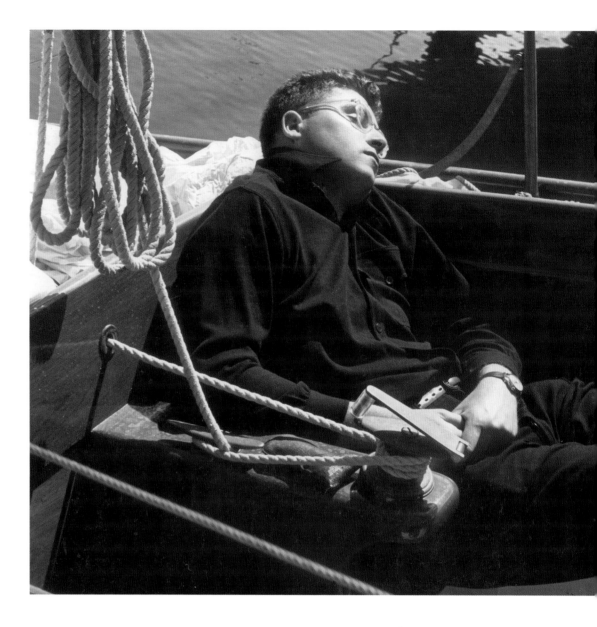

And he was very likable—he got to know a *lot* of people up there—and so we had a wonderful cruise."

As the film whirred in George's camera, the Kettenburgs encountered the Pacific Northwest, and Northwesterners met the Kettenburgs. The enthusiasm was mutual, despite a slightly rocky start, when George was introduced by a flustered member of the Royal Victoria Yacht Club as "George Kettering and his PPC from the Coronado—I *think*—Yacht Club"—a sobriquet that his fellow travelers refused to let him forget for some time. Their boat in 1948 was *Gossip*, sold in San Diego to Dr. Phil Smith, who was then commodore of Seattle's yacht club.

Above: During a hard season of relaxing on board the PCC *Bolero* in the Pacific Northwest in 1950, Gene Trepte naps next to the mainsheet. Right: George and San Diego friends rendezvous aboard PCC 9, *Gossip*, in Princess Louisa Inlet, British Columbia, 1948.

George, recalled yard foreman "Bud" Caldwell, "had a deal with the doctor that bought 'number nine' PCC to sail it at the regatta in Victoria, and then he'd bring it down—we'd cruise it and come down and deliver it to Lake Washington, where he lived." Leaving Paul behind to mind the store, George rendezvoused in the Northwest with a group of San Diegans. All of them, as it happened, would play significant parts in the future of Kettenburg Boat Works: George's son Bill, his daughter Jean and her husband Morgan Miller, Charlie Underwood (and his wife Ann), and construction foreman Bud Caldwell. The competitive woman skipper Dennie Barr brought her own family along as

George's "cheering section."

Among the figures in Northwestern yachting they encountered was Harold Jones, a personable playboy who owned a large Vancouver tugboat business and boatyard, whom they all came to know affectionately as "Jonesy." Gene Trepte recalled that "'Jonesy' says, 'Well, I'm gonna take you guys on a cruise. You've got your boats up here, and we're having a big cruise—you can come with me.' So we were rafted up alongside *Spirit*, in Friday Harbour."

There, along with the hospitality aboard the 72-foot yawl, "we were swimmin' all the time, and we'd have these clambakes on the beaches," Gene remembered, while "going to

all these wonderful coves and things." It was immensely satisfying for George, as for the first time he encountered adulation and celebrity—helped along by the racing reputations of the PC and PCC—denied him in San Diego as he faced the daily challenges of running his boatyard. "George had a wonderful way with people," and "just seemed to know everybody, and everybody liked George," remembered Gene. "He was just having a great time, I can remember. Because it kind of was a . . . new life for him, because he had worked so hard, and his wife was not much of a socialite at all." Eulalie, always more of a stay-at-home mom, remained in San Diego.

The Barrs rented a powerboat in 1950 and cruised alongside *Gossip* through landmarks like Princess Louisa Inlet, where the vacationers gazed up at peaks soaring from the water's edge to their glacier-fringed tops six thousand feet above. Miles up the fiord, they anchored near Chatterbox Falls, relaxed, and swam. And as they unwound, George could rest in the knowledge that the boatyard was in Paul's capable hands, and that just by racing and relaxing in the Northwest he was selling boats—with some help from his old friend

Kenny Baker, who was now taking some of the pressure off as their sales agent back in San Diego.

Gossip threaded tricky passages like the one into Princess Louisa Inlet thanks to her built-in Gray Marine Sea Scout engine, which spun what was advertised as the "special Petersen-Kettenburg two-blade folding bronze propeller." This innovation exemplifies another way in which George was a pioneer: he was among the first in the West to "build to the rules" set by the Cruising Club of America (CCA)—the

Above: Beneath the dramatic coastal mountains of British Columbia, *Bolero* leads two other PCCs to the line near Vancouver, 1950. Right: Flying her signal flags just after launch, a new PCC waits for her sails to be rigged.

organization that meted out ocean-racing handicaps to competing boats of different sizes. While a typical sailboat's propeller shaft runs down its centerline and pierces its keel (enabling the crew, when racing, to "hide" the drag from a two-bladed prop by temporarily positioning it vertically in the keel's shadow), the PCC lacked this advantage. Its shaft was mounted *alongside* the keel, eliminating whatever weakness might come from punching a hole through the deadwood, but losing the ability to mask the prop's drag. So, in its wisdom, the CCA took pity on disadvantaged boats like the Cal 32 and the PCC, offering them a favorably low handicap number. With the aid of the burly high school physics teacher and sailor Werner "Pete" Petersen, however, George designed a prop whose blades expanded outward when under power, thanks to centrifugal force. Under sail—once locked into place with blades positioned horizontally— the prop blades minimized drag by remaining tidily bunched together along the shaft, like the bud of a bronze flower. This little device sidestepped the rules and allowed the PCC to race—and win—with a very favorable handicap. As the designer Charlie Underwood Jr. put it, "the purpose of the rating rules is to 'even' the field, and to handicap the faster boats. And part of the job of the designer is to look for the ways to make the boat faster—in *spite* of the rule." As the CCA played catch-up with innovators like George, "the rules would change, and then the older boats would not be as competitive."

For the last of their three trips north, in 1950, "George got us all 'juiced up' again, and he said, 'Well, why don't we *all* go up the next time, and we'll get Dennie Barr'"—who, Gene recalled, had recently bought PCC 4, *Mickey*—"'and I'll take a 'spec' boat up there, and why don't you take the *Bolero* up there?'" George, the Barrs, and the Treptes flew north to meet their PCCs. These had arrived on three railroad flatcars in Seattle for reassembly by the brothers Charlie and Bob Ross, the

Kettenburgs' new northern representatives, at their boatyard, the Lake Washington Yacht Basin (known to local smart-alecks, according to Bill, as the "Lake Yottington Wash Basin.") So, Gene concluded, "we all put our boats in the water, and went as kind of a caravan on the way north to go to these various regattas—and then cruise afterwards." Gene was fortunate enough to miss *Mickey*'s stormy voyage south.

Just a few years before, several hundred spectators had watched George's daughter Jean break the customary champagne bottle across the bow of the first PCC, *Eulalie*, named after

the love of George's life, on May 19, 1946. Some onlookers had perhaps been attracted by the notice that "liquid inspiration will be supplied by the management"—this despite the fact that George himself almost never drank alcohol—but curiosity brought most to see the "long heralded" successor to the PC. "They have been threatening to unveil it for some time," the Los Angeles-based *Sea* magazine told readers late in 1945.

"The first PCC came out. She was fast but *ugly*—she had this awful squared-off stern—so he found a Mexican guy to buy it," recalled

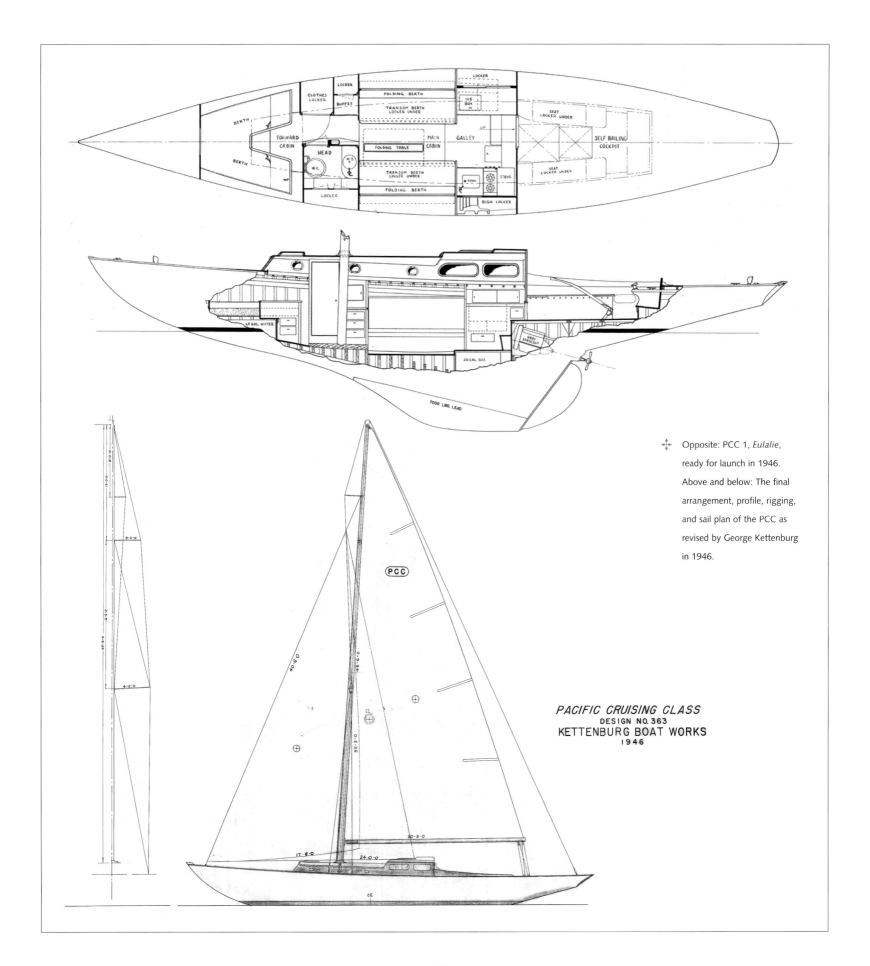

Opposite: PCC 1, *Eulalie*, ready for launch in 1946. Above and below: The final arrangement, profile, rigging, and sail plan of the PCC as revised by George Kettenburg in 1946.

PACIFIC CRUISING CLASS
DESIGN NO. 363
KETTENBURG BOAT WORKS
1946

Opposite: The first *Eulalie* (later named *Ray* and renumbered PCC 2) was distinguished by her cropped stern. A second *Eulalie*, PCC 1, was 18 inches longer and introduced the more graceful profile of the production PCC. Left: Having been framed and planked upside down on a jig, a PCC hull is rotated for completion. The first two PCCs were planked with Honduras mahogany on oak frames. The next fifteen were planked with Douglas fir on oak frames, and the last eight were planked with Philippine mahogany.

Gene Trepte; George swiftly "got her out of the country" away from public view, to the Acapulco home of an expatriate American. This original *Eulalie*'s slightly bobtailed stern, which prompted negative comments from both Gene and Joe Jessop, also illustrated George's efforts to design his boat for racing efficiency. Although Bill remembered that his father always thought this boat, carrying less weight aft, was slightly faster, the opinion of Joe Jessop, still the Yacht Club's chief Kettenburg booster, carried more weight; he thought her 44-foot,10-inch length looked too stumpy. Joe's opinion, which prompted George to settle on a slightly longer boat, illustrates another principle: good design wins races, but good looks win sales. Six

months later a more elegant new *Eulalie*—this one 46 feet, four inches long, and bearing the official hull number one—slid into the water.

At first glance, each of the 25 PCCs built looks much like other handsome yachts of the day, with the same graceful overhangs fore and aft that—when the boat was heeling—added waterline length to increase her speed. The decks alone offer a clue that the PCC was not a one-off, since the narrow, nine-foot, six-inch wide boat is decked with canvas-covered marine plywood instead of teak. The PCC was also clearly built for racing *and* cruising; her "completely equipped galley with unrationed elbow space"—in the words of an advertisement calling up shades of recent wartime rationing—

came with a set of plastic dishes. At a glance, the only unusual feature was her large cockpit, in which the crew worked from the pair of much-admired "grandfather seats" aft of the tiller, "and that's a novelty because in most boats they get tangled up with the skipper," as one sportswriter observed.

The principal distinction, however, was how light the boat was in comparison to her competitors: the PCC displaced 18,500 pounds, but her Island Clipper and Cal 32 competitors weighed in at approximately 19,800 and 22,000 pounds. Purporting to be baffled by why his new boat was so fast, George shrugged and offered a newspaperman the thought that "in the PCC's we seem to have hit just the right dis-

Above: An ad for South Coast's California 32, a very popular ocean racer and cruiser popularly known as the Cal 32. A prewar design, the Cal 32 was strongly challenged by the postwar PCC. Right: Cal 32 number 4 chases PCC 6, *Kitten*, which took first place in both the Ensenada Race and the Transpac Race in 1949.

placement for its size. The speed is the result." The boat, a reporter observed in *Sea* magazine, was "a compromise between the typical heavy ocean racing boat and the light 'racing' craft," and was so lean that one local newspaperman titled his story "Greyhounds of the Sea."

Bill Kettenburg remembered, with a smile, "going out, right after he launched it, and there were some well-established boats designed by Eastern designers that he had to compete with.

And this was pretty good-sized—46 feet—and a lot of money in those days," with an original base price of about $16,500. (George had hoped to keep the PCC under $20,000, but scarce postwar materials and labor would push the price up.) But, "in fifteen minutes he knew we had a winner; his boat took off, and just *pulled away*. . . . Everybody knew this was a hot boat."

One of these established boats was the elegant California 32, designed in 1937 by Nick

Potter, a talented émigré drawn to Los Angeles by movie money. Due to the interruption of the war, only seven of these beautiful yachts were built. Like the PCC, Cal 32s are 46 feet overall, with the same long overhangs, and 32 feet at the waterline—just inches longer than the PCC. The substantially heavier Cal 32 typified ocean racing sloops. With a taller rig and much more sail area, the Cal 32 had better off-wind speed and provided fierce competition from the

moment the PCC was introduced in the 1946 Lipton Cup Race. For that race, Gene Trepte had jumped at an offer to sail as a crew member aboard a Cal 32 in the challenge to be held off Catalina Island. He watched the new PCC from a distance, with curiosity that became admiration: "And so we're all over there, and by gosh, the old number one was a *fast* boat. And everybody said 'Look at those comfortable seats in the back—kinda like armchairs.' Everything

about the boat was so much better than the Island Clipper. So after that was over, when I got home, I talked to my dad. I said, Gee—we oughta build a PCC!'"

Gene's enthusiastic endorsement to his father, local construction magnate and yachtsman Walter Trepte, was hardly unusual, for no advertisement matches a trophy in selling a racing-cruising boat to a potential racer. The PCC's skipper Milt Wegeforth left the admiring Gene

in his wake, and, for the first time since a PC won the trophy in 1931, Sir Thomas Lipton's flamboyantly styled donation again graced a shelf at the San Diego Yacht Club.

Not long afterwards came a definitive test against the Island Clipper, the original inspiration for the PCC. The test was unofficial, remembered Ed Barr, who crewed for George that day, because "George was anxious to get the results in a non-public manner—being a consummate

The premier prewar Pacific open-ocean race had long been the Transpac, a legendarily wild 2,225-mile downwind run to Honolulu that had tested the mettle of West Coast designers, big boats, and sailors since 1906.

diplomat." A rendezvous was arranged inside sea buoy #5 off Point Loma between *Mickey* and an Island Clipper sailed down from Los Angeles, in order to settle the "heated barroom conversation" between partisans of either design: "Starting clear astern, the PCC sailed steadily over the top of the Island Clipper to windward. George, wishing to leave no doubt in anyone's mind, then crossed the Island Clipper's bow, jibed under his lee—coming up again from astern," and there, between the buoy and Point Loma, George tidily looped his rival. One reason the PCC was simply a better boat was "George's secret," as Charlie Underwood, his attentive design understudy, put it:

What we spent the most time working out was to get the best line—bottom lines—on the side of the boat . . . That's how the boat became a very fast boat . . . and that was only because of this original idea of placing the bottom on the side of the boat. Now the boat would heel over quite easily to a certain point, and then it would become stiff, and the reason that it won the Honolulu race is just because of that fact—that in a storm, it heeled over good, and the boat went over the waves nicely, when boats like the Island Clipper plowed through and nearly drowned!

San Diego's own newspapermen, never the most prophetic lot, were also catching on. They watched as "the speed and balance of the tautly-built, aristocratic" and "sleek and rangy" PCC were bringing them into contention for yachting's top honors off the West Coast. Interest in big-boat ocean racing was surging

now that racing's wartime suspension was over and racers had returned from the war. The premier prewar Pacific open-ocean race had long been the Transpac, a legendarily wild 2,225-mile downwind run to Honolulu that had tested the mettle of West Coast designers, big boats, and sailors since 1906. When the first PCC slid into the water, George speculated to a reporter that he was considering entering her in the revived postwar Transpac, but there was some debate among the committee about whether PCCs should be allowed. Bill recalled that "in the Honolulu Race, they almost didn't let the boat in the race, because they said it was 'too light displacement'" to take the rough conditions. Nevertheless, two PCCs placed respectably in 1947, and two years later Fred Lyon's PCC *Kitten* won the West's greatest ocean race outright. *Gossip*, with Bill Kettenburg among the crew, had her own turn at the Transpac in 1951, but detoured to hunt for a man who had fallen overboard from a competing boat. Light displacement was the prophetic, forward-looking aspect of the PCC's design that gave them a sharp racing edge in their early years. Between 1947 and 1977 several Kettenburg designs entered the Transpac 27 times, placing fourth or better 12 times—a remarkable figure for wooden boats, given the onslaught of lighter-displacement fiberglass boats and the ever-lighter custom fiberglass yachts that followed. The final Kettenburg Transpac contender, appropriately enough, was a PCC—almost 20 years old—that in 1977 finished less than 13 minutes behind the leader.

As the shadow of war receded, participation in the handful of small prewar ocean races nearer the coast also grew, and new races

began. In California, these included the Los Angeles Yacht Club's Channel Islands Race, the Farallon Islands Race off San Francisco, and a new race around San Clemente Island launched in 1946. In British Columbia, the Swiftsure was reorganized into a major race in 1947, while to the south in the "other" B.C., the first race from Newport to Ensenada—ancestor of all races along Mexico's Pacific coast—was run in 1948. PCCs won them all, and more besides.

Paul Kettenburg crewed on the inaugural San Clemente Island Race in 1946, in weather rough enough that he remembered that "there were six of us aboard—and there were only two of us not seasick!" Despite widespread predictions that victory would belong to a bigger boat, race day found her a half-day ahead, as *Eulalie* "skimmed the rough miles in almost unbelievable time, bounding across the finish line early on a Saturday night when the race was calculated for a Sunday finish," to the awe of one newspaperman. She proved that her performance was no fluke when a PCC took home the trophy again the following year. A string of Southern California races quickly fell to *Eulalie*, to the delight of George and his crew of family and employees, who campaigned her vigorously. She turned heads again as she won the 1946 Channel Islands Race, followed by victories at the 1947 Santa Barbara Regatta and the midwinter regatta in Los Angeles. As trophies piled up, buyers from across Southern California took up the racing flag, adding to the new class's victories well into the 1950s, when PCCs were gradually supplanted by boats that sharpened the divide between comfortable cruising boats and outright racers.

As the boats' racing reputation spread, so

PCC 9, *Gossip*, charges along under spinnaker in Hawai'ian waters, 1951. She finished seventh overall in that year's Transpac Race even though she changed course to search for a crewmember who had fallen off another boat.

did their geographical distribution. George's trips to the Northwest established Kettenburg's footing there. Their Seattle representative, Charlie Ross, sailed *Gossip* to win the 1950 Swiftsure Trophy, hurtling along in a wind that topped out at 55 knots, and repeated the feat in 1953; she was pushed into second place in 1949 and 1952 only by a newer Kettenburg design. And enthu-

siasm for the little company's products was finally spreading east. William Irwin sailed his PCC out of her Georgia home port to race against many of the best Eastern yachts in the Southern Circuit, or Southern Ocean Racing Conference (SORC)—a two-week regatta founded in 1941—and won it in 1950. That same year, Delaware chemical millionaire Henry

PCCs on the East Coast

Two of the 25 PCCs came east and compiled notable racing records that awakened East Coast sailors to the Kettenburg qualities. Both Henry B. "Hank" duPont, who kept his boats in Connecticut waters, and William Erwin of Atlanta, who kept his boat at Miami, bought PCCs and brought them east in 1950 to compete against the best designs of Olin Stephens, John Alden, Phil Rhodes, and other prominent naval architects.

The premier East Coast ocean race was then the biannual 635-mile race from Newport, Rhode Island,

across the rough Gulf Stream to the island of Bermuda. In the 1950 Bermuda Race a number of light-displacement boats challenged conventional wisdom on the need for heavy "cruising class" boats offshore. Hank duPont was a Bermuda Race committee member, and he knew what he was doing when he entered his new PCC, *Cyane* (PCC 17). Though of moderate rather than light displacement, *Cyane* was included among the suspects, and she impressed by finishing sixth in Class B and beating a number of prominent boats, despite

having run into a number of calms and light-air spots. "Henry duPont and Bill Stewart, *Cyane*'s owners, were well pleased with her. She's a tender boat in a breeze, but a fast and dry one," noted *Yachting* magazine.

Having proven herself, *Cyane* went on to compete again in the 1952 Bermuda Race, finishing third in Class B. From her berth at Pine Orchard, Connecticut, she returned to race to Bermuda again in 1954, '56, and '58.

In 1955 Hank duPont took *Cyane* across the Atlantic for some international competition. In July she sailed in the 350-mile Gotland Island Race on the Baltic Sea near Stockholm. The next month she crossed the starting line off Cowes, England, in the challenging 605-mile race to the Fastnet Rock off Ireland and return, arriving back in time to take third place in the second class. Having served duPont well in the most challenging Atlantic Ocean races of her day, the Bermuda and Fastnet Races, *Cyane* was retired from ocean racing and renamed *Spica* when he launched a new aluminum *Cyane* in 1959.

Bill Erwin's *Belle of the West* (PCC 19) made her first showing during the Southern Ocean Racing Circuit series early in 1951. The SORC included a number of races each year, including rough passages across the Gulf Stream from Miami to Nassau in the Bahamas or Miami to Havana. *Belle of the West* was again a leading SORC boat in 1952, and later that year sailed with *Cyane* in the Bermuda Race, finishing six boats behind her sister in Class B.

More than fifty years after their impressive showing against the best of the East, both of these boats survive.

Left: Henry duPont's *Cyane* starts the 1950 Bermuda Race, her first of five. Right: leaving the fleet behind, *Belle of the West* works to windward with her big genoa jib during the 1951 SORC in Florida.

Preparing for the 1950 Bermuda Race, *Cyane*'s crew practices with her new roller reefing gear on the mainsail. Left: As their crews prepare to bend on spinnakers, PCC 5 leads another PCC by a few feet at a turning mark. The PCC was exciting for round-the-buoy racing as well as long-distance competition. PCC 5 was national champion in 1957, 1960, and 1961.

duPont shipped a new boat east. He wrote a friend that "quite a few people on shore were looking through field glasses trying to figure out what PCC stood for" as he swept past them down Long Island Sound; "the more I sail *Cyane* the more thrilled I am with the way she handles under all sorts of conditions," he wrote to a friend. Shortly after his purchase, duPont sent his friend Kenny Watts, who made sails for PCCs, a sample of a new fabric, and suggested he try it for sailmaking. It was duPont's Dacron, the first satisfactory step away from canvas in boatbuilding history.

In 1950, duPont entered *Cyane* in the East Coast's version of the Transpac, the biannual Bermuda Race (sailed over the 635 miles of changeable water between Newport, Rhode Island, and Bermuda). That year, yachtsmen waited to see how the light-displacement yachts

introduced in Britain by Laurent Giles would stack up against American boats of varying displacements. *Yachting* magazine noted for the benefit of Easterners that "especially on the East Coast, the development of this type has lagged sadly. On the West Coast, however, the Kettenburg-designed PCC Class of light displacement sloops has been growing since its inception just after the war."

Among the 1950 Bermuda Race's mix of light and heavy displacements, *Yachting* found that the sturdy but light *Cyane* was "in a category by herself" as she took sixth in a class of noteworthy boats; the magazine deemed her "a tender boat in a breeze, but a fast and dry one. *Cyane* introduced others to the Kettenburg name: Olin Stephens, one of the most renowned yacht designers of the twentieth century, remembered that "my introduction to the Kettenburg name

was via Hank duPont." Olin recalled that she "seemed a surprisingly good all-around boat." While the small Kettenburg shop could not out-sell big Eastern naval architects like Stephens's own Sparkman & Stephens, Bill remembered that the PCC "really got us going in the bigger boat classes, because we were competing with the Sparkman & Stephens and the Aldens," whose boats stood against them in East and West Coast races.

One frustrated Pacific Coast competitor was the actor Humphrey Bogart, who with wife Lauren Bacall lent an air of celebrity to races in the late 1940s aboard his majestic Sparkman & Stephens-designed *Santana*. His yacht was handicapped very close to the PCC by the CCA rule, so the boats often finished within seconds of each other. Bogart insisted strenuously about the light-displacement PCC that "that boat isn't *fair*," Bill remembered with a laugh. "He had a

Sparkman & Stephens—a bigger boat—and Sparkman & Stephens was the 'blue chip' of the East. And here's my dad in the West, and we usually beat him boat-for-boat, and he didn't like that!" Bill explained that "his boat was a little bit bigger than ours, but we beat him: our boat was faster and a little bit smaller, so we corrected better." Smarting from his defeat in the inaugural Newport-Ensenada Race in 1948, Bogart growled to George Kettenburg Jr. that "this makes the fourth or fifth time those boats of yours have kicked water in my face," after PCCs finished first, second, fourth, and fifth. A newspaperman's record of their interaction captures George's self-effacing character: "'How many you have in the race?' 'Five.' 'Too bad yuh missed third place, too,' returned Bogey sarcastically. 'How come?' 'Well, laughed Kettenberg [sic], 'I should have brought in the boat I was sailing for third place. But maybe I'm not a very

good sailor. Anyway, I made a bad turn around the islands at the entrance of Ensenada Bay.'"

After one Ensenada Race, "Bud" Caldwell said, "I remember Lauren Bacall came over to the table and said to George, she says, 'Don't you get *sick* of winning?' She had a big smile on her face," however. But perhaps most humiliating to Bogart was the fact that he was beaten to Ensenada by a *woman*.

A traditional yachtsman like Bogart himself—or a yachtsman who imagined himself possessed of some of Bogey's onscreen machismo—might have been taken aback while strolling down the docks at the San Diego Yacht Club, had he glanced aloft at the unusual ensign flapping at the starboard spreader of *Mickey*. Ed Barr explained that "Mom conceived and adopted the three-cupped brassiere as her battle flag" to signify that Dennie Barr's PCC *Mickey* "had more" than any other racer—and presumably to give notice that yacht racing was no longer purely a man's world. A tough competitor, Dennie sailed *Mickey* in the inaugural 125-mile Newport to Ensenada Race in 1948. "Boisterous winds" between 20 and 35 knots trimmed the 97 boat-field to the most serious sailors, and the first to ride the wind into Ensenada, 21 hours later, was an 85-foot M boat. But once handicaps were factored in, Dennie—in a PCC hardly more than half as long—took first.

"The yacht club was almost entirely men" between the world wars, Paul recalled. "It was a gentleman's club, really. It wasn't until the later 'thirties and on up that the women became involved." One could correctly speak almost exclusively of yachtsmen up to this time, but a few women nationwide were coming to realize that their appointed stations in life could include boat cockpits. As the war parted women from their men, many entered the workforce for the first time to do their part in a world in which most jobs had been reserved for men. With young men absent, a few women like Dennie learned every aspect of sailing, became expert skippers in their own right, and didn't hand

back the tiller when ocean racing resumed after the war. Dennie never received the fame that came to redheaded Peggy Slater, who became known as one of the West's great sailors in her red-hulled Kettenburg racers *Valentine I* and *II*, but Dennie was a pioneering woman "big boat" skipper.

Dennie's son Ed Barr remembered one character-illuminating incident. During the 1950 Los Angeles Midwinter Regatta, "*Kitten* and *Mickey* were pitted against each other in a windward duel. Near the mark, *Mickey* was storming

along, raildown" on starboard tack. Fred Lyon's *Kitten*, winner of the previous TransPac, suddenly converged sharply on her port side: "*Mickey's* crew yelled, '*Starboard!*'—but Fred Lyon made no effort to give way. Dennie yelled to her crew, 'Where will we hit?' 'Center of their cockpit!' came the reply. 'Oh, *damn!*' With a sudden jerk, Dennie slammed the helm up to the quadrant limit—missing *Kitten's* backstay by inches."

Bound by her own code of honor, Dennie lodged no protest, though the torn tendons in

her right wrist left her with limited use of that hand for the next 36 years. She did, however, let the sailing fleet know in no uncertain terms that, "if he ever does that again, I will *not* give way!"

"After listening to the skipper say how alert the PCC is," expounded a Kettenburg brochure in the slightly patronizing tone of its day, "then get his wife to tell you how secure and comfortable the PCC is to sail." In Northern California waters in the early 1950s, men racing against Dennie seldom felt either secure or comfortable,

as she collected consecutive trophies for the boat-pounding, crew-exhausting "Buckner" round-trip race between San Francisco and the buoy off Bodega Head, and, in 1953, became the first woman to win the 125-mile Farallon Islands Race. As she remembered, "no one thought a PCC could race in that wind. All we did was reef and sail a broader course. We went farther—but we were much faster."

Whether skippered by women or men, the PCC's victories around 1950 rapidly enlarged Kettenburg's sales and reputation. A boat

designed in the West and built to tackle Western conditions could now be counted among the fastest of all wooden American ocean racing boats. Along with the quality of the champions who sailed them, the qualities George built into these sailboats led to their success. By deriving the hull's lines and construction from the light-displacement PC, George anticipated that light-displacement ocean racing yachts would be the wave of the future.

Left: Dennie Barr (right), Bill Frazee, and friends enjoy a cool afternoon sail in a PCC. More often, Dennie was at the helm in a hard-fought race. Above: Gathered around the Lipton Cup, San Diego Yacht Club winners show off their silver in 1952.

Chapter Seven

Kettenburg People

Some of the yard's heavyweights test the strength of a new laminated plywood cabin top, a postwar innovation at Kettenburg. Inset: The crew of PC 7, *Confusion*, poses with the PC women's series trophy at the end of the 1961 season.

The quality of the sailboats Kettenburg launched after the war is legendary—but what can be said about the people who ran the company, who worked there, and who bought their products? George Jr.'s awareness of the high quality of the company's people—his partners and workforce—must have been behind his decision to transform Kettenburg into a partnership in January 1949. The new partners all came from within the shop, and most were family members. Each one pursued a specialization that reflected the diversified and balanced direction toward which George envisioned his firm growing. Where one partner specialized in marine hardware, another worked at distribution; where one specialized in designing and building boats, another guided sales, and still another oversaw repair operations. Under this team was a labor force that worked in an environment in which nobody was confined to a single specialization; instead, people shifted departments to go wherever the company's needs dictated. This practice helped keep them light on their feet through the economic ups and downs of the postwar boating market and benefited the workers themselves by eliminating layoffs—and by keeping work life interesting and full.

F. ROSS

Ronald F. Ross's watercolor depicts a quiet, reflective moment at the Kettenburg yard in 1950.

In a city with a burgeoning Cold War military establishment, the procurement and distribution sides of the military contracts that had opened up to them during the war would prove crucial to the company's long-term success.

Left: Morgan Miller prepares to set the spinnaker of a PCC, 1961. Below: For tuna net fishing, Charlie Underwood designed handy, heavy duty 16- and 18-foot vee-bottom tenders, 155 of which were launched by the Kettenburg yard.

Outside this circle of partners and employees lay a final circle: the loyal customers—cruisers and competitors alike—whose habits in buying boats, in buying boating supplies over the Kettenburg counter, and in hauling their boats out in the yard, kept Kettenburg in business. On the inside, George retained 50 percent control—"he made the decisions," Morgan Miller recalled—and his five partners each controlled 10 percent of the company as it grew.

Morgan Miller—"Morg" to nearly everybody—was two decades younger than his boss and father-in-law. As a 12-year-old, he bought a Starlet with money won in a movie theater promotion, and the little boat hosted his first date with George's daughter Jean. They wed in 1946, after he spent the war training to fly with the navy. When Morg graduated from Stanford with an economics degree two years later, George persuaded him to set aside plans for graduate school in order to transform the boatyard's parts counter into a major retail operation. "He got out of Stanford," partner Bill Kettenburg remembered, "a couple of years before I got out of

school, and in about a thirty- by thirty-foot little room he started building a trade in boating materials—and that ended up to be a large end of our business."

Bill Kettenburg found himself propelled in the same direction, despite being an avid athlete in several sports. "My dad says, 'It's time to get into this business. Are you gonna be in athletics, or are you gonna be in the boat business?'" His father's strong advice to "go into the store—*that's* what we need." sent Bill, who with Morgan was the team's other "young guy," into supplying the firm's navy contracts. Bill went on to specialize in purchasing, and gradually he secured exclusive distribution rights for various brands of marine products, the first of which had already been arranged. Thanks to Charlie's 1945 design for Chrysler-powered net tenders—about 155 of which traveled through the South Pacific aboard San Diego's still-growing tuna clipper fleet—Kettenburg got the regional distributorship for Chrysler Marine products. In 1950, Morgan and Bill opened a large modern store on Carleton Street, which became one of the firm's

KETTENBURG BUILT **WORK HORSE** OF THE **TUNA FLEET** CHRYSLER POWERED

San Diego **HARBOR DAYS** *July* 20-21-22

main sources of profit. The store was perhaps the most up-to-date in the U.S. when it opened, and it grew into the nation's fourth-largest marine distributorship. At its height in the early 1970s, five other Kettenburg Marine stores were scattered across Southern California.

Upstairs behind his drawing board, Charlie Underwood found himself christened superintendent of construction and navy work, and he managed the cost accounting on each new boat. These were important jobs, but his brains and drive pushed him considerably further. In a city with a burgeoning Cold War military establishment, the procurement and distribution sides of

the military contracts that had opened up to them during the war would prove crucial to the company's long-term success. Workmen were already loudly at work fulfilling the first of a pair of contracts in 1952, blasting away with pneumatic chippers as they refurbished over a hundred rusty Second World War landing craft known as "Higgins Boats." As Paul succinctly put it, "all of a sudden they decided they were going to maybe have some more invasions" after the navy had scrambled to locate enough landing craft to equip General Douglas MacArthur's assault on the Korean coast at Inchon. For about a year, Paul remembered, "we had our yard just

Morgan Miller and Bill Kettenburg presided over the profitable Kettenburg marine supply store on Carleton Street in San Diego, seen here in 1952.

Left: The contract to repair more than 100 "Higgins Boats"— small landing craft—helped support the Kettenburg yard in the early 1950s. Here, most of the crew works on Higgins Boats in the background while others repair a tuna tender in the foreground. Above: The indispensable Charlie Underwood, 1954.

full of these things," 40 or 50 of which were jammed anywhere they could fit.

Under George's usually watchful eye, Charlie began flourishing as a designer. Although he always maintained that "my creative ability was discovered by George," Charlie dated his baptism as a designer to a 38-foot custom sportfisher he created in 1947. When a customer asked George for an inexpensive copy of a production powerboat he'd seen in a magazine, George passed the customer to Charlie, who

had to sell him on the idea of not spending that small amount of money and buying something that would be a pile of junk, but to let me design something for him that he would really be proud of . . . and that he

would always be able to sell for a good price, because of the particular design that I was gonna put on the bottom and sides of the boat. And after a considerable amount of work he said, "All right—go ahead and design it, and if you can make it so interesting to me that I'll pay more money for it, I'll let you build it." So, in the next three weeks, I designed a hull which was strictly my concept, not George's.

Charlie laid out the lines upstairs on the loft floor alone, to save money. Instead of devising the lofting out of a table of offsets calculated on paper, Charlie worked the other way round: he made his offsets by measuring the lines he had already drawn on the loft floor. Charlie had

evolved the new design during months of secret experiments as he and Bill Kearns constructed tenders for tuna boats, but he dreaded confronting his mentor. When Charlie finally showed him the drawings, "*that* is when George almost went into shock." The bottom was too radical a departure from the proven formula, and George was upset at not being consulted—but soon calmed down. He told Charlie, "There *may* be merit to your new formula. I'm going to let you go ahead with it—in order to prove who's right and who's wrong." But George warned that "*Your* name is going to be on all the drawings . . . I don't want to be responsible if it turns out bad!"

This hull would be the basis for future Kettenburg designs for fiberglass boats for navy

138

The friendly man in the Hawaiian surfers' shirt was one of the most public faces of the boatyard for 31 years—a fairly typical number of years for an employee. And if Bud gave customers estimates on painting their boats that proved too low, "when he found out that the cost was running over the estimate, he'd go down there at night, on his own time," recalled an admiring Paul, "so the yard wouldn't show a loss."

and civilian use. Thanks to Charlie's well-known production methods, the cramped shop was soon rolling out one PCC a month, and a PC every ten days. Between VJ day and 1952, Charlie's production lines launched 351 civilian and navy boats.

The Supervisor of repair work was Bill Kearns, Charlie's "right hand man" during the war, when his bachelor's degree and teaching credential in industrial arts made him a natural at reeling in the high-school students building the plane-rearming boats. According to his coworker Gary Keller, "I don't think there's anything that Bill couldn't figure out, or didn't already know. And if anybody had a problem down there—"Go to see Bill"—he'd solve it one way or another." The former woodshop teacher joined the firm in 1937 when servicing boats was already a main-stay of the business. The boatyard he came to direct gradually expanded to encompass both the land that the family owned and tidelands leased from the Port of San Diego. Taking nothing for granted, however, the partners built their improvements on land that they actually owned.

Bill Kearns also, recalled Charlie, "knew exactly how to talk to the customers and keep them happy." He was a realist who "had the ability to think of the customer's pocket book, and say: 'This is good enough.'" Like so many boatyard workers, his back also suffered from years spent shoving boats into place. Gene Trepte remembered: "I can close my eyes—he's at the one old railway, with that long stick with a spike. He was always shoving the supports—the bolsters—under the boats . . . to get the boats on that old cradle right." His widow recalled him "hunkering"—frequently meeting with customers in a squatting position, since those collapsed vertebrae made sitting or stand-ing quickly grow painful. But he was the go-to man on any project requiring imagination and skill, including such marginal maritime tasks as fashioning a gold-plated, teak-handled fire axe for a client.

The well-liked, knowledgeable but unobtru-

sive Kearns was teamed with an outgoing and likeable foreman, Alex "Bud" Caldwell, who enjoyed interacting with customers. Bud grew up sailing Starlets with Morg, and George's daugh-ter Jean remembered him as an unofficial Kettenburg family member. Bud started working at the boatyard on Saturdays when still in high school, where the two friends had shared Bud's colorful old Franklin—half painted in San Diego High School's white and blue, and the other half in Point Loma's maroon and gold. After flying for the navy, he started working full-time on PCs after the war. Bud took up surfing, teaching it to one of Morgan and Jean's sons. The friendly man in the Hawaiian surfers' shirt was one of the most public faces of the boatyard for 31 years—a fairly typical number of years for an employee. And if Bud gave customers estimates on painting their boats that proved too low, "when he found out that the cost was running over the estimate, he'd go down there at night, on his own time," recalled an admiring Paul, "so the yard wouldn't show a loss."

Bud later realized that his workplace was something out of the ordinary; "I said, 'My God!' I was in someplace special—y'know?" Most of the men who formed the labor force had similar feelings. "It was a great place to work," recalled Dick Palmer, hired as a painter in 1947. Dick became a carpenter and was eventually pro-moted manager in a career that stretched across 20 years of comings and goings. His career, like Bud's, epitomized the longevity of employees, their mobility between departments, and the company's habit of only promoting people to management from inside the shop. To Dick, "Kettenburg was a wonderful place—it was a small, family organization."

"The spirit of cooperation by both labor and management," agreed a navy representative in 1952, "has been outstanding." This was a rarity in one of America's more troubled labor periods, but one reason for Kettenburg's success was interdepartmental mobility for workmen. "A lot of the fellas," Bud explained,

140

had taken shop in high school, and they had the "knack," and they just kept improving, and loved what they were doing. And the nice thing about the company was—instead of being totally "specialist"—why, we'd get good at one thing, but then if that got a little slow, instead of lettin' the people go you . . . worked in almost all the departments in the production and in the repair, see? So when one was slow, you'd go and work in the other one . . . to where you could do most of the jobs.

This unusual labor practice of cross-training for different jobs began in the Depression, when there was almost no work—period. As Charlie Underwood noted,

rather than hire plankers to come in and plank, and finish workers to come in and do finish work—and so on—each individual worker was able to demonstrate his ability to do these various things, and gradually became proficient at many of the different jobs. . . . And rather than being all short-time employees, they were full-time *employees and did carpentry, painting, ways work, ways maintenance. Some worked in the machine shop—even though they were supposedly painters and carpenters!*

As a result, remembered Charlie, "George then had a very flexible group of people that could tackle almost any job."

And so even as the titans of labor and management struggled in postwar Detroit and elsewhere to strike a balance, attempts to unionize Kettenburg fell flat. "We had a break, and he talked," Bud remembered of a meeting with an unfortunate union organizer, who found that

"everybody was kind of against him before he even started." George's strategy was to consistently pay slightly above union wages, and his men were aware that flexibility in crossing department lines could work to their advantage. If a business downturn hit a shop like theirs, union contracts locked workers into a single trade. In that case, Bud recalled, "that's where you stayed, and you were out of work. So, the guys could all see that—so we never went union."

Boatbuilders also had in-house incentives for productivity. "When we came out with a new model," Paul remembered, he and Charlie would discuss it: "'Okay—the carpenter's gonna cost so much, the paint's gonna cost so much, the preparation will cost so much,' and so on; we set that all up. And then we went into production on the thing," which is where the workmen came in: "If they figured it was gonna cost a hundred dollars to do a job and they could do it for fifty—we split the fifty with them." The partners developed this bonus system to reward laborers for accomplishing their work quickly but within the quality standard. They rated each operation in terms of the time it demanded and paid employees extra for their efficiency in saving labor. Gene Trepte noticed that as the men built his own sailboat, "if they could beat those hours, they got a bonus."

"We got the best of people because they wanted to work for my dad. So, we had the 'Best in the West,'" Bill Kettenburg maintained proudly. The quality of the work in both the construction and repair sides of the business was well-known—and occasionally most apparent in the breach. Gary Keller watched a woodworker finish the side panel of a cabin, only to belatedly discover that the mahogany itself was flawed.

Apparently when the tree was downed, they had a "fall break"—it comes down, and there'll be a crack in the timber somewhere. And when they had this side all finished— planed!—and put it in place on the deck . . .

⊹ The yard's modern, well-equipped machine shop, 1951. This essential component of the yard supported both yacht construction and naval repair.

Right: PC champions pose with the George W. Kettenburg Perpetual Trophy for Annual Pacific Class Championship, 1961. They include Roger Bryan (second from left), Paul Kettenburg (standing center), and Doug Giddings (kneeling right).

the painter . . . spotted this fall break, and one of those two carpenters put in what you call a "Dutchman." They cut a piece of wood out—not all the way through—and put another piece of wood in there—just inset it, maybe a quarter of an inch, 3/8 inch, deep . . . and so matched the grain that when the painters stained and varnished you couldn't find that "Dutchman." I mean, these fellows were master carpenters.

The final group on which success hinged was the yard's customers. They were made up of both cruisers, in search of comfort primarily, and bare-bones racers, primarily in search of victory. One of the former noted that his sailboat sleeps six, but "drinks eighteen or more."

Customers frequently moved up to larger boats out of loyalty to the Kettenburg brand, based on their experiences with previous models. Jim Arness, the six-and-a-half-foot actor who played Marshal Matt Dillon on TV's *Gunsmoke*, is a case in point. He bought a K 40 "because it had a quarter-berth that he could fit into," Gary Keller said. There were many other first-rate sailboats on the market, "but he couldn't get in the quarter-berth. Or *any* of the berths. So he bought the K 40 on the strength of that quarter-berth. And he liked it so well—and he got interested in sailing—that he came back and bought a K 50."

Since almost half of K 50 owners had previously owned a less-expensive Kettenburg yacht, this tendency for repeat business was critical to their success. Charles Ross Underwood, who

followed his father into design work there, ruminated that "in the beginning Kettenburg sailboats were very competitively priced."

It was fundamentally a good product, but it was not the most "high end" on the market. When you look at the history of companies in the boat business, it has not been uncommon to see builders start out building good products at one end of the price spectrum, and continue to improve the quality, performance, feature content and style as they're "moving their customers up" to larger boats that sell for higher prices.

The very last members of the customers' circle who made Kettenburg succeed were those fire-breathing PC racers, whose victories continually offered great publicity. Postwar prosperity meant a dramatic surge in Pacific Class sales, and over half of all PCs were launched after the war.

Among the new racers were women, who were no longer a remarkable sight at the helm—although local newspapermen still referred to them with a touch of condescension as "skipperettes." Jean Godwin won major PC races just before the war, and after Dorothy Royce's brother gave her his PC, she won the PC Nationals in 1947. Peggy Slater, soon to emerge as a champion sailboat racer (and Kettenburg's own sales champion), bought a PC that year, and in 1948 the class instituted a regular race among women skippers. Other than relatively minor changes to the rig agreed to by the class association's members, their postwar PC remained

The final group on which success hinged was the yard's customers. They were made up of both cruisers, in search of comfort primarily, and bare-bones racers, primarily in search of victory. One of the former noted that his sailboat sleeps six, but "drinks eighteen or more."

the familiar prewar economical-but-fast racer.

Every champion praised the toughness of his, or her, racer. "We were comin' in at the weather mark—and it was *so* rough," Wally Springstead remembered of a postwar race at Newport, as he watched his crewman , standing before the mast, almost vanish in a wave up to his chest. "We went around the mark, and we started downwind, and got water *up to here* on the foredeck. We hit a wave, and went through the

next one. And we didn't sink—*God*, PCs are great boats!"

Racing resumed with a vengeance after VJ-Day for champions like Springstead (who took the class-wide George Kettenburg Trophy six times) and the redoubtable Giddings brothers. Some racing diehards like Doug Giddings swore that the more cruising-friendly postwar PCs were slower. George told Doug before he bought his postwar PC that the culprit was slightly heavier

Honduran mahogany, substituted for the old Philippine variety unavailable since the war. Paul, however, saw another reason behind the preference for older PCs: "Some of the hot racers grabbed them, and consequently everybody thought they were better boats. Everyone thinks they're a good sailor if they win—and if they lose, there's something wrong with the boat. *That's* the history of sailing."

Loyal customers quickly spread the PC's repu-

tation to the Pacific Northwest. With no room left to build them in the cramped metal building, four of the last PCs emerged in Vancouver, and the last three were finished in Seattle. The final boat, PC hull number 83, splashed into Puget Sound around the time that the 25th and final PCC slid into San Diego Bay in 1959.

George Kettenburg Jr.'s business partners, his employees (who "were kinda like his family," Morgan recalled) and loyal cruising and competing customers were shocked when George died just before Christmas in 1952, aged only 48. "George approached me," Charlie remembered,

and he said, "Charlie, I have a new problem that's worrying me . . . I'm worrying about the possibility of dying young." He said, "I don't know why I'm thinking that, because I feel fine." As far as I know, he had no physical problems at that time—he was a good athlete, he liked to—really liked to—sail . . . he loved archery, and he wasn't much for being pretentious. He . . . had simple needs: he loved his dogs and family, and the work he was involved in.

George was a regional archery champion, "a very powerful man; gee—he'd take a hundred pound bow—I couldn't even pull it back," Bud Caldwell remembered; "he could just take that bow and pull it back like nothing." But to the shock of Jim Underwood, Jr., "he just withered away" during his nine-month bout with cancer:

George had been going to a doctor, trying to cure up what he thought was a cold—nose kept running—and he changed doctors, and this doctor recognized his problem immediately and put him in the hospital. He had cancer in his sinuses. They pretty much disfigured him: cut his nose, laid it over . . . dug out the roof of his mouth, sewed the nose back on—the poor guy was just in misery. But he would walk out onto Shelter Island once a day, and he would stop by to see how I was doing, and encourage me, which I thought was pretty darn nice.

As an investment, George had gone into partnership with his former employee Jim, funding the latter's dream of building the first marina on Shelter Island. This new recreational development just outside the Kettenburgs' back door was part of the West's postwar proliferation of marinas, the rising tide of pleasure boating that lifted Kettenburg Boat Works itself. Shelter Island was no longer the sandbar that had provided meager shelter for the yacht club—and challenges for the club's young Starlet sailors, who used to race *over* it at low tide. In 1952 it was becoming a sprawling peninsula of dredged sand fringed with transplanted palms, still without a road or structure but linked to the mainland by a new causeway. Its development was the vision of San Diego's first port director, Joe Brennan, and after Joe's 1948 retirement it rose on the sandbar under the guidance of his successor John Bate. Both men recognized that part of San Diego's future prosperity would depend on the recreational resources their city could offer boaters.

Ironically, given George's swift decline, good

Left: George W. Kettenburg Jr., boat designer and builder and archery champion, 1904-1952. Right: With Point Loma in the background, Shelter Island takes shape in the 1950s.

KETTENBURG BOAT WORKS

fortune in timing had made the Kettenburg partnership possible, since George arranged for the partners to buy out his wife's interest with funds drawn on his own life insurance policy. "Everybody took out insurance, so I took it out in January—and one month later, I wouldn't have been able to get it," Bill recalled. According to Jim Underwood Jr., "Of course there was an investigation by the insurance company, who thought there was a kind of a fraud going on, but it was proved that George didn't know about his problem" at the time.

Near the end of George's life, he was able at last to let go of the strain of running the yard and spend more time with his family. Morgan recalled that George's grandson, three years old when George died, was a particular favorite, "and he used to come and pick him up with all his four dogs he used to have, in the car—he loved dogs—he'd come and pick him up, and take him for a ride almost every day." Morgan's wife Jean remembered that "they didn't have a very big house, but the house was just run by the dogs. He loved kids and dogs." While the inventive, self-taught designer George Kettenburg Jr. died a few days before Christmas, 1952, the best decade of the business he founded lay ahead.

"To show you how unaffected the guy was about *who* he was, and what his reputation was," Bud Caldwell told this story: "We'd come back from—I think we were on our way back from Santa Barbara, and the regatta—and we went into Avalon to get gasoline. And so we're tied up at the dock, and this guy on the dock says, 'Oh—it's a PCC! *I* know George Kettenburg!' And gave us this big spiel all about it and everything—and here he's talkin' *to* George."

Bud laughed uproariously: "And George never said a thing, and we left. After a while, he says, 'Well—I wouldn't want to ruin the guy's day!' . . . and *that's* the kind of guy he was."

Chapter Eight

Wooden "K Boats:"

The Family Boats that Won Races

K·50

LOA   50' 6"
LWL (under max. load)   34' 6"
Beam   13'
Ballast   9,000# lead
Sail Area — 987 sq. ft.
    in main and fore-triangle
200 gals fuel—200 gals water,
    space for an additional
    200 gals liquid
Choice of gas or Diesel auxiliary
Steam bent oak frames,
    mahogany planking.
Everdur bronze fastenings,
    stainless rigging.
Merriman hardware.
Two private staterooms

★

for further details
see our representatives:
San Francisco Area:
GLENN WATERHOUSE,
BERKELEY • THornwall 1-4882
Los Angeles Area:
PEGGY SLATER • TErminal 1-3100
Pacific N.W. Area:
DON STEWART,
MERCER ISLAND, WASH.
Great Lakes Area:
POHN BROS. YACHT CO.,
CHICAGO • MOhawk 4-5416
Florida Area:
WM. BURCHENAL,
CLEARWATER • 446-5995
East Coast Area:
ARNOLD C. GAY YACHT YARD,
ANNAPOLIS • COlonial 3-9277

or

KETTENBURG
2810 Carleton St.
San Diego, Calif.
ACademy 3-8161

⊹ Peggy Slater, champion sailor and champion sales person for Kettenburg
    yachts, at the launch of the first K 43 in 1963. Inset: Introducing the K 50.

K ettenburg Boat Works sailed smoothly through the 15 years following George's death—although occasional small squalls did come up in the relationships among the five partners. "After George passed away, I kind of became the lead partner," Paul said— with emphasis on "kind of." Despite the fact that he carried no more weight in decision-making than the others, Paul steered a challenging and sometimes frustrating course through the 1950s and '60s, "trying to keep all five of us going down the same road." Under Paul's direction, they succeeded in growing every aspect of the business that George Jr. had left to them. Their most visible successes were the string of wooden sailboats with "K" names, most of which were so well appointed as to make even George's PCC seem Spartan by contrast. Charlie Underwood was responsible for much of the design work on the K 38, K 40, K 50, and K 43 sailboats, while the understated Paul worked extensively on sales and on their hulls and rigs. Along the way they added the talents of a fiercely competitive, flamboyant, and very female sales representative: the champion sailor Peggy Slater.

The racing/cruising market for which they created their boats was then a peculiar ply of two ultimately incompatible strata that, during the 1950s and '60s, was already starting to delaminate. Sailors who primarily sought speed and those who primarily sought comfort found that their respective needs did not stay bonded well. Kettenburg's sales were based on what increasingly became apparent as a contradiction: evidence of competitive successes motivated some buyers, while other loyal luxury-minded customers climbed "up the ladder" to pricier sailboats. Paul and Charlie were increasingly aware

⊹ Peggy Slater aboard a new K 38. As the Los Angeles-area broker for Kettenburg yachts, she owned a K 38 and a K 43, both named *Valentine.*

"She was a *real good* sailor," Paul remembered, who "could out-sail 98 percent of the men in the area." The West's preeminent female sailor had already been the first woman to skipper a Transpac yacht, and she was on her way to amassing a lifetime hoard of 832 trophies and spending a stint as *Los Angeles Times* Woman of the Year.

that rising numbers of the latter were beginning to drive the sailboat market as recreational boat ownership across America doubled to seven million owners in the 1950s. San Diego itself saw the 1,481 recreational boats moored in their bay at the war's end *quadruple* in just over a decade, proportionally far outrunning even their city's expanding population. The city, in fact, soon had the highest number of boats per capita in the country. Kettenburg was in the right place with the right products, thanks to their sailboats' reputation for combining speed, comfort, quality, and beauty.

As sunny Southern California's population soared, the region also started leading America in innovations on recreational boatbuilding's production side. Young engineers 85 miles north in Orange County, from which South Coast had arisen to trouble George in the PC days, were beginning work that would lead to large sailboat hulls made of fiberglass, an entirely new material. Charlie Underwood mastered it very early, as Kettenburg premiered his popular fiberglass outboard runabout in 1955. But the fiberglass revolution was beginning to undercut Kettenburg and every other builder invested in wooden construction.

In the meantime, however, Kettenburg Boat Works benefited from another aspect of Southern California's new cultural leadership: in 1953 Paul named Peggy Slater—one of only two women yacht brokers in the country—as their all-important sales representative in the Los Angeles market. By Peggy's estimate, her efforts came to account for 85 percent of Kettenburg's sales, while the combination of her outsized personality and string of victories demonstrated to the world that women were in sailboat racing to stay.

"She was a *real good* sailor," Paul remembered, who "could out-sail 98 percent of the men in the area." The West's preeminent female sailor had already been the first woman to skipper a Transpac yacht, and she was on her way to amassing a lifetime hoard of 832 trophies and spending a stint as *Los Angeles Times* Woman of

the Year. Peggy recalled of her 15 years with Kettenburg that "we had a perfect relationship. They built the finest racing boats on the Pacific Coast, and I wanted to win races. They were proud of their work, and had many craftsmen who had worked there since their youths, each with a personal joy in his craft."

Their joy became her job: to sell each potential buyer the dream of owning a shiny new wooden Kettenburg racing/cruising sailboat—despite the fact that racing often more closely resembles what another Kettenburg owner described as "standing in a cold shower tearing up thousand dollar bills." Peggy employed her unique ability to simultaneously present the boats' racing strengths to men and their "family" aspects to women. She was hired because "people had a tendency to buy boats that their wives would enjoy," in Paul's words, and she found her womanly expertise relied on in "laying out the interiors so that the women would like them." Gary Keller remembered her as "kinda demanding, because she wanted things *right*. Of course, she didn't have to demand too hard on Paul. He'd make 'em right, 'cause she was a good salesman for us—*and* she was a good racer." Peggy recalled driving down from San Pedro to Point Loma weekly, where she met Paul,

and we checked the progress of the boats on order and made my requested changes or additions. Over lunch we discussed new designs and which of his boats were winning races. . . . After each launching was completed and the crowds had roared away, I spent a day shaking down the new boat. I rigged all the sails, used all the instruments, checked the tune of the rig and sailed her on all points. I always returned to Kettenburg with a list of minor items to be corrected prior to delivery.

"A new trouble-free boat made everyone happy," Peggy concluded. As sales rolled in, the partners were happy too.

The first K 38, *Tomboy*, took to the water in 1949. The K 38 was intended to fill the gap between the Spartan PC and the ocean racer-cruiser PCC.

"She decided she wanted a boat that she could sail herself, so she bought a K 38," and Paul stood by as Peggy christened her *Valentine* in 1953, on a blustery Valentine's Day. (After a hailstorm broke moments later, the reception crowd got progressively drunker and louder inside the metal building. Paul's son Tom, then six years old, remembered thinking something like "What've I gotten myself into?" about this first exposure to the sailing fraternity's rough edges.) When the new K 38 had been introduced four years earlier, the national yachting press and even local newspapers took notice. *Yachting* informed

readers across the nation in 1949 that "this design will fill in a gap that has heretofore existed between the PC and the PCC." The newest member of the Kettenburg product line, planked with navy-surplus Douglas fir, had a base price of $11,000, versus the PCC's price of about $20,000. The new sailboat "certainly has a good deal of eye appeal"—rather more, the reviewer might have noted, than the "Beetle Swan," a memorably-named 12-foot catboat introduced at the New York Boat Show two years earlier. The Swan was the first production fiberglass sailboat, the unimpressive harbinger of a coming revolution.

George "supervised when I built my first personal project," Paul said, as he and Charlie worked on the first K 38 in a corner of the shop floor, squeezed by Charlie's assembly lines for the PC, fish boat, and PCC. Concerned about how inflation was forcing the latter's price up, George had assigned Charlie to create a new boat: "Well, now we have to have something to start down about $11-or-$12,000 as a base price, without sails." said Charlie. "He really liked his lines on the PCC, and so did everyone else. And so this would be a smaller sister to that boat." Charlie worked out the table of offsets on a calculator and arrived at a scaled-down design that would capture the same lines, but at five-eighths of the cubic capacity of the PCC's hull.

The one thing that George did was increase the width of the boat at the keel, so there could be a heavier timber in that area. Which changed the reverse curve and a little portion of the bottom, but it didn't spoil the run—and the rest of the waterlines—and worked out very nicely. Now Paul . . . was gonna be the one who was gonna get this first boat. So he had a lot of input as to exactly what he wanted in there for an interior arrangement, and also on the sail area, and sail plan rating.

Paul chose a name for their new 38-foot class that intentionally echoed the aviation-conscious public's awareness of another fast Southern California design—Lockheed's P-38 Lightning. Like every future Kettenburg sailboat, the K 38's hull design and construction was bred out of the PC, by way of the PCC. The later K 40 design would stretch that hull and beam a bit and add more freeboard—the distance between water and the top of the gunwale being important for customers who preferred to spend drier days at sea, and who wanted more interior space. The luxurious K 50 stretched the hull ten feet further, while the K 43 shrank the essential shape back down. "Our designs were all pretty

The simple, spacious interior of the K 38.

much based on San Diego and Newport Harbor conditions," explained Paul; "this was our market." They were simultaneously proving to be very serviceable designs for Puget Sound, "because there they had pretty much the same conditions," those usually gentle breezes he termed "light air."

Paul recalled the genesis of the firm's 40 K 38s somewhat differently. As he told it, it was born from annoyances that the recently married Paul endured on a weekend cruise to Catalina in August 1948, after racing off Los Angeles. Paul and Dorothy's not-terribly-romantic 22-mile voyage to the island demonstrated to them both that the PCC "was a little too big for only a husband and wife to handle easily" and, as Paul said, "too much boat" for ordinary sailors. "So I sat down and figured out: Now—if we shrunk this down to here, and moved *this* into here," he could shrink the PCC "down to a size that would be comfortable for the two of us."

I got back home, and I talked with my brother George, and I said "Gee, you know,

we really enjoyed usin' your PCC, but I think I'd like one just a little bit smaller." . . . So, I told him about what I had kinda dreamed up, and he says, "Gee—Well, go ahead and build one; see what happens." . . . So Charlie and I got together, and we lofted the boat. And my brother George was there, and he kinda stood over us and saw to it that we . . . didn't do anything that he didn't agree with—and got the thing all lofted and . . . built a boat. The two of us, together. And got the boat goin'.

"While we still hadn't launched the first boat, three or four other people came in and wanted to place an order for 'em, before the first one was even in the water!" It was Dorothy who suggested a name: "Tom's mother, about in the middle of the night, shook me, and said 'Hey—I got an idea. Why don't we name the boat *Tomboy*?'" The prototype of every future

151

Kettenburg sailboat would bear that name, and Paul campaigned successive *Tomboys* in races to support sales. As he raced, he took advantage of his yachting affiliations to informally research the market, and he carefully analyzed each new boat's performance.

In addition to sales, Charlie remembered Paul as having an aptitude for machine shop work, and especially for rigging, enjoying the chance to get "on the boat with the man who did the deck hardware and rigging, and step the mast with him, and put the deck fittings on, and get the boat lookin' pretty for launching." After launching, it was up to Paul to study each new design with one hand on the tiller, because their design process itself was based fundamentally on "feel"—a difficult-to-quantify combination of calculations based on their experience of what had worked previously, plus awareness of what was happening worldwide that he gained by keeping up with the yachting magazines. Paul explained that for the K 38, as with earlier boats, "the basic hull design was all done on the loft floor": "What we'd do is get up there and lay out with battens on the floor the way we thought the waterline ought to look, then prick it up from there and build the cross-sections off of that."

In later designs, Charlie Underwood drew hull lines in scale beforehand to save time on the loft floor, but design fundamentals remained unchanged. Paul and Charlie were conservative designers cautiously working out the principles of George's discovery that light-displacement construction could work well in ocean-racing sailboats. They did it without recourse to aids like scale model tank testing, which many other professional designers were using. "We don't use synthetic materials until they have been tried and proven," Charlie explained of their cautiousness: "too many boats, slapped together with some new product, fall apart before the owner has even had time to pay for it." As Gary Keller observed, "when Paul designed and had a boat built, there wasn't any going back and making

changes; he had it all 'up here'—he knew what he was doing." Proven ways, carefully improved upon, seemed best.

As an apprentice architect in the 1960s, "Charlie Junior" watched his father work with Paul. "The process was well-organized," he says. His father, in collaboration with Paul, produced a set of initial lines drawings, then exterior plan and profile drawings, and finally the working drawings used to develop the boat itself. His father and a helper then lofted the boat, producing

the pattern-making for the frames and jigs and fixtures that were developed for manufacturing wooden boats. As soon as the hull was produced on the hull jig, it was then rotated into position, and construction of the interior and mechanical installation began. From there, the deck was fabricated and installed on the hull, and the finish carpentry, mechanical, electrical, and hardware installations were completed. Simultaneously, the spars were constructed and finished in the loft. With wooden boats there was a tremendous amount of skilled labor in paint and varnish work. It always seemed to appear that five days before launch the boat was a long way away from completion.

In retrospect, as the younger Underwood recalled, "the boats usually were finished on time—which is somewhat unusual in the boat business."

Charlie's father was sophisticated in managing construction time and costs, but lacking tank testing, their design method sometimes led to undesired results—particularly in handling. "They were very nice little boats, 38s, but they weren't very good in a breeze, 'cause they leaned over," maintained Gene Trepte, while Bill Kettenburg remembered that, compared to PCCs, "they were more tender and they had a lot more motion to 'em. I was never seasick in a PCC in my life, and I was seasick on a K 38!" The low freeboard—which could make for wet sailing on

K 38s—was raised on later designs. But one negative result of evolving the same basic hull design was that handling challenges endemic to the PCC were only magnified in the K 38. The sportswriter who observed on the trial run of the first PCC that "a teething infant could steer the *Eulalie* with one little pink finger," obviously hadn't sailed her in a blow from astern or abeam. Paul and Charlie continued to grapple with how to best control their light-displacement boats downwind. In each successive design, with a focus on improving balance, they maintained their traditional steering configuration, in which a tiller steered a rudder that was hinged on the aft edge of the keel. Others, like Charles "Bill" Lapworth, a young naval architect living in Orange County, were beginning to rethink rudder placement and control.

The challenges of downwind handling aside, the K 38 stood up well in both light and heavy airs. Its small size and minimal wetted surface helped it out-ghost heavier competitors in light and fluky breezes. And while one little K 38 demonstrated how well it stood up to heavy weather by making the long downwind passage to Hawaii, another showed it in the pair of barracuda that the commodore of the Los Angeles Yacht Club "caught" in his boat's companionway as he drained water after a gale-swept race to San Clemente Island.

In a market where racing trophies still shaped sales numbers, competitions remained crucial, and nowhere more so than in the expanding postwar Pacific Northwest market. On the bridge of his ship far off British Columbia's coast in 1951, one Canadian naval officer was startled to see a new boat forging seaward through a chillingly cold dawn as "sleeting rain and a dull swirling mist cut visibility to a few hundred yards." He recalled: "We sighted a yacht with K 38 on the sail, rail down, double reefed with storm jib, headed for Japan. A single numbed figure crouched immovable at the helm as she plunged on and on. We wheeled and came alongside within hail and told the stunned night

Morgan Miller shows off a Sweet Sixteen. Charlie Underwood designed the shapely little fiberglass sportster, and the yard launched the first one in 1955.

watch that he was almost twenty miles beyond the mark!"

Moments later, *Ono*'s chilled and doubtlessly disappointed crew scrambled on deck, shook out the reefs, hoisted a jenny, and tore away for the coast to chase the pack in the Swiftsure Race. Nineteen fifty-one was a rare bad year for K 38s in the Pacific Northwest's most famous sailing competition. The previous year *Ono* led the fleet of a dozen boats, and had been the only craft to escape damage in 50-knot gusts, despite being the smallest entry. The PCC *Gossip* took Swiftsure that year, but *Ono* won it outright in 1952, slicing through exceptionally heavy swells that drenched (and thinned out) her competitors. *Ono* won again in 1958, after one last *Gossip* victory, and in 1954 Charlie Ross triumphed in another K 38, *Totem*. By 1959, when *Rebel* won the race for Doug Sherwood, the K 38 was established as the first modern light-displacement one-design class to compete in northwestern waters. The second, however, was close

behind; Bill Lapworth's fragile but ultralight-displacement wooden Lapworth 36 racers, launched in Orange County, entered Swiftsure in 1954.

Yachting had informed its readers back in 1949 that the new K 38 appeared to be "a satisfactory compromise between an out-and-out racer and a comfortable cruiser," but by the time the last of the 40 K 38s was launched in 1959, racing sailboats able to bridge the comfort gap were becoming tough to find.

Americans had looked closely at a new fiberglass car, the Corvette, in 1953, and a few daring souls desperate to impress girls bought them. Off Point Loma in June 1955, the Kettenburg crew enjoyed speeding around in Charlie's newest prototype boat, a pioneering production fiberglass runabout named the Sweet Sixteen. The little boat's hull, Charlie said,

> had much more concave flare in the sides
> than you could possibly get with wood—and

it always had been my desire to produce a boat as shapely as a Sweet Sixteen, but it was an impossibility with wood. Now I had to start with wood, however, in order to build this shape—the male plug, that is—so I could build a female mold over that male plug.... By the time I had gotten this far, my partners got together and said to me, "Charlie, there's no sense in you payin' all the money for this adventure in fiberglass; we have to know about it too. So why don't you let us share in the cost of this material . . . and we may sell a couple?"

Kettenburg would sell more than 500 of these stylish outboards, which could be had complete with wraparound windshield and optional mahogany deck for $1,400. Therein lay the rub: theirs was a relatively small shop sitting on expensive bayside real estate. A $700 fiberglass boat like their entry-level Saucy Fourteen could have been built in any part of the country and

"The little boat's hull," Charlie said, had much more concave flare in the sides than you could possibly get with wood—and it always "had been my desire to produce a boat as shapely as a Sweet Sixteen, but it was an impossibility with wood."

✦ The Sweet Sixteen came in a classic runabout style (left) or a variety of other open and canopy styles.

The K 47 Motorsailer

For comfortable cruising or weekends afloat, some mariners preferred to combine the pleasure of sail with the comfort and reliability of a powerboat. William Hand had popularized the motorsailer in the 1920s, and a new generation of motorsailers appeared after the Second World War. Paul Kettenburg designed the company's version, the K 47, which was introduced in 1959. With a length of 46 feet six inches and beam of 13 feet six inches, the K 47 featured mahogany planking over steam-bent oak frames and fiberglass-covered plywood decks. The wide trunk cabin offered good space and headroom

To suit client preferences, the K 47 came in two styles.

The sloop-rigged K 47 had 926 square feet of sail as well as a 95-horsepower Mercedes Benz engine. A little more sailboat than powerboat, the sloop had its helm aft and slept four in two cabins.

The ketch-rigged K 47 had 898 square feet of sail in its split rig and a 125-horsepower Chrysler Crown engine. With its flying bridge amidships and owner's stateroom aft, the ketch slept six and was more powerboat than traditional sailboat.

Three K 47s took to the water in 1959: a sloop and two ketches.

Left: James Shannon's *Jimava*, K 47 number 2, shows the sloop configuration of the Kettenburg motorsailer. Below: The ketch version of the K 47 had a powerboat's flying bridge rather than a sailboat's conventional wheel aft.

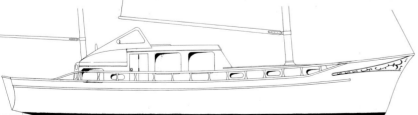

delivered by truck. They also received a compliment that cut into their profits: fiberglass's inexpensive "knock off" ability encouraged theft. Charlie recalled that "in the first year, it was stolen several times by people who borrowed a boat and molded over it." In 1958, with hundreds of fiberglass runabouts and sailboats built, Kettenburg was forced to halt fiberglass production. They were faced with crushing price competition from corporations like Ohio's Glasspar, which grossed $12 million the following year as it sold 16,000 boats, popped off molds in six plants across the country—one of which was in Orange County. In the short term, Paul and his partners made the right choice in leaving fiberglass behind; by about 1961, Americans suddenly realized that they were drowning in a sea of new fiberglass runabouts, and the market self-destructed as people bought used ones instead. But in the world of sailing, Kettenburg Boat Works and most other builders of wooden sailboats did miss the boat, which would set sail from neighboring Orange County.

Nevertheless, on a summer's day in 1959 three hundred happy onlookers gathered on Point Loma to watch the christening of *Tomboy II*, the first of the new 40-foot wooden K 40s. Five years in the making, the K 40 was beamier and had the masthead rig of all future Kettenburg sailboats. Company advertisers played up its family appeal, billing it as "The Family Boat that Wins the Races," and described the design as "traditional"—an odd but fitting term. There was nothing radically new about the K 40, whose fine qualities came instead from the firm's practice of refining and evolving the essential Kettenburg design in an upscale direction. The same ads described the storage space aboard as "a ladies' delight," and in the decidedly sexist world of 1950s boating, the fact that the design "wins over the skipper's lady" was somehow mentally kept in balance with the fact that sales were driven primarily by a lady skipper. Peggy was joined in her efforts by Glenn Waterhouse on San Francisco Bay and the Ross

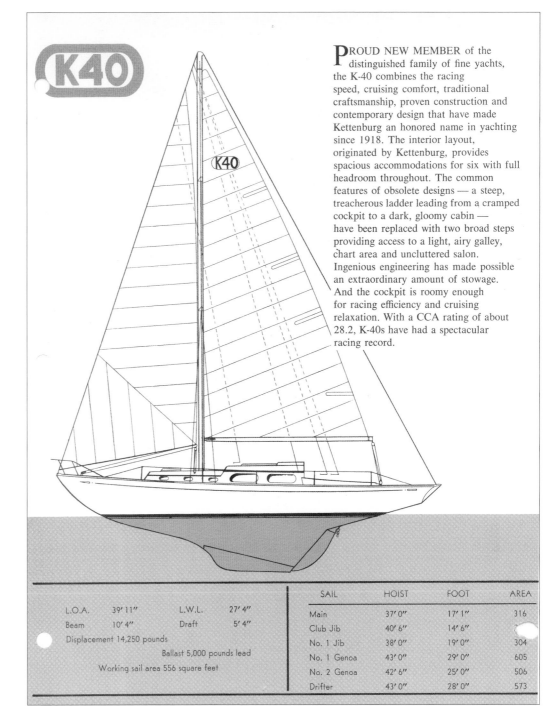

PROUD NEW MEMBER of the distinguished family of fine yachts, the K-40 combines the racing speed, cruising comfort, traditional craftsmanship, proven construction and contemporary design that have made Kettenburg an honored name in yachting since 1918. The interior layout, originated by Kettenburg, provides spacious accommodations for six with full headroom throughout. The common features of obsolete designs — a steep, treacherous ladder leading from a cramped cockpit to a dark, gloomy cabin — have been replaced with two broad steps providing access to a light, airy galley, chart area and uncluttered salon. Ingenious engineering has made possible an extraordinary amount of stowage. And the cockpit is roomy enough for racing efficiency and cruising relaxation. With a CCA rating of about 28.2, K-40s have had a spectacular racing record.

L.O.A. 39′ 11″   L.W.L. 27′ 4″
Beam 10′ 4″   Draft 5′ 4″
Displacement 14,250 pounds
Ballast 5,000 pounds lead
Working sail area 556 square feet

SAIL	HOIST	FOOT	AREA
Main	37′ 0″	17′ 1″	316
Club Jib	40′ 6″	14′ 6″	
No. 1 Jib	38′ 0″	19′ 0″	304
No. 1 Genoa	43′ 0″	29′ 0″	605
No. 2 Genoa	42′ 6″	25′ 0″	506
Drifter	43′ 0″	28′ 0″	573

Brothers in Seattle, who had sold the company's earlier boats. Now, however, sales representatives in Chicago and Florida were also taking orders as the firm prospered. In the previous year the sales team sold 140 sailboats and runabouts—a third of them to buyers within San Diego County—and the $300,000 they brought in was welcome indeed.

Peggy's best-known customer was, in all

In 1959 Kettenburg introduced the wooden K 40 as a traditional family sailboat.

Peggy's best-known customer was, in all except his profession, a familiar Kettenburg "type." Marshal Matt Dillon on TV's *Gunsmoke* was played by Jim Arness, remembered by Paul as "one of the greatest guys I have ever known."

except his profession, a familiar Kettenburg "type." Marshal Matt Dillon on TV's *Gunsmoke* was played by Jim Arness, remembered by Paul as "one of the greatest guys I have ever known." When Paul picked him up at the airport, for example,

by the time the poor guy got up to the gate, there must have been thirty women around

Working to windward under her big genoa jib, *Tomboy II* gives her crew a comfortable ride in her spacious cockpit. Designed 30 years after the PC, the K 40 was the first Kettenburg sailboat to carry a masthead jibstay.

there. *They would hold a piece of Kleenex or whatever they had in their purse and say, "Oh, Mr. Arness—can we have your signature? My granddaughter in Timbucktoo would just love your signature." He sat there for about fifteen minutes signing his name, with a big smile on his face. I said, "Jim, don't you ever get tired of that?" Jim's reply was, "When they stop that, I'm through!"*

Jim named both his Kettenburg sailboats *Sea Smoke*, following Peggy's suggestion that this term for the mist rising from wintry seas nicely echoed the name of his TV series. The boatyard was not above a few custom touches for a celebrity customer, and Gary Keller was responsible for one: "The head had an aluminum handle—a hollow aluminum handle with a yellow bicycle grip on top for the pump, to pump the salt water through. . . . Well, we took the yellow handle off, and got a plastic six-shooter, and stuck it down in the hollow aluminum handle, and taped it to the top." Peggy and her client were first aboard, "and when he saw that in the head," grinned Gary, "he gave a 'whoop'—you could'a heard him at the other end of the yard!"

When Jim moved up to a K 50, Peggy and Paul and his wife Dorothy sailed to Catalina with him on Paul's *Tomboy III* to talk over potential "extras" for his next Kettenburg product. "I don't think I have ever spent a more enjoyable weekend in my life with *anybody* than with him. He was the easiest-going person—he was just like a big Great Dane. If you wanted to go swimming, *he* was ready to go swimming," unlike customers of equivalent fame or wealth, whom Paul had come to believe had expectations for "everyone to be doing just what *they* wanted to do."

Like every K 40, Jim's boat was a racer at heart. Kept just an inch shy of 40 feet overall to comply with the Cruising Club of America's measurement rule, she was beamier than their earlier sloops and featured more freeboard, as the CCA favored when it doled out ocean racing

handicaps. Kettenburg for many years was a leader in "designing to the rules," which essentially had to do with balancing the goal of maximum performance against rating handicap penalties.

One K 40 took the thousand-mile race between Los Angeles and Mazatlan in 1961. A glance at the finish of the 130-mile race between Newport and Ensenada the year before shows a peculiarity of these long-distance ocean races, which had become Kettenburg specialties: as often as not, the victor had to puzzle out the fact that he'd won. Thanks in part to good navigational choices, at sunset skipper Don Stewart pushed the new K 40 *Bravata*—a Class D boat—up among a pack of six big Class A yachts. As the sun came up, his crew squinted astern at their celebrated competitors. With increasing excitement, Stewart pointed them out in turn: "that's *Chubasco*; that's *Barlovento*. Know what? We just won this race!" Their K 40 had beaten the biggest fleet in history, and sailed into Todos Santos Bay with 345 competitors trailing behind.

Like every port at the end of a long-distance race, Ensenada held opportunities for victors and vanquished alike to put their days of deprivation

and cold behind them. Gary Keller smiled as he recalled that "Hussong's was *the* famous watering hole in Ensenada after the race." After a race prior to 1961 in which Paul, Bill Kearns, and Charlie Underwood crewed on another K 40, Bill Kettenburg and his wife drove down to join them:

We got down there and, "Gary—you gotta see Hussong's." (I'd heard so many stories about it. And—I'm not gonna drink.) And we go down there, and I'm waiting outside Hussong's. Bill would come out...and I run into Bill. "Well, when're you guys ready to go?" He says, "I dunno. Have you seen Paul?" "No, he hasn't been out yet." . . . So—"Well, I'll go get him." And he dives into this milling mob around the bar, and the floor's all wet with margaritas—spilled margaritas, y'know, it smelled to high heaven . . . anyways, here comes Paul out of the crowd: "You seen Bill?" "He was here a minute ago—he's in there lookin' for you." "I'll go get him!"

And so on.

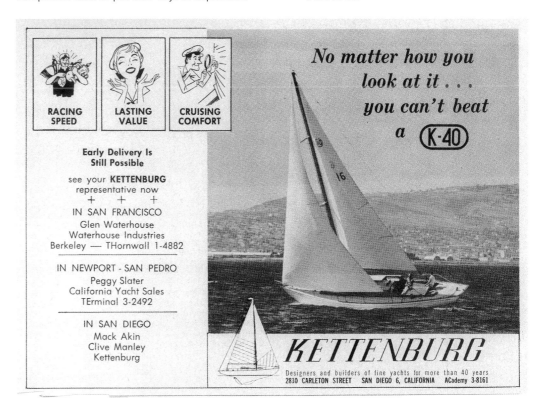

The results of the 1961 Transpac Race, however, revealed a disturbing trend. Trophies were spread among three K 40s and three Lapworth 36s, the largest class of light-displacement sailboats. And sailors reported that K 40s had some of the tracking problems endemic to traditional designs, as in strong following seas the rudder's placement so near the boat's center made for unruly handling.

While many yachtsmen were celebrating the K 40 as Kettenburg's best sailboat, in 1962 the attention and envy of most was grabbed by the new K 50, the biggest and most luxurious sailboat the firm produced. The gracious 50-footer with the houseful of glass was indisputably "a family yacht in conception," and essentially a luxury cruiser, although it did win a major race to Tahiti.

Serious racers like Doug Giddings and Gene Trepte had reservations about the K 50's competitive potential, but bought them anyway. Doug confessed that "it wasn't a very fast boat. In handicap races it never did anything. But it was a real, *real* fun boat," ideal for cruising with his young family, and for a bit of racing. Doug was an unusually casual participant in one San Clemente Island Race:

I decided, on this particular race, "The heck with following the fleet," so when we started out we kept going south all by ourselves, on the starboard tack, until I figured I might be able to make San Clemente and put over on port tack—and boy, we had a good wind. So we got near San Clemente Island the following morning. No boats around. I said, "Oh boy—we've lost them; we're last. So, okay— let's just enjoy the rest of the race." So we went around the island . . . just sailing for the fun of it. Got back to Point Loma and [Port Director John] Bate was there. He said "Congratulations!" I said, "What do you mean?" He said, "You're the first boat to finish!"

Opposite: *Tomboy III*, the first K 50, introduced the new class in 1962. A boat this size steered with a wheel. Above: The interior of James Arness's K 50 *Seasmoke* had a western feel in its spacious saloon. Left: *Tomboy III* emerges from the shop. Note the stylish new sign above the door.

For the first time, however, tuning a Kettenburg sailboat up to race-winning form required extensive modifications. Gene prodded Paul and Charlie into altering his K 50 as it was under construction, so he could capture the coveted Ahmanson Trophy off Los Angeles.

In the sad days at the end of 1963, just after President John F. Kennedy was killed in Dallas, Paul and Charlie introduced the K 43—their "condensed" K 50. It was still not clear that wooden boats themselves were about to sail into the sunset. Paul explained that "we wanted a comfortable cruising boat that would accommodate two or three couples, and one that would also be competitive under the old racing rule." Like Paul, Bill Kettenburg, Gene Trepte, and Charles Ross Underwood have all looked back on the K 43 as their favorite K boat, partly thanks to the presence of classic racer/cruiser elements, from the highly evolved Kettenburg hull on up. The interior layout was born in front of a fireplace, where Peggy Slater and famed Los Angeles-area sailmaker Kenny Watts swapped ideas, and when it came to the cabinetry, Charlie Underwood's design added still more luster to his firm's reputation for quality woodwork. In 1965, a new K 43 cost $32,900—about nine times the cost of Ford's sporty new Mustang convertible.

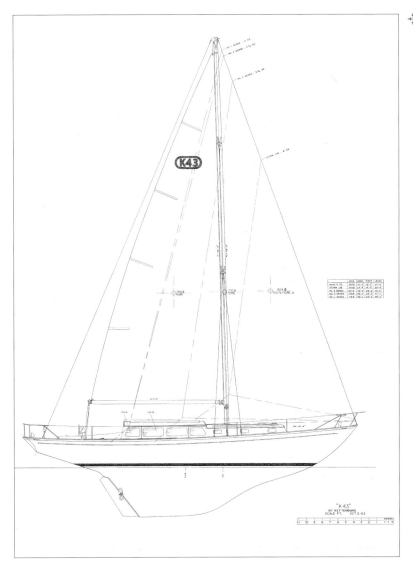

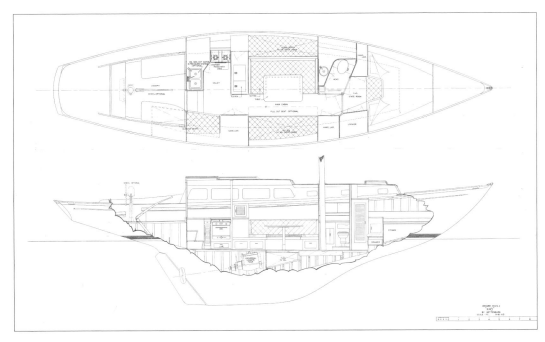

Opposite: The first K 43 draws a crowd after her launch in 1963. Left: The shapely K 43, with its deep keel, tall rig, and large cabin windows, was Paul Kettenburg's favorite design. Below: The K 43 was designed to be a comfortable cruising boat for two or three couples.

This was certainly no bargain, but the price was commensurate with the boat's quality and the firm's established upmarket position. According to Charles Ross Underwood, his father and Paul both "felt that it was important to keep the traditional style of the Kettenburg products, so they kept building the wooden decks [and] the wooden cabin sides—but in hindsight, that wasn't the right move. So at that same time, you had Islander, Ericson, Cal going totally fiberglass," which "drove the cost down—and the price down." Compared to Kettenburg's elegant yachts, the plastic products of those Orange County firms "didn't have that same wonderful style, and charm, and all the rest of it—but the market went to all-fiberglass." Paul recalled what

⟷ Left: Paul Kettenburg (left) and the production foreman inspect the keel of the first K 43, set up on the framing and planking jig in September 1963. Right: Caulking the hull of a K 38 or PCC in the late 1950s. Bottom: Profile of the K 43 with spade rudder like the Cal 40's, a design that was never built.

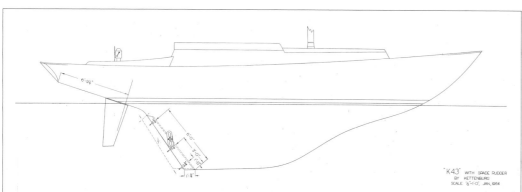

"K 43" WITH SPADE RUDDER
BY KETTENBURG
SCALE ½"=1'-0", JAN. 1964

happened next: "We were building the K 43, and fiberglass came into being, and our sales just practically *stopped* on it—because people thought they *had* to buy a fiberglass boat." Production ceased abruptly in 1967 with the 19th K 43.

Rolled up together in the MacMullen Library & Research Archives at the Maritime Museum of San Diego are plans for two very different K 43 hull profiles. One depicts the sailboat as produced, with its traditional keel arrangement. The

In 1966, Cal 40s also swept almost every trophy in the Bermuda Race. Lapworth changed yacht design and construction forever by combining his ideas about building light with the fin keel and spade rudder that had previously appeared only on much smaller boats, and on the custom boats of the very rich. And, of course, there was the fiberglass hull. What followed was a brief era in which production fiberglass sailboats like the Cal 40 competed at the highest levels in racing.

Bill Lapworth's new fiberglass Cal 40 became the ocean racing machine of the mid-1960s, and a real challenge to Kettenburg designers. Here, Cal 40 number 2, *Conquistador*, races off Miami in the midst of her winning SORC season in 1964.

alternative design shows the same boat with a spade rudder fully detached from the keel. The rudder is reminiscent of that on a new Southern California competitor, the Cal 40, designed by Bill Lapworth and launched in 1963, shortly before the first K 43 splashed into San Diego Bay.

Bill Lapworth of Newport was five years younger than Paul. As one of naval architecture's new generation, he was a university-trained theoretician of light-displacement yacht design, and a love of fast sailboats was his only similarity with the high-school-educated Paul and Charlie. Lapworth's first Cal 40 customer took the plans for what was intended to be a one-off design to two builders, who turned it down. He then drove south to Point Loma to call on Paul: "When I told him who did the design he threw me out of the office. He wouldn't have anything to do with it!" Perhaps the implication is that Paul, like most wooden builders, was blind to the future of boatbuilding—or it could simply be that Paul carried a grudge against the reputedly arrogant Lapworth. The customer next took the design to Jack Jensen, an engineer in Costa Mesa with no professional boatbuilding background. Jensen agreed to build it on condition that he construct 10 to absorb his mold-making costs. Instead, he ended up building 16 times that many.

The Cal 40 was a pioneer, and one trophy after another fell to this first class of large fiberglass sailboats. The early boats did suffer a few structural problems: the interior bulkhead tabbing of their hulls had a nasty tendency to fail at inconvenient moments, and the hull itself might occasionally "oil can"—or flex in and out—alarmingly. And there were inconveniences, as one would expect in any pioneering design; "the windows on all Jack's boats leaked like sieves," Lapworth confessed. But not even leaky windows stopped Cal 40s from winning the Southern Ocean Racing Circuit in 1964, or Transpac the following year, and again in 1966, 1967, and 1985. In 1966, Cal 40s also swept almost every trophy in the Bermuda Race. Lapworth changed yacht design and construction forever by combin-

ing his ideas about building light with the fin keel and spade rudder that had previously appeared only on much smaller boats, and on the custom boats of the very rich. And, of course, there was the fiberglass hull. What followed was a brief era in which production fiberglass sailboats like the Cal 40 competed at the highest levels in racing.

The Cal 40's long winning streak was finally laid to rest by the coming of the International Offshore Rule (IOR) in the early 1970s—a rule intended to allow boats from many countries to compete together—but the coup de grace was delivered by the procession of expensive one-off custom fiberglass designs that continue to dominate racing. Bill found himself regretting what he had done to help eclipse comfortable racing/cruising craft like the K boats. "It isn't a family thing anymore—and it's not even the kind of thing you can do without a lot of young bucks that are boat bums," Lapworth complained. "A lot of these fellows," he grumbled, have "never been to sea in a good boat that's comfortable and seaworthy." In other words, in a K boat.

In those times of intense market competition, the pressures of operating America's sole remaining mass-production wooden boatbuilding business told on Paul. So did the strains of balancing the concerns of his partners: "We were actually five *equal* partners, as it ended up. Everyone thought that this was impossible—for five equal partners to be able to run a business. Fortunately, each one had his own job, and each one could complement the others, and we worked really as a very close-knit group."

Unlike his gregarious brother, Paul was "a little more aloof—not because he was 'uppity,'" insisted Bud Caldwell, but because his was the more introverted personality. While "George didn't care about pressure, he just enjoyed totally what he was doing," Paul instead found racing competition stressful. "He was *good*, but I know it really put the heat on him," Bud recalled; "it was hard for him to take all the pressure" of racing and of running a business that was much

Oregon's Wallowa Lake

Scanning TransPac's Horizon

Valentine's Day Launching

larger than in his brother's day. "I had an office and a secretary, and I *still* spent most of my time in the yard," remembered Paul; "anybody that wanted to see me down there, they had to be in there before nine o'clock, or after four. Because the rest of the time, I was out in the yard." Tom Kettenburg remembered his father coming home exhausted, slumping into a chair, and falling asleep—then later lying in bed frustrated at being unable to get back to sleep again. The tightly wound Paul found an intense hobby to help him relax, like the archery and movie-making that had helped George Jr. When their father had died in 1953 (less than a year after his namesake son), he left his youngest boy his love for repairing cars. "I remember I took two beat-up Model Ts and made one good one out of them," while the boy was helping his brother build boats in their backyard. Dennie Barr O'Bryan always called Paul the company's "Motor Mack"—an engineer who loved engines. Ten years after his father died, Paul brought that passion for tinkering back to life. In 1963, he bought what was left of a 1912 Maxwell Special—a car a year older than he was—and got hooked on automotive restoration. "My wife made me build a new garage for the cars," Paul admitted to a reporter; "that's my occupation from eight to eleven most every night."

Others found different ways to relieve the stress of competing within the fiberglass walls that had suddenly sprung up around them. Peggy Slater, characteristically, thought that sailing her wooden K 43 single-handedly to Hawaii would be just the thing to help her relax. She dreamed of it even while her *Valentine II* was ready to be launched a few minutes before the stroke of midnight on Valentine's Day 1965. Peggy remembered the christening as "a splendid affair, with many flags, red roses frozen in a huge ice heart, and a lethal punch that had been 'thinned' with champagne." Three years later,

Peggy Slater's K 43, *Valentine II*, is ready for launch on Valentine's Day 1965.

however, Peggy found herself alone, stone cold sober, and living an entirely different side of sailboat ownership: "I was nineteen days at sea on my solo voyage to Hawaii, and my dream vacation sail had turned into a nightmare."

While back in Los Angeles, Peggy had used *Valentine II* as a sales tool, "taking customers sailing or to lunch or dinner aboard," she guiltily felt as if she was "using Babe Ruth to play with a pinball machine." So she planned her single-handed adventure, and ordered a Los Angeles firm to weld a wind-activated steering vane in the shape of a heart—the heart-shaped self-steering vane, taken together with her boat's bright red hull and bronze cherub figurehead, suggests Peggy's distinctive tastes, not to mention her eye for self-promotion.

During her passage, this steering device failed, leaving her to steer constantly or to adjust her sails to balance the boat while she rested. After 19 days in the open ocean, Peggy clambered forward in 35-knot winds to rig a jib as she headed into the notorious Molokai Channel. A wave smashed across the bow and "the jib and I were washed into the sea, which quickly wrapped the sail around me like a straitjacket." For 12 hours she hung alongside the strong Kettenburg hull, where, "held by my stretched-out lifeline, I was in no danger of the boat leav-

ing me, but I could not get back aboard. Trapped inside the sail and dragging beside the boat, I fought desperately in the darkness and the cold," struggling too against the pain radiating from a broken hand.

"I was alone on turbulent seas, 2,000 miles from home, and no one could help me," she recounted. "Each time the boat headed off the wind, the bow dipped below the seas and I was dragged underwater. Each time, I prayed that the boat would come back in time for me to catch my breath. As the hours dragged interminably through the black night, I pictured *Valentine* driving up on some reef."

Her struggle paid off: with her good hand, Peggy tugged once more on the snap-shackle that held her trapped. "This time it broke easily, weakened by previous usage. Suddenly my sail straitjacket began to move. I flexed my muscles to relieve the cold and stiffness and waited for one wild swing of the defective steering vane. As the boat heeled sharply and the rail dipped in the water, I managed to swing an arm and leg over the rail. Grimly I held on until a second wild knockdown put the rail under six inches of water."

"I was back aboard!" she crowed, but she was not yet in the clear. Peggy deliriously steered seaward and unintentionally evaded Coast Guard rescuers for three more days as she hallucinated about being saved by a tall, strong Western actor—who really *was* her client and friend. She remained embarrassed years later to talk to reporters about this single-handed adventure gone haywire, but she would tolerate no criticism of her K 43: "I have the means to own just about any boat in the world—and *this* is the one I have."

Even a vessel as well built as a K boat could merit the classic definition of a yacht: "a hole in the ocean lined with wood, into which one pours money." The owners of the new fiberglass boats soon found that their own holes in the ocean also sucked down plenty. Fiberglass, however, was opening sailing up to a much wider group of people than could afford the splendid wooden K boats.

Chapter Nine

Writing Kettenburg's Final Chapter

Paul Kettenburg and Charlie Underwood inspect the first K 41,
Kettenburg's first and only fiberglass sailboat design, in June 1966.
Inset: Helen Kearns christens the first K 41.

Today, what was once merely unmodern-looking has become classic, like the MG TF sports car Morgan Miller was driving at the time. The years have proved kind to both the MG TF—introduced to the market alongside the racy new Corvette and dismissed then as handsome but dated— and to the fiberglass boat with the wooden interior and cabin sides.

On any weekend on the water in early 21st-century Southern California, several of the region's most treasured "woodies"—bearing that distinctive K marking on their mainsails—will leap back to life. On San Diego Bay, one can even witness a fairly savage race between PCs decades older than many of their owners, kept in competitive trim by a merry band of passionate grass-roots acolytes. In other words, there is a surprising amount of life in these cherished old boats yet— despite the fact that the Kettenburg firm itself collapsed in 1994.

Eight years earlier, a 52-year-old businessman and sailor named Thompson "Tom" Fetter stepped aboard the yard's own newly restored PC, *Tradition*, and pushed off from the dock for her inaugural cruise. Kettenburg's last owner projected something of a "Norman Rockwell-esque image," enhanced by Effie, his little Sheltie who happily perched herself aboard. Tom's simple actions—unbuttoning the sail cover, running up the mainsail emblazoned with PC, and feeling the breeze in his face—*ought* to have given him pleasure. But not even a beautiful boat, a sunny

spring afternoon, and a canine companion could switch off the distractions in his head. "I had pictured that I would be able to have it at the dock there, and I could go down afternoons, and go for a 'beer can' sail." But restoring *Tradition* in-house had proven something of a costly boondoggle, and his worries wouldn't let him relax. Tom was fated not do a lot of sailing on George Kettenburg Jr.'s most famous design.

"I sailed on it *once*, in all the time I had it. And I had my dog on it—and she slipped and fell off." So Kettenburg's last owner, ingloriously smelling of wet dog, turned *Tradition* around; he never sailed her again. "I just could never take the time. Kettenburg was a seven-day-a-week, 12- or 14-hour-a-day thing. You just couldn't get rid of it—in the middle of the night you'd just wake up worrying about it." He sold *Tradition* itself, fittingly enough, during the frantic cost-cutting that characterized the last throes of Kettenburg Marine. Tom's eight years at the helm ended the Kettenburg company 76 years after George Kettenburg and his father started it.

Back in the late 1960s, profitability in the company's new boat design and construction, its staple, symbolic line, was slipping bafflingly out

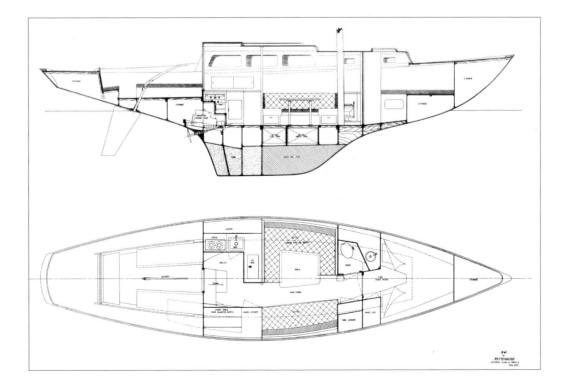

Left: *Tomboy V*, the first K 41, shows off at sea. More cruiser than racer, the K 41 rarely beat the Cal 40 in races, and the distinctive wooden cabin sides made the K 41 a more expensive boat. Right: The comfortable arrangement of the K 41.

of reach. "It's going to be a good, hot boat," Paul had prophesied in 1966 of their firm's first foray into fiberglass sailboats. But instead, their K 41 seldom if ever beat Bill Lapworth's radical fiberglass Cal 40, and their boat's sumptuous (and expensive) wooden cabin sides and trim looked dated by contrast with the all-fiberglass competition. Today, what was once merely unmodern-looking has become classic, like the MG TF sports car Morgan Miller was driving at the time. The years have proved kind to both the MG TF—introduced to the market alongside the racy new Corvette and dismissed then as handsome but dated—and to the fiberglass boat with the wooden interior and cabin sides. But when interviewed in recent years, Paul sighed. "None of us particularly liked working with fiberglass. And we couldn't figure out how to make money at it."

The K 41 was the last production sailboat designed and built at Kettenburg. The younger Charlie Underwood, who drew the boat's lines while apprenticed to his father, remembered: "The market was *really* changing rapidly then. And it was changing because of the introduction of fiberglass into construction." Kettenburg plowed head-on into a wave of cheaper competitors from companies like Cal, Ericsson, Islander, Coronado and Columbia, most of which were located near Costa Mesa in Orange County. Kettenburg's first and only fiberglass-hulled sail-

boat was launched in July 1966, several months later than anticipated. While Charlie had experience in developing fiberglass runabouts and designing hulls for navy boats, his son recalled that it was in the painstaking care given to the hull tooling that his father's perfectionism "really shone": "Anyone who is in the business of developing fiberglass boats will tell you that the fairness of the hull is a direct reflection of the accuracy and structural integrity of the tooling. I know that Charlie took criticism for the amount of time and money that it took to develop the hull mold," but on *Tomboy V*'s launching day her dark green sides offered a near-perfect mirror for

Above: Paul Kettenburg developed the sail plan for the K 41. The boat's bow was adapted from the K 40, Paul and Charlie collaborated on the hull design, and Charlie designed the rest of the boat. Left: *Tomboy V* gleams before launch. Kettenburg rightly claimed its hulls were smoother and stronger than any other comparable fiberglass boats on the market.

onlookers' faces. "It would be hard to find a more flawless fiberglass hull," Charlie reflected. Advertised as the "strongest and smoothest in the industry," the new hull offered a few twists on Paul and Charlie's old design themes, most notably in a detached spade rudder inspired by the Cal 40.

When interviewed four decades later, Paul still had mixed feelings about that rudder. "Instead of the rudder being out on the back end of the keel, we put a spade rudder in it. Spade rudders had come into—*hah!*—popularity." Spade rudders did have reputations for making boats wild to steer, and they demanded constant tending in cruising, but the configuration offered more downwind control in racing. Virtually no new large sailboat has been launched without one in the decades since.

Like every K boat since George's day, the K 41's design was a team effort. Paul contributed the design of the rig and worked out the sail plan with his friend, the sailmaker Kenny Watts. About the hull, he explained to a newspaperman that "we took the bow lines directly from the K 40 but made changes in the hull sections aft of amidships," to turn it into a sleeker, better-performing design. "I worked out the hull lines," explained Charlie Underwood, reworking them after he received feedback from Paul, Kenny, Kermit Seeley, and other friends of Paul's. Charlie developed the cabin's exterior profile, its interior finish and trim, and calculated the sales price, making the concept a reality at a new facility a few miles inland in Santee. The company optimistically opened the new plant early in 1967 to build the hulls and to house the office where they anticipated developing and designing future sailboats.

Looking up from his drawing board, the younger Charlie Underwood watched the design process up close, as his two strong-willed elders occasionally engaged in "spirited debate" about elements of the their latest sailboat's design. "I was doing the drawing on that boat with a *lot* of guidance—that was really my first project—and

Above: Charlie Underwood outside Kettenburg's fiberglass production facility in Santee, California, 1967. Left: Paul Kettenburg and David Grimes inspect the spade rudder of a K 41, 1969. Charlie Underwood added this feature of the Cal 40 to the K 41.

Paul and my dad were debating the width of the side decks on the house. And Paul felt that from the crew's point of view they would rather have a wide side deck to sit on while they were 'hiking out.'" But "my father's point," Charlie maintained, was that "part of what sold these boats was that there was so much perceived room in the interior, and they were open and light, and . . . if we go make 'em narrow again, we are—in so many words—we're going *backwards*." This was "kind of a standoff situation" between the two men, but in this case the senior Underwood's idea won out and the boat ended up with the wider house. In the balance between outright racing and the big interiors favored for comfortable cruising, comfort had been outweighing racing speed at Kettenburg since 1962's K 50. But with the benefit of hindsight, the younger Charlie Underwood believed the K 41 could have been more financially viable had the deck been fiberglass, and the boat priced low like its competitors—and had it been faster.

Another controversy between the two designers reveals more about competitive drawbacks of the K 41: greater weight was one of the factors that slowed it down. Gary Keller, who worked out the boat's mechanical and electrical layout and helped Charlie develop the production line, remembered that Charlie

and Paul came head-to-head one time, in the production of the K 41, down near the end of the run—it was starting to taper off. Paul had gotten "on" Charlie about the laminations in the hull—I don't know how many extra laminates down in there, because he was afraid in that portion of the hull that it needed more strength. . . . Paul kept badgering him: "Hey, lighten up on that fiberglass, Charlie!" . . . But the . . . very last hull we molded, it was done on "spec"—we didn't have a buyer for it. And Paul got his way. He lightened up the fiberglass. Well, that boat went like stink. I mean—he increased the speed, in lightening it up like that!

Gary recalled "coming back in one Sunday, having sailed this last K 41—and I was amazed at the speed of that thing—we were coming in, and coming up behind one of the company boats that was owned by a very prominent yachtsman." This particular yachtsman was quite proud of his K 43—a bigger boat with a longer waterline and a lot more canvas—that should, theoretically, have been faster. But Gary "took him on his leeward side, and I walked past him like he was backing up!" The memory made him cringe: "you *don't* fly by a customer like that. I didn't realize who it was until I was coming up real close on his quarter—well, anyway, I turned

⊹ Left: Charlie Underwood Jr. began work at Kettenburg drafting the K 41 with his father's guidance. Above: Charlie Underwood (left) and Gary Keller, with a new K 41 hull in the new Santee plant, 1967.

Left: Charlie Underwood and Paul Kettenburg inspect the wooden plug for the K 41's fiberglass hull production, 1966. Right: A K 41 sails alongside *Columbia*, an Olin Stephens-designed 12 Meter yacht that successfully defended the America's Cup in 1958.

around and put my back to him." Scrunching down in his seat, Gary fretted, "*Damn!* If he sees who's in this thing . . . !"

Gary needn't have worried, and in competition the K 41 would not be remembered as a particularly successful design. The younger Charles Underwood first "took serious notice of the difference in performance between the K 41 and the recently developed Cal 40" when racing off San Diego as a crew member aboard a K 41. Compared to the Cal 40, designed "to the rule" with much less overhang, a longer waterline, and lighter weight, the $29,975 K 41 was slower and cost more than its competitor, priced at about $28,000. While fans of the elegant Kettenburg wood interiors disdained the all-fiberglass Cal 40, the K 41's higher price took a toll on sales. And it was painfully apparent that their new boat lacked the speed to compete well; weight was one inhibiting factor, but not the only one. The firm stopped building these last production sailboats after completing 29—an impressive number, but ultimately a disappointing finish to decades of memorable Kettenburg yachts.

Ultimately, in Gary Keller's opinion: "there was *no way* Paul would sacrifice quality for price. And that's one of the reasons the line ended. Because along came fiberglass boats, and every new . . . racing season, new rules would come out, and the fiberglass boats could very easily be revised to meet the new rules—we called 'em 'rule beaters'—and that's what people wanted: 'Tupperware'—throwaway boats. The hot racers would buy a new one every year."

Increasingly, too, the wave of new fiberglass sailboat designs from small Orange County firms were commissioned from specialized naval architects, like the two Bills: Lapworth—whose

Ultimately, in Gary Keller's opinion: "there was *no way* Paul would sacrifice quality for price. And that's one of the reasons the line ended. Because along came fiberglass boats, and every new . . . racing season, new rules would come out, and the fiberglass boats could very easily be revised to meet the new rules—we called 'em 'rule beaters'—and that's what people wanted: 'Tupperware'—throwaway boats.

designs became synonymous with Cal boats—and Tripp, who did the same for Columbia. Specialists were pushing sailboat evolution *fast*, introducing ever-more-powerful rigs and lighter, higher-performance hulls that rapidly made the market more competitive. As Paul and Charlie played catch-up, other builders allied with "name" designers were going national with sales more successfully. Better sales ensured them better economies of scale, enabling them to drop prices still further. And all-fiberglass construction allowed competitors to create much less expensive products than the K 41, with its signature wooden trim.

The Kettenburg boatyard did, however, launch one last splendid "one off" wooden

time, Paul and Peggy Slater negotiated with a customer, and the K 46 *Hidalgo* slid into the water on her way to a successful racing career. The younger Underwood would soon leave the yard for firms where he could work further on his design and product-development skills, because the handwriting was on the wall: Kettenburg's new boat design was coming to an end under new ownership.

"Paul called all the employees to the back of the yard, and stood up on a box," remembered Gary Keller, as Paul announced in 1968 that the partners had decided to sell. Although Gary and the other shaken listeners appreciated Paul's assurances that their jobs were guaranteed, "we were all in shock" at the fact that their old firm's

succeeded in persuading their partners not to sell the land itself—a decision that proved financially beneficial for them in the long run. But for Paul at least, "it took the load off" to hand the company's fortunes to others; he worked for ten more years as Kettenburg's president after the corporation took over in January 1969.

The family firm that Whittaker absorbed had been reorganized as Kettenburg Marine in 1965, when the five partners re-divided equal ownership among themselves and added key men like Bud Caldwell and their invaluable accountant, Fred Neumeister. About 140 employees worked for them in 1967: in the profitable chandlery built up by Morg and Bill; in Bill Kearns's boat repair yard; and in Charlie's naval repairs, on

"They bought us for all our expertise," explained Bill Kettenburg, "because we did *every-thing*. There wasn't anything—from navy boats, to sailboats, to power boats, to repair, to wholesale distribution, to export, to retail stores, design—you name it, we were in it."

sailboat in 1968. The owner of an earlier Kettenburg model was considering ordering a custom racer from Olin Stephens's East Coast design firm, Sparkman & Stephens, famous for both class boats (including America's Cup-winning 12 Meters) and one-off racers. Instead, he went with Kettenburg. The younger Charlie Underwood was proud to be given charge of the design: "I proposed to Paul and Charlie several concepts that would improve the performance of the successful K 43 hull shape—enlarged to 46 feet—by changing the design of the underbody and keel. Essentially we would add what was called a 'bustle' from the keel to the rudder fairing at the leading edge, and shape the keel so that it would angle aft toward the bottom."

While these improvements added significant cost, Paul and Charlie decided that they also added performance, and these final evolutions of their old hull design were incorporated. One last

new master would be the Los Angeles-based Whittaker Corporation, a *Fortune* 500 company with roots as an aerospace valve maker and a value of $753.4 million. "I wasn't really *for* selling, because I was the youngest," remembered Bill Kettenburg, but "Paul was getting older, Charlie was older, and Bill Kearns was older. And nobody had ever retired from Kettenburg—they all died." Bill too was looking to separate himself from running the distribution side of the firm before the same fate befell him: "I flipped a coin to either buy a Kettenburg 43, or build a house up in the mountains." The mountains won. "We felt," explained Paul, "that we were all getting along in years, and something could happen to any one of us, and that could be a *real* problem." Tom Fetter—whose involvement spanned both ends of this last chapter of the Kettenburg business story—negotiated with Paul on behalf of Whittaker. The "young guys," Morg and Bill,

whose profits the firm would increasingly depend. Since the Korean War, the yard had secured many contracts for small boat repair for the navy, and these plus a number of prototype navy projects provided the firm's bread and butter. When he helped purchase Kettenburg in the late 1960s, Art Miley was group contoller for Whittaker's Marine and Leisure Time Division. He remembered the Kettenburg firm as a "solid, small and well-managed company—no 'smoke and mirrors' at all—what you see was what you got. The company had changed in the last few years before this, getting out of the boat-building business and becoming primarily a supply and repair business."

Art explained that "Whittaker was a conglomerate, and conglomerates by their nature acquire a diverse number of types of companies—and they had decided to acquire a large number of pleasure boating companies."

Whittaker Vice President David Grimes, a San Diegan and avid fisherman whom Gary Keller remembered as "a real gentleman," had proposed acquiring a group of companies centered around the theme of marine and leisure activities. When Whittaker snapped up Kettenburg, they had already swallowed up the Costa Mesa fiberglass sailboat builder Columbia, as well as Coronado, another Southern California fiberglass sailboat builder. Trojan in Pennsylvania, Bertram in Miami, Desco—which built shrimp trawlers in Florida—and Italian yacht-builder Riva filled the other stalls in Whittaker's Marine and Leisure Time stable.

"They bought us for all our expertise," explained Bill Kettenburg, "because we did *everything*. There wasn't anything—from navy boats, to sailboats, to power boats, to repair, to wholesale distribution, to export, to retail stores, design—you name it, we were in it." In 1969, they were the biggest repair facility in the West for small pleasure craft and industrial and navy boats, taking in about two hundred boats per month. With several sources of income—and despite the K 41's sales troubles—the company's overall sales had doubled between 1960 and 1967, reaching $3.3 million. Kettenburg's name reached its zenith under Whittaker in the 1970s, when they repaired more boats than any other American boatyard. A magazine writer gushed that "there is scarcely a yachtsman on the Pacific Coast, and in many other areas as well, who hasn't at one time or another been in contact with Kettenburg produced boats, Kettenburg marine hardware, Kettenburg brokerage houses, or had his boat hauled out at Kettenburg's, so broad has been the coverage of this name in the boating field." Kettenburg had become, as another magazine writer put it, "a name synonymous with the boating business in Southern California."

Whittaker, however, wasn't interested in reviving Kettenburg's sailboat design and construction fortunes, although they recognized the firm's reputation for quality new boat construction. Instead, as Tom Fetter said, "one aspect of

The company's managers after the sale to Whittaker Corporation: Art Miley (left), Dave Grimes, and Tom Fetter, ca. 1970.

the marine and recreational business that we didn't have a handle on was hardware and repair," which made Morg and Bill's ventures especially attractive. At the chandlery's height under Whittaker, they operated a half-dozen stores scattered across the lower half of the state, as far north as Oxnard. They supplied wholesale parts throughout Southern California, and Bill set up sales of products to Mexico, Taiwan, Singapore, and Hong Kong—this back when Asian boatbuilders relied on brand-name American parts. Tom confessed, however, that the fact that Whittaker was Los Angeles-based made acquiring Kettenburg a bit more attractive to Fetter, Grimes, and Miley: "Grimes and Art Miley and I wanted to live in San Diego, and Kettenburg was a San Diego company, and so we felt that we would sort of rationalize and justify—to *some* degree—our location here."

Whittaker's primary purchasing technique was to snap up companies by swapping them for Whittaker stock, whose high price-to-earnings ratio was one result of their corporation's high-tech aerospace aspect. By pooling the earnings of an acquired company back into Whittaker's own earnings "you would just rocket the stock up"—quite legally at the time—and Whittaker stock soared skyward on a kind of artificial high.

But when articles appeared in *Barron's* in 1968 questioning the validity of "pooling of interests"—the shifting sand underpinning Whittaker's soaring stock value—it "just decimated the stock prices of conglomerates," remembered Tom. "They all just plummeted after that."

Whittaker stock, which had commanded $70 per share during negotiations, hurtled downward, disgusting stockholders like Bill Kettenburg; he and his partners grumbled that they could have economically wallpapered rooms with their stock certificates. As Art Miley recalled, "I ended up selling my stock in Whittaker, and I had options of, I think, $100 a share" but "probably sold 'em for thirty bucks a share." The younger Charlie Underwood recalled his father saying that his stock went from over $24 per share to $2. Frustrated but patient, his father held on to his stock until it staggered back up to $24, well after the rest of his partners had dumped theirs.

Not only was stock volatility an issue, but the theory behind conglomerates like Whittaker was itself flawed. As Art explained, the theory "says that if you have a 'template' that's successful in running a business, you can apply that template to . . . other businesses, and they're all going to come out as cookie-cutter, well-managed, well-run companies. Well, that whole theory came to be flat-out considered not true! In the early '70s the conglomerates were *really* out of style; they ended up divesting themselves of most of the companies that they bought."

Just over a year after buying Kettenburg, Whittaker hired a CEO who, faced with $332 million in debt and plunging stock prices, joined the rush to divest unwanted subsidiaries and began gradually selling off a quarter of their 135 acquisitions. Pressured by the new CEO in 1971 to move up to Los Angeles, Fetter, Grimes, and Miley demurred and left Whittaker, but Tom kept an eye on Kettenburg as the beleaguered giant sold its other recreational boating companies to a Bahrainian buyer in 1985. As Tom recalled, "Kettenburg became kind of an orphan, at that point. The other boat companies were all gone—the rationale for 'em was gone, and Kettenburg was just left there."

Along the way, Whittaker had discovered there was no institutional management in place to run Kettenburg or the other boat companies, because they had bought virtually all of them from graying founders. They also discovered just how difficult it was to coordinate their operations efficiently with each other.

The last hurrah for boatbuilding itself at Kettenburg came after Whittaker united its Columbia and Coronado sailboat lines, closed their Costa Mesa plant, and moved manufacturing to a new Virginia factory in 1975—then discovered that they had thrown away their West Coast market share. Australian designer Alan Payne's new Columbia 9.6 Meter had a typical molded fiberglass hull and deck, but its interior was drab at best. Around Christmastime 1975, while visiting his son in Orange County, Charlie Underwood took a phone call. It had been over five years since K 41 production had ceased, and he and Ann had moved to Florida, to build trawlers for Whittaker. His bosses asked him to return to San Diego to study Payne's interior, which Charlie thought "lacked personality, and

was quite austere, and wasn't very acceptable on the market—at least on the *Pacific* Coast. Now some people are not really concerned about the interiors—just like to race the boat—and I figure Payne did a great job at designing that boat. However, as far as making it a Kettenburg standard of interior, it missed by ten miles!"

Paul and Charlie were asked to remodel the boat up to their old standards of beautiful interior woodwork as a special "West Coast Edition," under the Kettenburg name. In San Diego, Charlie looked over the interior, accompanied by three dark-suited Whittaker executives:

> *The Senior Executive Vice President of the whole corporation . . . said, "Now, Charlie, what can you do? I hope you just have to put a few trim pieces on, or somethin' like that, to make this look better." And I said to him, "Well, it all depends on whether you're just tryin' to hit the bottom of the market with a 'price boat,' or if you really want to make this a decent interior." And he said, "Well, what do you mean?"*

As Charlie pointed out the superior trim of other boats for sale on the lot, Paul walked up: "'Why don't you take him along and show him some *real* boats? Show him what you did on the K 50 and the K 43.' He said, 'You always made great interiors, and we knew that we'd better not try and match your work . . . but we knew *you* could.'"

These were kind words indeed from an old partner and sometime rival. Charlie told the Whittaker men,

> *"Well, if you want me to fix this, the only thing—'trim piece'—that I can take off and make it work is...gut* this *interior, and start over from scratch." . . . "And stop the production at Columbia on this boat, until we get somethin' straightened out—so we don't just have a bunch of junk to sell." Well, that's when one guy said, "Oh, no!" And I said to the Executive Vice President, "Who the heck is that guy, anyway?" He said, "He's the Vice President of production at Columbia Yacht!"*

With great effort, as Paul recounted proudly, "we made it into a boat that you could live in," but ultimately "it wasn't really a Kettenburg boat."

The boats, renamed K 32s, weren't exactly sow's ears, but even so, Kettenburg's modifications to interiors and rigs still couldn't turn them into silk purses. Gary Keller called them "nice little boats, but by no means a racing boat," and they received decidedly mixed reviews on their debut in 1977. Priced higher than average for a fiberglass sailboat in their size range, their wood interiors added weight. They weren't commercially successful, and were too little, too late for Whittaker. Charlie, initially positive and enthusiastic, set up manufacturing in the new Kettenburg boatyard near Oxnard, California, where he moved with his family. But ultimately, he decided it was "the most mixed-up and wasted effort in Kettenburg history," and finally retired, disgusted, in 1978, with Paul retiring shortly thereafter. The doors closed on Columbia itself the following year.

With great effort, as Paul recounted proudly, "we made it into a boat that you could live in," but ultimately "it wasn't really a Kettenburg boat."

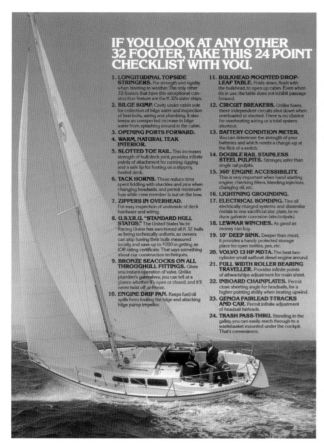

IF YOU LOOK AT ANY OTHER 32 FOOTER, TAKE THIS 24 POINT CHECKLIST WITH YOU.

1. **LONGITUDINAL TOPSIDE STRINGERS.** For strength and rigidity when blasting to weather. The only other 32-footers that have this exceptional construction feature are the K 32's sister cans.

2. **BILGE SUMP.** Cavity under cabin sole for collection of bilge water and inspection of keel bolts, wiring and plumbing. It also keeps an unexpected increase in bilge water from splashing around in the cabin.

3. **OPENING PORTS FORWARD.**

4. **WARM, NATURAL TEAK INTERIOR.**

5. **SLOTTED TOE RAIL.** This increases strength of hull/deck joint, provides infinite points of attachment for running rigging and a safe lip for footing on a slippery, heeled deck.

6. **TACK HORNS.** These reduce time spent fiddling with shackles and pins when changing headsails, and permit minimum fuss while crew member is out on the bow.

7. **ZIPPERS IN OVERHEAD.** For easy inspection of underside of deck hardware and wiring.

8. **U.S.Y.R.U. "STANDARD HULL STATUS."** The United States Yacht Racing Union has sanctioned all K 32 hulls as being technically uniform, so owners can skip having their hulls measured locally, and save up to $200 in getting an IOR rating certificate. That says something about our construction techniques.

9. **BRONZE SEACOCKS ON ALL THROUGHULL FITTINGS.** Gives you instant operation of valve. Unlike plumber's gatevalves, you can tell at a glance whether it's open or closed, and it'll never twist off or freeze.

10. **ENGINE DRIP PAN.** Keeps fuel/oil spills from fouling the bilge and attacking bilge pump impellor.

11. **BULKHEAD MOUNTED DROP-LEAF TABLE.** Folds down, flush with the bulkhead, to open up cabin. Even when it's in use, the table does not inhibit passage forward.

12. **CIRCUIT BREAKERS.** Unlike fuses, these independent circuits shut down when overloaded or shorted. There is no chance for overheating wiring or a total system shortout.

13. **BATTERY CONDITION METER.** You can determine the strength of your batteries and which needs a charge-up at the flick of a switch.

14. **DOUBLE RAIL STAINLESS STEEL PULPITS.** Stronger, safer than single rail pulpits.

15. **360° ENGINE ACCESSIBILITY.** This is very important when hand starting engine, checking filters, bleeding injectors, changing oil, etc.

16. **LIGHTNING GROUNDING.**

17. **ELECTRICAL BONDING.** Ties all electrically charged systems and dissimilar metals to one sacrificial zinc plate, to reduce galvanic corrosion (electrolysis).

18. **LEWMAR WINCHES.** As good as money can buy.

19. **10" DEEP SINK.** Deeper than most, it provides a handy protected storage place for open bottles, jars, etc.

20. **VOLVO 13 HP MD7A.** The best two-cylinder small sailboat diesel engine around.

21. **FULL WIDTH ROLLER BEARING TRAVELLER.** Provides infinite points of athwartships adjustment for main sheet.

22. **INBOARD CHAINPLATES.** Permit close sheeting angle for headsails, for a higher pointing ability when beating upwind.

23. **GENOA FAIRLEAD T-TRACKS AND CAR.** Permit infinite adjustment of headsail fairleads.

24. **TRASH PASS-THRU.** Standing in the galley, you can easily reach through to a wastebasket mounted under the cockpit. That's convenience.

Left: Introduced in 1977, the K 32 was designed by Alan Payne as the Columbia 9.6 Meter and fitted out with a suitably stylish wooden interior by Kettenburg. Above: Paul Kettenburg at the helm of a K 32. Above right: Paul Kettenburg in the K 32 interior he designed with Charlie Underwood. Right: Paul Kettenburg, before his retirement at the end of 1978.

To Tom Fetter in 1986, "it looked to me like Kettenburg was an opportunity: there was a seller, who didn't want to keep it—namely Whittaker—it was a business I knew and understood, and I had contacts within the company, and so it looked like a good deal." Quite a few people besides Tom would come to regret that assessment, but he was nothing if not self-assured. "It's gonna be a family business again!" he proclaimed to Gary Keller, who now ran Kettenburg's highly profitable marine electronics division. As Fetter promoted family and friends, he also developed a reputation among some for acting without listening to those who had been with the firm for decades. Gary remembered one of the original Kettenburg partners emerging from Tom's office fuming, "I don't know why I'm

One smart move in the gathering financial gloom proved to be Fetter's purchase of a former Safeway store near the boatyard on Rosecrans Street, which his daughter Margi and Bill Kettenburg converted into one of the largest and finest marine hardware stores in the world. Kettenburg's retail, wholesale and export aspects had made up 56 percent of company profits the year before Tom bought it.

still here—Fetter won't listen to a damn thing I had to say!" But buying Kettenburg also seemed like good business from Tom's standpoint as a lifelong San Diego sailor who had long serviced his own ketch at the Kettenburg yard, and whose daughter "JJ" was an Olympic sailing medalist. He was also working his way up through the yacht club ranks to commodore, the exalted position that Paul and the PC-racing brothers Joe and George Jessop had held. In classic 1980s style, Tom put together a highly leveraged deal, borrowing 90 percent of the purchase price of $7.5 million.

So, Art Miley asked rhetorically, "why did a reasonably successful small company go out of business?" In his opinion, Fetter merely "happened to be there when the bow went under," as the waters of insolvency closed around the old company. In Art's estimation, the causes came from outside: "Tom got caught with a 'double whammy': the Stock Market crash, and the navy cutting back on its business." Tom and his wife Jane—his vice president—made money in 1986 and 1987, the year Morg retired from running the stores. Bill, the last Kettenburg to retire, called it quits shortly thereafter. But on "Black Monday" in October 1987, the stock market plunged 22 percent—a greater drop than the one that precipitated the Great Depression. As capitalism's hot flash temporarily withered the discretionary spending that drove the recreational boat market, the navy simultaneously strove to make its procurement practices more efficient. The service cut back radically on repairs, which had reportedly supplied 65 percent of Kettenburg profits for several years.

As the navy pulled its haul-outs of its small boats from the boatyard to the navy yard, the

advantage of the company's navy master ship repair contract also melted away. It had ensured them a niche business among much larger competitors on San Diego's waterfront—until the navy began to aggregate repair contracts over six or twelve months on individual ships. Navy work dried up.

One smart move in the gathering financial gloom proved to be Fetter's purchase of a former Safeway store near the boatyard on Rosecrans Street, which his daughter Margi and Bill Kettenburg converted into one of the largest and finest marine hardware stores in the world. Kettenburg's retail, wholesale and export aspects had made up 56 percent of company profits the year before Tom bought it. But there was competition here too, in the form of a young company that opened its first store in 1975 after a decade as a mail-order rope business, changed its name to West Marine in 1977, and spread rapidly across the West.

By the end, Fetter's five Kettenburg Marine stores competed directly with West Marine's 13 stores, and Tom had invested in expensive new warehousing. Trapped by the economics and unable to work out an alternative, Tom ultimately had to sell: "I sold everything I could get my hands on to pour the money into Kettenburg. And so I sold the land after I had bought it, and the money got flushed into Kettenburg—and flushed down the toilet, so to speak. Anyway, we struggled . . . and I was in the Special Assets Group—sort of the 'reform school' for problem loans."

A friend of Art Miley's told him that "in the latter months of Kettenburg when they were really on their way under, he saw Tom's light in his office on many nights late at night, as Tom was there trying to work out *something* to keep it going." Tom felt forced to liquidate, and, as he surmised, "I probably shortened my life expectancy, with all that stress." He later rebounded to business success with a small empire of local car washes and gas stations.

The memory of being at the helm of a beloved sinking ship, however, remained bitter—especially when he had just achieved his dream of becoming the San Diego Yacht Club's commodore.

Tom recalled, with a shudder, one of the hardest things he ever had to do. At a Wednesday luncheon at the yacht club in February 1994, he stood and announced, as commodore, that the 76-year-old business bearing Paul's family name was closing. Paul, an active staff commodore himself, sat stonily in the audience. At its height under Whittaker, Kettenburg Marine had employed about 300 people; 10 percent were of Mexican descent, reflecting labor's changing face in Southern California. The last 28 employees were laid off in February 1994, and the yard was leased.

Kettenburg Marine, like notable Eastern wooden boatyards from Nevins to Luders, failed to establish itself as a viable fiberglass boatbuilder. The new material, which held so much promise for ordinary sailors, snuffed them out as the economy globalized, and the newest threats to American recreational boat manufacturing shifted to sailboats shipped over from Asia. Ironically, however, the loss of wood as an everyday building material has led true, die-hard enthusiasts back to evaluate the work of every wooden builder. And Kettenburg's inverted wooden churches, with their grace and speed, have began attracting long-overdue notice.

Chapter Ten

Life After Death for Kettenburg Sailboats

The 2004 launch of the restored *Orion*, PC 68, originally built in 1948. Inset: The restored *Wings* (PC 8) sails again, with the restored bark *Star of India* under sail in the background.

As the business itself was sinking beneath the waves, however, interest in Kettenburg boats was rising, centered around the aging but graceful PCs. Their virtues as a relatively small and economical purebred racer stood them in good stead as time flowed around them. As Morgan Miller said, the PC "was kind of the backbone of everything" that happened at the boatyard, and it remains so today.

In the early 1960s, Gary Keller was one of those taken with the grace of the aging PCs, already several years out of production. On occasional Sundays he sailed his own boat toward the Coronado Islands, 16 miles distant. With "a fair wind, I could get about halfway to the Coronados, and I'd turn around and come back," he explained, since "the wind would lay down around five." One Sunday, however, Bill Kearns invited Gary to join his family on a borrowed sailboat—a PC. "We started out, and we're talking. We're going like stink—I didn't realize how fast we were going. And we're talking, and I look up, and I'm *three-quarters* of the way to the Coronado Islands. I never went more than half in that other boat I had. I said, 'Gee— Boy, Bill, we'd better turn around and get back!'" "Naw—we got plenty of time," Kearns assured him.

In the 1960s, two Southern Californians stepped up to protect the old boats from time's ravages. In Marina Del Rey, the yacht harbor of Los Angeles, Hilyard Brown pioneered the fleet-saving technique of splining the aging boats' seams, filling them first with wood and later with fiberglass rope soaked in epoxy resin. In San Diego, another who used that technique was Bud Caldwell, who rescued his first dilapidated PC from Newport around 1958, while he was foreman at the yard. He recalled that "we took our two boys and went up and bought it from this guy, and sailed it down here. And it was leakin' *so bad*. The kids were real little and we wondered why they were so quiet—and they

were in the bilge wading around, havin' a ball!" Morgan remembered Hilyard and "Bud" as "both sort of 'PC spokesmen' from the '60s on. They helped people learn to sail and repair their boats, time after time. They took newcomers sailing and talked them into buying. . . . They were the heart and soul of the two fleets. After Hilyard got too old to sail, the Marina Del Rey Fleet kind of dissolved," and one by one the boats have returned south, thanks primarily to Bud at first, and later thanks to Richard "Rish" Pavelec and Jack Sutphen.

But age and attrition still took their toll, and San Diego's PC fleet dwindled to fewer than half a dozen competitors by the mid-1980s. But interest was growing, in part because of the contrast between the reliable but dull world of fiberglass and the grace of the PC. "Tupperware boats," Paul snorted about fiberglass-hulled sailboats, "are silly-looking things that don't interest the people who like PCs."

Of the people who like PCs, Rish Pavelec has emerged as the most passionate. When he was a heart researcher in 1990, he had only been sailing a few times when he was persuaded to go out one Sunday aboard what his wife Cissy

⊹ Opposite: Richard "Rish" Pavelec in the cockpit of his restored PC *Dawn*. Above: Launched as PC 16 in 1934, *Dawn* was restored for Rish Pavelec in 2004.

described as "just some old wooden thing." He went reluctantly, but along E Dock at the San Diego Yacht Club the couple strolled past six or seven PCs, most in bad shape. Although, as Rish explained, "I grew up in a universe of fiberglass hulls," he was immediately enamored with the PC, whose appearance seemed to offer "exactly what a sailboat should look like." The boat he stepped aboard that day was "suffused with a patina of smell, sight, touch and sound" that evoked "something old whose special qualities have been carefully nurtured and appreciated down through the years. In the PC's case, this

care has lasted long past when the original purpose of cutting-edge competitive racing faded into memory." He began hunting for a PC for himself, and after months of work, launched the restored *Puff* in 1991. For Rish, saving as many as possible of the remaining examples of "a boat that was born and built here" became his life's work, and he has owned seven.

The primary midwife of the physical rebirth of Kettenburg PCs in San Diego has been C. F. Koehler, a shy, bearded boatwright who was restoring four PCs when he spoke to a reporter in 2001. "You have a time machine," he

explained, "when you have one of these boats." The hulls of these time machines are lightly built, prone therefore to having their cracked original ribs sistered beyond recognition, not to mention harboring every disease common to aging wood. While not strictly "authentic," restorations by infusing epoxy and fiberglass rope may have saved the fleet—and, as Koehler put it, "authenticity is a bunch of crap" when what matters most, in his opinion, is keeping these boats alive and competing. C. F. "tells the truth and says it like it is," remarked Pavelec; "most people don't want to hear that."

One of the invalids laid up at Koehler's yard at that time was the 1931 *Wings*, the oldest surviving PC. When she was donated to the Maritime Museum of San Diego as an early Christmas present (and tax writeoff) in 1983, she was "all but wood rot," according to Rish. The cash-strapped museum put her in storage at Kettenburg, but when Kettenburg Marine breathed its last—and all *Wings*' original hardware had been "mysteriously lost, stolen or destroyed"—the Museum transferred her to outdoor storage, of which it had precious little. In 1998 the board of trustees met and "asked why the Museum was paying so much to store a boat that they could not afford to restore. Because money was tight and because they had other, more important, obligations, the board had decided to just cut the boat up in order to get out from underneath the debt." They hadn't reckoned, however, on one board member. Trustee Paul Kettenburg met with the Museum's director, Dr. Ray Ashley, told him of Pavelec's enthusiastic restoration of *Puff*, and suggested that the Museum should give him *Wings*. But Rish, too, was a Museum member who privately wanted very much to see the boat in the Museum's fleet. In 2002, "I started doing some

Veteran 12 Meter sailor Jack Sutphen became a PC convert in the 1980s and helped buy up older boats to be restored and added to the renewed San Diego fleet.

Competitors at the 1993 PC National Championship included Jack Sutphen, sitting at right.

research and sending out feelers to see if restoring the boat was going to be possible. I contacted Ray and asked, 'If I get this vessel restored—would you want it back in your fleet?'" The question went to the Museum's board, which issued a resounding "Yes!" and he signed what was left of Wings back to the Museum, going to work on a letter-writing, speaking, and telephone fundraising campaign. Thanks to time, money, materials, and effort donated by Pavelec, the Museum, Koehler, and the Kettenburg family, Wings sailed again in 2003. She now occupies a place of honor mounted high in front of the Museum like a gigantic trophy. Visitors regularly walk up and admiringly pat her shapely flanks.

Along with Pavelec, another major figure of the PC revival was a much older, weatherbeaten sailor named Jack Sutphen, who holds a place in the America's Cup Hall of Fame. Shortly after meeting Dennis Conner, then the helmsman of the successful 1974 Cup defender Courageous, Jack was signed on as Conner's trial-horse skipper—racing a former Cup champion, to test new materials and technology aboard Conner's

boat—a role he filled for six America's Cup races. (When Dennis was a boy in San Diego, he sailed in Wings, and the first championship he won in any boat was the PC Nationals.) Jack first visited San Diego in 1979, began sailing weekly with Joe Jessop, and found himself racing PCs in 1990.

His first ride in a PC was with the Hartley family on Wings in 1980—an introduction to the truly casual spirit of PC racing at the time. Invited to a "beer can race," he brought his pocket timer—but kept it in his pocket after meeting the crew: nine people and a dog, preparing water balloons to launch at their rivals. Their forebear, City Councilman Paul "Pappy" Hartley, "was very adept at steering it with his feet so he could hold a beer can in his hands," as one of the hundreds of kids he took out sailing recalled. Jack Sutphen is one of the reasons the standard of competition has risen; he has since won seven fleet championships.

Jack and Bud worked closely to buy PCs that came up for sale around Los Angeles. Jack funded Bud to go north, look them over, begin restoration, and then sell them to worthy San Diegans to build up the fleet. "We want to make

sure that the people who have PCs really want them, because we want the boats to stay in good repair," Jack explained. Like Pavelec, he's owned and re-sold seven PCs. "Unfortunately for the L.A. fleets," said Jack, "anytime one of their boats was for sale, the San Diego group bought them."

"PCs are known for the fact that they all go sailing at the same speed, but like other one-designs, you can do little things to make them go faster," Jack explained. "Since it's not a technical boat to sail, you can bring your family, and soon your kids make great crew."

Joe Jessop, still sailing in his eighties, remained their advocate. "In the declining years of the poor ol' PCs," remembered Gene Trepte, "Joe Jessop got on my back, and said 'Gene—why don't you get into the PC fleet? They're a great boat, and they're goin' off the face of the earth unless somebody saves 'em.' And we only had a couple of 'em there" at the Yacht Club. As the 1994 America's Cup races drew the international yachting spotlight to San Diego, Gene and Jack Sutphen chatted casually but persuasively with the owner of a New York-based Herreshoff

In beauty and function, Wheeler swore that the sailboats are "as near perfection as one can get," for "the care and craftsmanship used in constructing each boat equaled or exceeded that done anywhere else."

The gleaming mahogany cabin trunk and sleek folding-handle winch of the restored PC *Orion*.

Orion (PC 68), built in 1948 and restored in 2004.

Nick Lee restored a K 38 in 2006.

S-Class yacht. The following April, 65 years after Joe Jessop had raced the PC into the spotlight in Hawai'i, San Diegans witnessed a one-race, winner-take-all "rematch" between the classes. Once again, the PC won, but "the story goes," said Pavelec, "after a few beers in the bar, some of the players decided that they should race again." As in 1931, the adversaries were so evenly matched that the S boat beat them. Joe Jessop lived long enough to hear about it, and only his 95 years kept him from jumping back into a cockpit.

One more testament to the PC's importance as an icon for Southern California sailors came in 2004. With Paul's blessing, Carl Eichenlaub, the boatwright for the U.S. Olympic sailing team since 1976, reopened old PC plans almost five decades after the last one was built. Surrounding himself in sawdust and reusing the keel from an unsalvageable PC, the two-time Lightning champion built the first new PC in 45 years. It was a gift for a historic occasion: the first woman commodore of the San Diego Yacht Club would receive from her father Carl a resurrected version

of the most historic San Diego sailboat.

The revival of interest in Kettenburg trickled beyond the PC class to the K 38, and beyond Southern California too, when Steve Barber of Berkeley bought a K 38 in 1999 and grew curious about it. He called the San Diego Yacht Club and asked, "We got these Kettenburg boats. Anybody down there got Kettenburg boats?" Since then, Steve bought and restored two more K 38s, and channeled interest and enthusiasm for every Kettenburg model through his Kettenburg Boat Owners Association Web site. In the 1990s, according to Steve, retired naval officer George Wheeler "traipsed up and down the entire West Coast of the U.S. and Canada looking for K 38s." Wheeler not only composed a poem about his favorite boat, but he also encouraged buyers to snap up every Kettenburg boat, maintaining in 1996 that "there were no bad models." In beauty and function, Wheeler swore that the sailboats are "as near perfection as one can get," for "the care and craftsmanship used in constructing each boat equaled or exceeded that done anywhere else." He

insisted—with a touch of hyperbole—that as a group they were "the finest sailing yachts ever designed and built on the West Coast," whose "incredible balance, near-silent, easy motion and speed make them a joy to sail."

George Kettenburg's last design, the PCC, also got a new champion. Alerted by Steve Barber, "the urgency of the moment" pressed Washingtonian Neil Atwood into buying *Eulalie*— or what was left of her—in 2004. He had never sailed a PCC, but having owned the last PC built had whetted his appetite. *Eulalie* had, however, sat uncovered for two years high and dry in the high desert in a Salt Lake City industrial park. If not moved, "she would literally be cut up with a chainsaw, and hauled away." Atwood mused: "From my point of view, the timing was wrong, the logistics were wrong, and the financing was wrong. However, this was George Kettenburg's former boat, and there *is* only one Number One." After long negotiations, he faced the boat itself: "the hull had dried out so much that you could literally stand on one side of the boat, and look through the hull below the water line to the

Left: Neil Atwood bought and restored *Eulalie*, the first PCC. Above: A group devoted to the preservation of Kettenburg boats poses next to *Selene*, PCC 3. Front row (left to right) Bud Caldwell, Jean Kettenburg Miller, Morgan Miller, Wally Springstead, Jack Sutphen, Tom Sterling, and Rish Pavelec; back row (left to right) Steve Barber, G. W. "Bill" Kettenburg III, Tom Kettenburg, Neil Atwood, and Gene Trepte. Right: Steve Barber on board his K 38, *Dyad II*, 2006.

other side." After restoration, however, "*Eulalie* sails like a dream. She is fast, powerful, graceful, and easy to sail. All of my expectations were met and exceeded. And I feel better knowing that I have saved a yacht that made a significant contribution" to ocean racing history. Of the ten PCCs that George formed into the first PCC yacht racing association in 1948, five remain active today, thanks in part to Neil's enthusiasm in rejuvenating the organization. Gene Trepte, rather older than he was in 1948 when he was a fire-breathing PCC racer and charter member of the original association, came back aboard as an honorary member.

In the first decade of the 21st century, as one steps aboard a restored wooden sailboat from "PC Row" at the San Diego Yacht Club, it's not hard to remember that stepping aboard was all it took to kindle these restorers' love. The breeze puffs lightly, almost imperceptibly; the sails fill, and one of the 47 surviving PCs slices through the water again. It's a testimony to the esteem in which all of their aging "woodies" are held in Southern California. Although surrounded by modern yachts, the first sailboat class designed to race on Southern California waters holds an honored place. "Perhaps the most important thing about the PC is that it is a joy to sail," said Jack Sutphen; "it's just the feel you have when you have the tiller in your hand." Speaking for his family and partners, an old man in a plaid shirt gave the best explanation of the lasting appeal of every Kettenburg sailboat: "We designed 'em as something that *we* would like to sail," said Paul. "It turned out that a lot of other people liked the same thing we did." And as he spoke, among the dozens of hull models and plaques hanging behind him in his home office hung a little sign that suggested "People Matter."

✛ Representing the popularity of restored Kettenburg
   boats, the 2007 Kettenburg Regatta included the
   range of production boats from PCs to K 41s.

Endnotes

Abbreviations

AM–Art Miley

BK–Bill Kettenburg

CAU–Charles Arthur Underwood

CRU–Charles Ross Underwood

DG–Doug Giddings

GK–Gary Keller

GT–Gene Trepte

JUJ–Jim Underwood Jr.

PK–Paul Kettenburg

SDHS–San Diego Historical Society

SDYCHC–San Diego Yacht Club History Collection

TK–Tom Kettenburg

PREFACE

Page 8, "What follows, springs from": PK, video interview with Steve Barber, Scott Wild, and Rish Pavelec, with TK, January 3, 2002, 9. Copies of this and all other correspondence, documents, and interviews, except where noted, are in the Kettenburg Boat Works Collection of the MacMullen Library & Research Archives, Maritime Museum of San Diego.

Page 8, "Today, this family company": The New England Solo/Twin race is a double-handed 77-mile race from Narragansett Bay to Cape Cod's Elizabeth Islands, around Block Island, & back. The sailboat portion was won in 2006 by the PCC *Totem II* (hull #14), presently the only PCC in the East. Three sailboats finished, including *Totem II* and a 1920 cutter—the only two wooden sailboats entered, "Wooden Boats Triumph in Offshore Race," *Classic Boat* (October 2006).

Page 8, "But you would at least have": Olin Stephens, email to author, July 18, 2006. Stephens came to know San Diego yacht architect Greg Stewart on ratings committees, came to visit him in San Diego, and sailed on Frank Taliaferro's PC #63 *Puff*.

Page 8, "Kettenburg Boat Works was truly": The U.S. Census reports Peoria's 1920 population as 76,121, and San Diego's as 74,361.

CHAPTER 1

Page 14, "In a sense": The author is indebted for much of the substance of this chapter to TK and his unpublished "A History of the Kettenburg Family in Pittsburg, Pennsylvania, 1832-1912, and Early Years in San Diego, California, 1912-1914, with Emphasis on the Activities of the Second George William Kettenburg (1868-1953)," n.d. (1997); for further information, see "The History of the Kettenburg Family" in *Pittsburg and Her People*, vol. 4 (Pittsburgh, 1908); except where otherwise indicated, copies of documents and interviews cited in these chapters are in the MacMullen Library & Research Archives at the Maritime Museum of San Diego.

Page 14, "Although he loved to travel": BK, interview with the author, May 8, 2006, 2; "Bill" is also George William Kettenburg. "Mr. Kettenburg" is here used to distinguish his grandfather, whose life spanned the years from 1868 to 1953; he retired from managing Kettenburg Boat Works in 1935, see Gunnar Anderson, "Through Three Generations: The Kettenburg Log," *Sailing* (June 1974): 32.

Page 14, "His grandfather had emigrated": PK, video interview with Steve Barber, Scott Wild, and "Rish" Pavelec, with TK, January 3, 2002, 7; TK reports that when he died in 1892, his 23-year-old son may actually have kept the plumbing business going for a few years, since it is listed in the 1899-1900 Pittsburg city directory, although Tom concludes this continuation of an unloved job is unlikely. He probably started his electrical generating business in 1896 or 1897, as it is listed in the 1900-1901 Pittsburg directory, TK, "History," 5, 7; "Pittsburg" was the common spelling of the city's name when the Kettenburgs lived there; the terminal "h" became official in 1911.

Page 14, "As his neighborhood electrical": George married Amelia Eyth in 1894, and their first two children died in early childhood. Their surviving children were Robert (an engineer who never became involved in the boat business), born 1896; George William, born January 1904; Julia, born 1905; Ella, born 1906; and Paul Albert, born 1913 in San Diego, Carol Kettenburg Dubbs to author, July 17, 2006; PK, interview by author, October 9, 2003, 3. Additional travel by Mr. Kettenburg with elements of his family included a 1910 trip to Europe and South America, and trips around the world in 1926 and 1930.

Page 15, "Perhaps partly in frustration": TK, "History," 14; when new, their English Daimler had cost a very substantial $6,600. PK, interview with Bob Wright, May 25, 1985, San Diego Historical Society, 2. In that interview, Paul recollected that the family crossed the country by car in 1912, but his children believe they came by train; The architect was William S. Hebbard, best known for his partnership with pioneering San Diego modern architect Irving Gill; PK 1985, 1.

Page 15, "When the family settled": Pittsburg's 1910 population was just under 534,000.

Page 17, "Many local pleasure boats": On San Diego's early relationship with the U.S. Navy, see Bruce Linder, "1917-1922: The Decisive Years in San Diego's Relationship with Its Navy," *Mains'l Haul* 38/39 (Fall 2002/Winter 2003): 4-13; on local yachting in 1912, see Terry Shewmaker, "*Silver Gate* and the San Diego Yacht Club," *Mains'l Haul* 41 (Winter 2005): 4-13.

Page 17, "The mountains that walled": San Diego Chamber of Commerce Minutes, 1931, quoted in Abraham Shragge, "Aircraft Carriers and the Development of San Diego Harbor Since 1930," *Mains'l Haul* 38/39 (Fall 2002/Winter 2003): 58.

Page 17, "The seven little boatbuilding firms": 1912 San Diego *City Directory;* this racing class was known as the Chula Vista One Design, after the yacht club for which it was built; most were badly damaged in the floods of 1915, Willis "Clem" Stose, interview by Edward S. Barr, February 3, 1973, SDYCHC; Billy Edwards, "Lark and Ripple Lose in One-Design to Southwind," article from unidentified newspaper, August 12, 1924, 1924 scrapbook, SDYCHC; see also Thomas G. Skahill, "Fellows & Stewart Inc., Boatbuilders," *WoodenBoat* 173 (2003): 46-57.

Page 17, "*Butcher Boy*'s builder": On San Diego's tuna industry, see August Felando, "California's Tuna Clipper Fleet (Parts 1-3)," *Mains'l Haul* 32 (Fall 1996): 6-17; 33 (Winter 1997): 16-27; 34 (Summer 1997): 28-39, and "Into the Valley of Death, 38/39 (Fall/Winter 2003): 18-27.

Page 18, "William A. Hand Jr.": "Talk With Our Naval Architects," *Motor Boating*, June 1912, 31-32; *MotorBoat*, August 10, 1912, 23; William H. Taylor, "William A. Hand Jr., Yacht Designer," *Yachting*, February 1953; WoodenBoat Magazine, *The Designs of William A. Hand Jr.* (Brooklin, ME: WoodenBoat, 1985); Jerry Kirschenbaum, "William Hand: The Evolution of an Architect," *WoodenBoat* 28 (1979): 58-67.

Page 19, "Since gasoline engines were": On the 1915 race and the 1929 Harmsworth Trophy race, see D. W. Fostle, *Speedboat* (Mystic: Mystic Seaport Museum Stores, 1988); on specific naval architects cited throughout, see Lucia Knight and Daniel Bruce MacNaughton, *The Encyclopedia of Yacht Designers* (New York: W. W. Norton, 2005).

Page 19, "George Kettenburg Sr.": PK 1985, 2, and October 9, 2003, 3.

Page 19, "This assertion, made by a 14-year-old": PK, October 9, 2003, 3; PK identifies the neighbor who sold them *Joiselle* as Dr. Foster; PK 2002, 2; the plans may have been those for Hand's 22-foot "V-Bottom Racer" in *MotorBoat,* March 25, 1910, 26.

Page 19, "As sometimes happens": Richard Crawford, *Stranger than Fiction: Vignettes of San Diego History* (San Diego: San Diego Historical Society, 1995); PK notes "Poggy" as Ella's nickname in PK 2002, 5, and 2003, 10.

Page 19, "When his father and brother installed": Edward Barr, note to author, October 1, 2006; *Poggy* was completed in either 1919 or 1920, TK, "Kettenburg Boats Timeline" September 22, 2003, 1; while it appears that *Poggy* was re-engined with an OX5, *Poggy II* was definitely given a Hispano-Suiza, which according to Paul rated 220 h.p. "Hissos" powered the French SPAD fighter as well as training aircraft like some models of the Curtiss JN4 "Jenny." References to her 35 m.p.h. speed are in "Speedboats in Close Contests," clipping from *San Diego Tribune*, August 11, 1924, untitled *Union* clipping, August 14, 1924, and Dick Barthelmess, "With the Rocking Chair Fleet—Ashore & Afloat," date unknown, all in scrapbook labeled "San Diego Yacht Club, S. B. De Silva, 1923-1924," SDYCHC.

Page 21, "Time spent together": PK, 1985, 3-4.

Page 21, "The Kettenburg Boat Works": BK, 2; PK, interview by Karen Scanlon, June 19, 2003; PK 1985, 5; Richard Hershey, "Richard B. Hershey," typescript, ca. 1987, 5, courtesy Harry Hershey. The 13 ½-foot runabout was powered by a 4-cylinder Hallet, which TK believes was a 12-h.p. motor.

Page 21, "From the beginning": Underwood, 3, 6.

Page 21, "Dick had already built model boats": Underwood, 2.

Page 22, "They launched and hauled out boats": Hershey, "Richard B. Hershey," 1.

Page 22, "Curious Portuguese neighbors": Hershey, "Richard B. Hershey," 1, 5; TK, "Kettenburg Boats Timeline," 1-2.

Page 22, "Along with hiring Dick": Richard Henderson and Robert W. Carrick, *John Alden and His Yacht Designs* (Camden, ME: International Marine Publishing, 1983), 283-88, 424.

Page 22, "This was my brother's first experience": Hershey, "Richard B. Hershey," 3; punctuation and capitalization altered; PK 1985, 5; Sun boats were planked in cedar, PK 2002, 2; the $1,200 figure is from "Kennedy [sic] Boat Firm Creates Big Boom Here – Factor in Increase of Craft Sport Along Coast," clipped from unknown ca. 1927 San Diego newspaper, Richard Hershey scrapbook, courtesy of Harry Hershey.

Page 22, "Competitors, too, had begun": "Kennedy [sic] Boat Firm"; see also TK, "Of Ship Chandlers, Sunboats, and Streetcars," unpublished typescript, 1997; Stose, 14, SDYCHC.

Page 26, "Photos taken then": Charles La Dow, "Kettenburg Marine: The Story of an Enterprise," unpublished typescript, 1988, 3; John Springer, "'Greyhounds of the Sea' – Sleek, Slick PPC [sic] Boats Have Startling Speed," *San Diego Union*, October 17, 1948; Morgan Miller, BK, and Jean (Kettenburg) Miller, interview with author, March 22, 2004, 2-3.

Page 26, "George Kettenburg Jr. was never": JUJ, interview with author, October 10, 2005; BK, 3; Morgan Miller mentioned George's sensitivity to secondhand smoke in conversation with the author, February 9, 2005; all interview subjects agreed that boatyard toxins caused George's cancer; "Building Another Beauty," *San Diego Daily Journal*, January 24, 1946; BK, 3.

Page 26, "As a sailor he quickly grew": BK, video interview with Fred Lewis for television program *The Heart of San Diego*, broadcast June 13, 2005.

Page 26, "In the light breezes": BK, 6. The description is of sailing a PCC.

Page 27, "George's primary gifts": George Jessop, quoted in "Sailing Around by 'Salty' [Lawrence Fenstermaker]," *San Diego Sun*, September 15, 1934; PK 1985, 5; Gordon T. Frost, "Remarks at Commissioning of George Kettenburg, Jr. – New San Diego Yacht Club Race Committee Boat," May 21, 1972, SDYCHC, 2; Miller, BK, and Miller, 14; Alex S. "Bud" Caldwell, interview with author, July 17, 2006, 4.

CHAPTER 2

Page 30, "The dark-haired young sailor": The world's first airline briefly operated a flying boat between Tampa and Petersburg, Florida, in 1912; Ryan's was the first airline to operate for longer than a year. According to PK, engines sold to Ryan had already been fitted with an adapter that had made them usable in speedboats, which had to be removed. PK, interview by Robert Wright, May 25, 1985, San Diego Historical Society, 3.

Page 31, "It was not the exoticism": Ryan sold his interest in the firm prior to building the "Spirit of St. Louis," but remained temporary plant manager during its construction. Ev Casagneres, *Spirit of St. Louis: The Untold Story* (Historic Aviation, 2002). George Kettenburg Sr. bought the land that became the boatyard about 1927; PK, video interview by Steve Barber, Scott Wild, Tom Kettenburg, and Rish Pavelec, January 3, 2002, 2.

Page 31, "The power of those war-surplus": $1,500 is the lowest cost cited for a "Hisso"-powered runabout in "Kennedy [sic] Boat Firm Creates Big Boom Here – Factor in Increase of Craft Sport Along Coast," clipping from unknown newspaper (1926 or 1927), Richard Hershey scrapbook, courtesy Harry Hershey.

Page 34, "What the elder George Kettenburg was": The competitors were all classed as 610 cubic inches; "Speedboats in Close Contests," clipping from *San Diego Tribune*, August 11, 1924; untitled *San Diego Union* clipping August 14, 1924; "Jones' Poggy Shows Speed," date and newspaper unknown; and Dick Barthelmess, "With the Rocking Chair Fleet—Ashore & Afloat," date unknown, all in "San Diego Yacht Club, S. B. De Silva, 1923-1924" scrapbook, SDYCHC. Observations about bleachers are drawn from photographs. PK believed his father's enthusiasm for speedboats had drawn him to join SDYC. PK, interview with author, October 16, 2003, 10; the elder

Kettenburg remained business manager until retirement in 1935, retaining some managerial role until Paul returned in 1943, PK 2002, 10.

Page 34, "Racing success drew many": "Clem" Stose, interview with Edward S. Barr, February 3, 1973, 15, SDYCHC.

Page 35, "The boatyard's handsome work speedboat": *Husky* was powered by a four-cylinder Stirling, according to Hershey, "Richard B. Hershey," ca. 1987, courtesy Harry Hershey, 3; PK remembered it as powered by a Scripps engine, according to his son, TK; *Husky* remained the yard's workboat into the 1960s, CRU, email to author, June 2006.

Page 35, "Maybe George wouldn't bring him in": PK told him that in the summer of 1930 these men loaded their 20-foot outboard with raw alcohol near Rosarito, PK, interview with TK, January 15, 1997.

Page 35, "If alcohol is a drug": Hershey, "Richard B. Hershey," 1-2.

Page 35, "The *Goose*'s Libertys": Hershey, "Richard B. Hershey," 1-2, punctuation altered. While Hershey described these engines as 500 h.p., PK described them as 400 h.p. The boat was delivered without engines according to PK, 2002, 13-14, a fact that calls Hershey's recollection of the Kettenburgs' involvement in muffler installation into question.

Page 35, "One time, recalled Paul": PK, 2002, 14.

Page 37, The government men were": Hershey, "Richard B. Hershey," 1-2, italics added and punctuation altered.

Page 37, "The last boat built": Hershey, "Richard B. Hershey," 1-2, 4-5. *Johnnie* was remembered as a rumrunner when owned by Schmidt's successor, mortuary owner Legler Benbough, John and Barbara Ogden, interview with Barr, August 13, 2000, SDYCHC; she reportedly ended her career as a San Francisco-area rumrunner, according to later owners quoted by Pavelec, 2002 interview with PK, 9.

Page 37, "My dad noticed an ad": CRU also notes that Jimmy became a master carpenter, "Charles Arthur Underwood–Eulogy," October 20, 1998; Jim Jr. recalled that his father's heart condition darkened his personality; after his retirement about 1946, Mr. Underwood raised tropical fish commercially at home until his death in 1954, JUJ to author, July 1, 2006; another family story was that Jimmy quit rather than work under his son, after a consulting company recommended that Charlie take over to bring production costs under control. The angered Jimmy walked home to Pacific Beach, about ten miles, CRU, email to author, October 17, 2005.

Page 38, "Charlie Underwood agreed": CAU, personal history recorded October 1987, 2.

Page 38 "Another special skill": In addition to colors "unavailable anywhere else" at the time, he developed paint-related products including paint and varnish removers, a knifing putty (to build up the "racing finish" on hulls), and marine oil, CAU, 2.

Page 38, "Despite his fiery temper": Gerry Driscoll, interview with Ruth Held, February 14, 1991, 10, SDHSHC; JUJ, interview with author, October 10, 2005, 3; Wallace Springstead, interview with author, April 14, 2006, 4; Loch Crane, telephone conversation with author, January 6, 2005.

Page 38, "Underwood's reputation spread": JUJ, 2; his father's well-known do-it-yourself lessons were actually part of an intentional policy toward young yacht club members that he and George created, according to CAU, 2.

Page 38, "Racers and rumrunners built": ca.-1927 prices appear in "Kennedy [sic] Boat Firm," which discusses "put-puts" and notes that runabouts and speedboats could be had with "Hisso" or Scripps engines; it mentions a 34-foot cruiser built for H. E. Blumberg; according to Hershey, *Aljo* was later sold to Bud Beckwith of La Jolla, for whom the company added a cabin; he renamed her *Cigarette*, Hershey, "Richard B. Hershey," 3; *Aljo* was 26 feet long, and powered by a 220 "Hisso," according to a photo caption prepared by Charles La Dow.

Page 38, "By this time, George's speedboats": CAU, 32.

Page 40, "Not long before *Johnnie*": PK 2002, 2; the $25,000 figure is the top price noted in "Kennedy [sic] Boat Firm," published while *Agilis* was under construction in 1926; Robinson had purchased *Poggy II*.

Page 40, "Robinson named this new boat *Agilis*": Fellows is quoted by Hershey, "Richard B. Hershey," 2-3; punctuation modified.

Page 42, "Increased demand for Kettenburg boats": PK 1985, 11.

Page 42, "In 1929": Benjamin W. Labaree, William M. Fowler Jr., John B. Hattendorf, and Jeffrey J. Safford, Edward W. Sloan, and Andrew W. German, *America and the Sea: A Maritime History* (Mystic: Mystic Seaport, 1998.)

Page 42, "When the Stock Market crashed": *Agilis* became a rumrunner known only as "A1772 out of L.A"; another firm removed her aft cabin, moved her bridge forward, and gave her twin Libertys and a coat of dull gray; on the apparently knowing participation of the Kettenburgs in equipping rumrunners see CAU, 13, 15.

Page 42, "Paul Kettenburg recalled": PK 1985, 6.

Page 42, "When Prohibition was repealed": CAU, 15; Josephine Israel, "Ahoy! Skippers!" *San Diego Union*, 22 September 1935.

Page 43, "Charlie and the rest": CAU, 13, 15; see also Hershey, "Richard B. Hershey," 2; in 1936, George played host at San Diego Yacht Club's new

archery range; he may have been a principal impetus behind its construction; Israel, "Ahoy! Skippers!" *San Diego Union*, January 26, 1936; Crane, 2005 conversation, he worked for the yard for about six months, sometime between 1934 and 1936; Charlie recalled making 35 cents per hour in this era, CAU, 15.

Page 44, "George's loyalty to his workforce": JUJ, 2005, 3.

Page 44, "Although its membership dwindled": "Overhaul Season Here but Yacht Activities Continue on S.D. Bay," clipping from unknown newspaper, February 9, 1938, scrapbook, SDYCHC; CAU, 15-16.

Page 45, "Loyal customers saved the day": Springstead, interview with author, April 14, 2006, 3; Springstead, interview with unknown interviewer, October 9, 2000, SDYCHC.

Page 45, "As George scrambled to find": *Joanne* was designed by Daniel M. Callis, an architect of yachts and commercial vessels who moved to the Los Angeles area about 1921; "Ready to Launch Local Freighter at Kettenburg's," probably *San Diego Union*, (November?) 28, 1932, in PK scrapbook, courtesy TK; the largest vessel built at the yard was a bottomless 90-foot "pirate ship" built in 1971 for the Seven Seas amusement park in Texas, "Would You Buy a Bottomless Boat from this Company?," *Whittaker NOW!* (March-April 1974), courtesy TK; Springstead, 2000; Charles Springstead (who named *Joanne* after his daughter) grew peas for Associated Seed Growers, but, according to his son, the freight-hauling career of *Joanne* ended after one trip, due to Mexican regulations that favored shipping by railroad. Springstead ordered the boat in partnership with N. H. Ruby, whose name appears in "Ready to Launch" and "Plain Water Will Christen New Boat," probably *San Diego Union*, hand-dated 1932, in PK scrapbook; Ruby, not Springstead, is identified as owner in "New Freighter at San Diego," *Pacific Motor Boat* (October 1932): 27; Springstead, 2006, 2; Springstead 2000; *Joanne* was later leased to the U.S. Coast and Geodetic Survey, which valued her all-weather qualities, Springstead 2000; her horsepower rating appears in "Ready to Launch"; BK, in Morgan Miller and Jean (Kettenburg) Miller, interview with author, March 22, 2004, 6; "Plain Water"; she was launched November 28, 1932; PK (her first chief engineer) recalled her being built for cost plus 3 percent; the newspaper clippings cited give her cost variously as $30,000 and $45,000; TK, "The *Joanne*— Kettenburg's Biggest Boat," unpublished typescript, 1997, contains additional information about engines and construction.

Page 45, "As the Depression settled": PK 2002, 3; price from "Kennedy Boat Firm"; PK also described Star boat racing and related facts on October 16, 2003, 6; that George's Star boat was *Miss II* is noted in "Angela, Trilby and Sundart Class Leaders," *San Diego Union*, May 28, 1928; capitalization altered; E. J. Sprague Jr., *The San Diego Bay Star Fleet: 1925 to the Present Day*, 2 vols., (San Diego: author, 2007).

Page 45, "Joe came up to George": PK 2002, 3; PK, October 16, 2003, 9.

Page 46, "But, he said he thought": Gordon T. Frost Sr., interview with Charles Bishop, 1998, 3-4, SDYCHC; Frost recalled that Kettenburg also sold his plan sets for $5 to raise money for a junior program; in his last interview on the subject, in 2000, Frost stated the Kettenburg Starlet's cost with sails as a much lower $125, but this may represent his memory of what Ruski was charging; Kettenburg quickly raised the price to $300, according to their September 1930 ad in *Pacific Coast Yachting*.

Page 46, "That was the beginning": Frost's quotes are drawn from three different occasions in which he told the story, "Remarks at Commissioning of George Kettenburg, Jr.–New San Diego Yacht Club Race Committee Boat," May 21, 1972, 2, SDYCHC; comments from 2000, quoted in Iris Engstrand and Cynthia Davalos, *San Diego Yacht Club: A History* (San Diego: San Diego Yacht Club, 2000), 65; also "we put the numbers in a hat and drew for the boat we were to get. My brother Al, who was ten years old, and I … got #8 and Jerry Torrance got #7. A short time later Grant Stone and Bob Sharp, as partners, got #9 and began to sail with us"; four Starlets were built by students at local high schools in the 1930s, according to clippings in SDYCHC scrapbooks.

Page 46, "To a boy": Bob Sharp, May 8, 2000, 4, SDYCHC.

Page 46, "And, Gordon continued": Doug Giddings, interview by Doug Werner and Andy Bofinger, January 20, 1999, 15, 6, 10, SDYCHC; on Starlet racing and rituals, see SDYCHC scrapbooks.

Page 47, ""But the Great Depression rendered": JUJ, 2.

CHAPTER 3

Page 50, "Twenty-five-year-old George Kettenburg Jr.": The author is indebted to PC owner and historian Richard S. "Rish" Pavelec for much of the substance of this and the following chapter. Some were previously published by Pavelec, with this author's assistance, as "The Rise of the Kettenburg PC" in *Mains'l Haul* 41 (Winter 2005): 14-21.

Page 50, "The effects of newfound prosperity": Curtis Zahn, "Oh for a Life on the Bounding Main! Yachting is work, but it's fun, too," *San Diego Union*, July 4, 1937.

Page 50, "To reach these businessmen": *Yachting* and *Pacific Skipper* named Jessop one of the West's ten best skippers in 1935, PK, interview with the author, October 16, 2003, 8.

Page 51, "Joe was the ablest sailor": Josephine Israel, "Ahoy! Skippers!" *San Diego Union*, November 1935.

Page 52, ""Joe himself was a champion sailor": Joe Jessop, quoted in Kate Bast, "A Good Guess that Endured 65 Years: The Pacific Class," *Sailing* (November 1994): 67; the Star class was introduced in 1911.

Page 52, "During the summer and fall of 1928": The earliest source on competing designs considered by the San Diego Yacht Club is A. E. Childs, "Evolution of the Pacific Coast One-Design Class," *Pacific Coast Yachting* (September 1930): 21-22; other sources include Samuel Dauchy, "The Pacific One-Design Class," *Yachting* (August 1934): 57, and Harry B. Wilford, "The P.C.'s Conquer New Territory," *Pacific Skipper* (February 1937); Charles La Dow names Charles Springstead among the "interested parties" discussing designs, although his son doubts his involvement; Wallace Springstead, transcript of interview by unknown interviewer, October 9, 2000, SDYCHC; *Pacific Coast Yachting* (December 1929): 16; the Universal Rule, adopted in 1904, focused on length and sail area but also governs displacement, overhangs, draft, freeboard and other elements through the imposition of penalties. The formula determined that 18 percent of the product of length, times the square root of the sail area, divided by the cube root of the displacement, equaled the boat's rating. This rule was supplanted around 1928 by the International Rule, which created the "meter boats." It had emerged after 1907 from the International Yacht Racing Union (IYRU), created to settle differences among various rules. The Six-Meter designation, for example, has nothing to do with length—they are typically between 10 and 12 meters long—but is the product of a complex formula. The IYRU is now the International Sailing Federation.

Page 52, "The Bar for one-designs": Maynard Bray and Carlton Pinheiro, *Herreshoff of Bristol: A Photographic History of America's Greatest Yacht and Boat Builders* (Brooklin, ME: WoodenBoat Publications, 1989), 154; the S-class was Herreshoff's design #828; see Kenneth Upham and George Hanson, *History and Register of the S-Boat* (Saunderstown, RI: K. B. Upham, 1994).

Page 52, "Starling Burgess was developing": Quoted in Frank Haven, "One Design for Living: Coast Yachtsmen Turning to Locally Designed Boat," *San Diego Sun*, December 20, 1934; Wilford, "P.C.'s Conquer New Territory"; "The Atlantic Class orders, fortunately, were easy to cancel, due to the demand" elsewhere for the design, Jessop, "A Successful One-Design Class," *Pacific Skipper* (January 1935), in 1935 scrapbook, SDYCHC.

Page 54, "In 1919 Herreshoff designed": Bray and Pinhero, *Herreshoff of Bristol*, 154, 155; Diana Esterly, *Early One-Design Sailboats* (New York: Charles Scribner's Sons, 1979), 95-99.

Page 55, "W. Starling Burgess had recently reestablished": "The Atlantic Coast One-Design Class," *Yachting* (November 1928): 78; Maynard Bray, Benjamin A. G. Fuller, and Peter Vermilya, *Mystic Seaport Watercraft* (Mystic: Mystic Seaport, 2001), 85; Llewellyn Howland III, "The Burgess Legacy, Part IV," *WoodenBoat* 74 (January/February 1987): 42-52;

Page 57, "They also considered jettisoning": Jessop, "A Successful One-Design Class," in 1935 scrapbook, SDYCHC; 25 meters appears to the author to be an odd amount of sail area for a Nordic yacht to carry; it appears in

Pacific Coast Yachting (December 1929): 16. Sanctioned sizes of square-meter yachts were 15, 22, 30, 40, 55, 75, 95, 120, and the huge and unwieldy 150 square-meter sizes. The best-known size today is the 30 square meter.

Page 57, "Despite looking eastward": San Diego Marine Construction launched Shock's *Vileehi* in June, 1930; the involvement of an unnamed Los Angeles architect in the club's considerations is mentioned by Childs, "Evolution," 21; that the architect was Shock is noted in Jessop, interview by unknown interviewer, March 22, 1985, SDYCHC, and La Dow, "Kettenburg Marine," 7; La Dow quotes Jessop as reporting that Shock and another designer, Phil Thearle, built models for their proposals in La Dow, draft article "From Hobby to Enterprise: The Story of Kettenburg Marine," 1987, Tom Fetter collection; see also Thomas G. Skahill and Charles Shock, "Edson B. Shock: Naval Architect," *WoodenBoat* (July/August 1993): 60-68.

Page 57, "Joe Jessop knew George Kettenburg Jr.": PK, interview with the author, October 16, 2003, 7.

Page 57, "In the fall of 1929": Jessop, "Successful One-Design," and as quoted in Haven, "One Design for Living"; PK, October 16, 2003, 7; The East Coast origin of the sails is noted in PK, 2002, 4; La Dow, "Kettenburg Marine," 8.

Page 57, "As with most creation myths": Edward S. Barr, "*Wings* and the PC Story," *Mainsheet* (August 2003); the napkin story also appears, misdated 1931, in Bill Center, "PCs Continue to Ply Nicely in San Diego Waters," *San Diego Union-Tribune*, August 11, 1992; although Barr's published account of the napkin tale is uncredited, in a 2005 conversation with the author he stated that his mother, Kettenburg client and confidant Dennie Barr O'Bryan, told him the story; Wilford, in "P.C.'s Conquer New Territory," misrepresents the date of this conversation as "late in 1930," well after PC #1 was already sailing, but because he knew the principals involved, his story may be substantially true; punctuation altered.

Page 57, "Perhaps the most satisfying account": PK, October 16, 2003, 7; Hershey supervised construction of several subsequent PCs under George's supervision and was later put in charge of their production, Richard Hershey, "Richard B. Hershey," ca. 1987, 2; he was succeeded in 1938 by Charlie Underwood, as noted in his recorded monologue, October 1987, 17.

Page 58, "In January 1930 George was showing": The January 1930 drawing is noted as Kettenburg's design #63 in "The Inter-Club Team Races at Honolulu," *Pacific Coast Yachting* (July 1931): 9; PC #1 launching date is from anonymous, "Newest One-Designer," clipping from unidentified San Diego newspaper in Hershey scrapbook, hand-dated March 5, 1930; length of construction time is from Ken Bojens, "Off the Main Line," *San Diego Union*, September 14, 1946; the author knew the Kettenburgs, who presumably told him this information; an incorrect February 1929 date for design and construction is offered in Kenneth "Keno" Hallawell's typescript "History of the San Diego Yacht Club 1886-1942," 6, SDYCHC; Jessop related a peculiar story about her construction to Kate Bast: "We weren't naval architects, so

we had to do some guessing when building it. For example, we left an eight-inch-wide by two-foot-long hole in the keel and put a wooden plug in it. The boat was a little tender on the water and needed more weight, so we pulled out the plug and put lead in its hole," Bast, "A Good Guess," 67; PK, video interview with Steve Barber, Scott Wild, and Rish Pavelec, with Tom Kettenburg, January 3, 2002, 9; Mr. Kettenburg's nicknaming habit was noted by Morgan Miller in a conversation in March 2007; he was nicknamed "J. P." after financier J. P. Morgan.

Page 58, ""Apparently borrowing": Childs, "Evolution," 21; the designation of PC as "Pacific Class" had become established by the 1934 *Yachting* article, Dauchy, "Pacific One-Design," 58; after racing success in the Hawaiian Islands in 1931, it was reported that "the name of the class has been changed to the 'Pacific One-Design Class,'" omitting "coast" now that the design had spread offshore, "Inter-Club Team Races," 11.

Page 58, "The 'interested parties'": Childs, "Evolution," 21; PK 2002, 4; PK states that the following day they sold four PCs; PK 2002, 21.

Page 60, "A few months later": The ad showing the PC price at $2,100, including sails, appears in *Pacific Coast Yachting* (September 1930), and the article in the same issue; many years later, PK recalled that the first four actually sold for $1,800, plus sails, while Jessop recalled the first PCs selling for $1,850—but he and the other three San Diegans who raced in Hawaii in 1930 sold their boats there for $2,150, supposedly their replacement cost back home, PK, interview with Karen Scanlon, June 10, 2003; Jessop, "Successful One-Design," 4; Doug Giddings recalled spending $1,750 including sails for PC #10 in 1935, DG, interview with the author, October 31, 2005; by the February 1939 issue of *Sea,* the advertised price had risen to $2,550; oddly, it dropped to $2,250 in the same magazine the following month—a discount perhaps attributable to typesetter's error, given that Richmond is spelled "Ricmond" in the same ad (it may also reflect competition from the newly-introduced Rhodes 33); by the February 1941 *Sea,* the price had risen to $2,950, while an unidentified ad, probably from around 1945, lists it at $3,750, apparently also without sails; with the exception of 1930, advertised prices specify "less sails"; This rough comparison of prices echoes that of Walton Hubbard Jr., "A True One Design Class," undated magazine article from unknown publication, 1934 scrapbook, SDYCHC; La Dow, "Kettenburg Marine: The Story of An Enterprise," unpublished typescript, 1988, 11; the bartered boat was PC #8, *Wings*, traded by Edward Depew for the lot where George settled his family, Pavelec, "PC News," *MainSheet* (August 2000): 20.

Page 61, "As we sailed by Kettenburg's": Springstead, 2000, 1.

Page 62, "As a result, my father went": Springstead, 2000, 1; Jessop had ordered PCs #2, 3, and 4; one odd result of this transaction was the construction of PC #2 *after* PC #5.

Page 62, "It was customers": PK stated that Jessop had considerable input into the cabin interior, and the cockpit's size and layout, PK, October 16, 2003, 7; Jessop, "Successful One-Design"; Bast, "A Good Guess," 68.

Page 62, "Since consistency among the boats was": Jessop, "Successful One-Design"; see untitled rules of the PC Class Racing Association, July 6, 1938, 3, SDYCHC, and Childs, "Evolution," 22; "The all purpose Racing-Cruising Sloop," Kettenburg Boat Works brochure, ca. 1940, copy at Maritime Museum of San Diego; the figure appears in Jessop, "Successful One-Design."

Page 62, "While one of Joe's goals was": Childs, "Evolution," 22.

Page 62, "PC's are Fast!": "All Purpose Racing-Cruising Sloop."

Page 62, "Advertisements could not ensure success": Jessop, interview by Bob Wright, November 10, 1990, 9.

CHAPTER 4

Page 66, "Out of the blue": "The all purpose Racing-Cruising Sloop," Kettenburg Boat Works brochure, ca. 1941; for photocopies of this and several other advertisements and articles consulted for this chapter, the author is indebted to historians Richard S. "Rish" Pavelec and Gene Trepte.

Page 66, "To sell a racing boat": Joe Jessop, "A Successful One-Design Class," *Pacific Skipper* 2 (January 1935), in 1935 scrapbook, SDYCHC.

Page 66, "It seems to have been": No hull #6 was completed. That boat had been intended for Robert Mann, who disdained the number as unlucky. Mann purchased #7 instead.

Page 66, "The parties agreed": Jessop, quoted in Elaine Davis, "PCs, If You Please: West Coast Woodies Have Found the Magic Formula for Longevity," *Waterfront* (December 1988): 14A.

Page 66, "First, however": "The All Purpose Racing-Cruising Sloop"; PK credits Jessop's navy connections with the trip to Hawaii, PK, interview with author, October 16, 2003, 5; Kenneth "Keno" Hallawell, "History of the San Diego Yacht Club 1886-1942," ca. 1942, 7, SDYCHC; information about this race series comes, except where noted, from "The Inter-Club Team Races at Honolulu," *Pacific Coast Yachting* 9 (July 1931): 7-11; San Diego skippers and hull numbers in this regatta at Honolulu Yacht Club were Jessop with Charles Wilson and Jack Nuttall in *Blue Jacket* (PC #2), A. E. Childs with Harry Uhler, Jack Bottomley, Albert J. Jones, and Gordon Hitchcock in *Tiana* (#3), George Jessop with Arthur Kelly and Roswell Yates in *Jean* (#4), and Mann with Jack Snell and Charles McKenzie in *Jade* (#7). Sailing the S boats were Harold Dillingham, Millard Allen, Robert and Ernest Mott-Smith, Jack Walker, A. W. T. Bottomley, Harold Ernman, Tom Balding, R. W. Atkinson, Eddie Hunter, Charles Wicher, C. Weeber, Albert Afong, Alice & Charles Hite, E. W.

Bogardus, Robert Purvis, James Woolaway, Paul Winslow, and Charles Henderson.

Page 69, "The shaken San Diegans": Statistics cited in "The Inter-Club Team Races at Honolulu," 7; the sail area reported for the PC varied over time, apparently due to changes permitted by the class rules; 353 square feet is also cited in A. E. Childs, "Evolution of the Pacific Coast One-Design Class," *Pacific Coast Yachting* (September 1930): 22, and Harry B. Wilford, "The PC's Conquer New Territory," *Pacific Skipper* (February 1937), and advertisements in February 1939 and March 1941 issues of *Sea*, as well as an advertisement from unknown publication probably from 1945, "Custom Built Boats," as well as "New Type Racing Yacht Unveiled by Kettenburg," *San Diego Union*, May 19, 1946; 385 square feet is cited in Samuel Dauchy, "The Pacific One-Design Class," *Yachting* (August 1934): 58, and Curtis Zahn, "Those Perennial PC's," *Sea* (June 1943); the last Kettenburg brochure to include PC specifications, "Here is Your Sailboat," late 1950s, lists the sail area as 395 square feet.

Page 69, "Lasting benefits came": Quoted in Frank Haven, "One Design for Living: Coast Yachtsmen Turning to Locally Designed Boat," *San Diego Sun*, December 20, 1934.

Page 70, "The excited returning racers": "The Inter-Club Team Races at Honolulu," 11. On unfulfilled plans for future matches against other racing classes, see also Jessop, "Successful One-Design Class"; Dauchy, "Pacific One-Design": 58; former commodore of Chicago's yacht club and a founder of the North American Yacht Racing Association, Dauchy had a second home in San Diego; Harry Wilford maintained in 1937 that "The four boatless San Diego men had not been home an hour before they had all ordered new boats," but other accounts dispute this, Wilford, "The P.C.'s Conquer."

Page 70, "The Lipton Cup win": "George Jessop Sails *Scamp II* to Lipton Cup Victory," *San Diego Union*, August 8, 1931; "Scamp Wins U-T Trophy," clipping from *Union*, ca. 1935, SDYCHC; *Scamp II* was apparently the name temporarily assigned by Kettenburg to PCs not yet sold, in this case hull #9, later *Ni-Ni-Nie*; PK remembered *Scamp II* as the name assigned to his postwar hull #43, PK, video interview by Steve Barber, Scott Wild, and Rish Pavelec, with Tom Kettenburg, January 3, 2002, 7.

Page 70, "Joe Jessup kept": This was hull #10, *Windy,* Doug Giddings, interview with Doug Werner and Andy Bofinger, January 20, 1999, 7, SDYCHC; Wallace Springstead, interview with unknown interviewer, October 9, 2000, 2, SDYCHC.

Page 70, "George Kettenburg Jr.": DG, interview with author, October 31, 2005, 1.

Page 70, "As his crew": PK, 2002, 7. JUJ, interview with author, October 10, 2005, 1, and letter to author received April 20, 2006.

Page 72, "Honing his sailing skills": Josephine Israel, "Ahoy! Skippers!" *San Diego Union*, April 24, 1935; JUJ, 1.

Page 72, "My memory of George": DG, 1999, 17; they were disqualified; the incident is noted in "George Jessop Takes Second Race in *Wings*," *San Diego Union*, August 19, 1935.

Page 72, "He didn't blow up": DG, 2005, 2.

Page 72, "Win or lose": DG, 2005, 2.

Page 72, "PC racing took place": DG, 2005, 1; Giddings credits Joe Jessop as the chief booster of the Saturday series.

Page 72, "The PC class did something": DG, 1999, 3.

Page 73, ""In this comparatively casual": Zahn, "Those Madcap San Diego Mudhens," from unidentified 1937 magazine (*Sea?*), 16-17, SDYCHC.

Page 74, "We're racing out in the ocean": DG, 1999, 3; before experimenting with toilet paper, the Giddingses wrapped their spinnaker with thread; because this race headed south from the yacht club, with a southwest wind a spinnaker was immediately useful; DG to Thompson Fetter, ca. 1987, Tom Fetter coll., 4; Don Giddings was also well known as Point Loma High School's football coach.

Page 74, "Don Giddings also": "Former Winners Absent," *San Diego Union*, ca. 1939, Giddings scrapbook.

Page 74, "Joe Jessop and his brother": "Joe vs. George, Again," *Pacific Skipper* 2 (January 1935), SDYCHC.

Page 74, "As the new design": "'Ni-Ni-Nie' Annexes Union-Tribune Trophy," *Pacific Skipper* (February 1936), SDYCHC.

Page 74, "The view from the boat works": "Dredge at Work on Yacht Basin," *San Diego Union*, November 6, 1934; Jessop, interview with Jim Mills, May 28, 1993; PK, interview with author, November 20, 2003.

Page 77, "The muddy shallows": JUJ, 4; Giddings sometimes took advantage of a loophole in the rules by intentionally running aground when the current was taking the boat aback, pushing off with the spinnaker pole once the wind came up, DG, 1999, 9.

Page 77, "At least one PC owner": DG, 1999, 9.

Page 77, "Leisure boating in Southern California": *San Diego Union*, July 11, 1934; Zahn, "Oh for a Life on the Bounding Main! Yachting is Work, but it's fun, too," *San Diego Tribune-Sun*, July 4, 1937; despite the 1926 defeat of countywide bonds intended to fund Newport Harbor's development, the following year the city voted $500,000 toward the project. In 1933 the federal government stepped in with $1.14 million, which Orange County supported with $640,000; Ed Giddings, "Pacific Class (PC) Association News," *Sea*, ca. 1940, Giddings scrapbook; DG, 1999, 17.

Page 77, "After this success": Giddings 2005; "Local Yard Delivers Yachts," unknown newspaper, February 20, 1939, SDYCHC; *Joy Too* was built in 1938 for Waterhouse; Coxhead's PC was *Lady Berkeley*, Glenn Waterhouse and Woodbridge Metcalf, "Five Hundred Miles on the Nose," *Sea* (December 1946): 13-14; Hunt, Willis, and Coxhead are first listed as distributors on a February, 1939 *Sea* ad.

Page 77, "Perhaps at the invitation": Haven, "400 Yachts Await Regatta Race Program," *Sun*, August 5, 1935; Jerry MacMullen, "What's the Use of Racing?" *Sea* (April 1939): 22; Waterhouse and Metcalf, "Five Hundred Miles," 13; Zahn, "Yachting News," *Tribune-Sun*, July 23, 1941; Wilford, "P.C.'s Conquer New Territory."

Page 78, "As PC competition blossomed": CAU, "Table of Contents" to audiotapes, October 18, 1987, 1.

Page 78, "Walt Hubbard was": DG, 2005, 7; GT, interview with the author, March 10, 2005, 8.

Page 78, "His South Coast": Gerry Driscoll, interview by Barry Moscowitz and Charles Bishop, June 23, 1999, SDYC, 18; Tom Skahill, "South Coast Company: The Life of a Full-Service Yacht Yard," *WoodenBoat* 193 (2006): 78-91.

Page 78, "George Kettenburg was so successful": GT, 2005, 7; Pavelec, personal communication, 2005; Hubbard built PC hulls #13, #15 and #17; South Coast's launching of #19, and (unrealized?) plans to build #22, are noted in "They Blew Their Tops," *Sea* (May 1937): 12; Walton Hubbard Jr., "A True One Design Class," *Sea* [?] n.d., in 1934 scrapbook, SDYCHC; Wilford, "P.C.'s Conquer," Dauchy, "Pacific One-Design," 58; Hubbard may have planked his PCs in a heavier wood than George's more water-resistant Philippine Tanguille (Tanguile) mahogany, which may have slowed them slightly; Tanguille mahogany is mentioned in a Kettenburg brochure and ads from ca. 1940-41; Postwar PCs were planked with more readily available Honduran mahogany, before Phillipine wood became available again, PK, 2002, 8; Milton Wegeforth, interview with Ruth Held, February 13, 1991, 6, SDHS; GT, 2005, 7.

Page 78, "Speaking as the designer": CAU, self-recorded reminiscences, October 1987, 12; Charlie's assertion that Rhodes used the PC's lines drawing is apparently unfounded; indeed, Richard Henderson relates it closely to Rhodes's 1937 Lake One-Design intended for Great Lakes use, see Richard Henderson, *Philip L. Rhodes and His Yacht Designs* (Camden, ME: International Marine Publishing, 1981), 139-49.

Page 79, "The rip off": Rhodes designed Albatross, Eagle, Falcon, and Gull sloops for construction by Hubbard, see Henderson, *Philip L. Rhodes and His Yacht Designs*, 362.

Page 79, "In 1938": Rhodes 33 hulls are 33 feet 8 inches long overall, 22 feet 4 inches at waterline, with 386 square feet of sail area; Allen Farwell Trane, ed., *Newport Harbor Yacht Club* (Newport, CA: 1991), 390; the designer,

Underwood, who may have been underinformed, insisted that they "could round the transom and add three inches to the sheer amidship, use the same lines and produce a boat called the Rhodes 33. And that was an outright steal," CAU, 12; the Rhodes 33 price is in an ad inside the back cover of the February 1940 *Sea*; the PC was advertised at $2,250 in the March 1939 *Sea* and $2,950 in the March 1941 *Sea*; DG, 2005, 2.

Page 79, "The Rhodes 33 smashed": CAU, 11; "Speed and Comfort—get both with a Rhodes '33 [sic]," *Sea* (December 1940): 3; Skahill, conversation with author, 2005; CAU 12; DG to Fetter, 2-3, spelling corrected; Frank Pickard, "Yachtsmen Demonstrate Superiority: San Diego Skippers Best 'Outsiders' in Competition," *San Diego Union*, September 20, 1939.

Page 80, "Duels between the classes": DG, 2005, 7.

Page 80, "The shop introduced": *MainSheet*, January 18, 1940; Zahn, "With Yachts in Local Waters," *San Diego Tribune-Sun*, September 4, 1937; Gartzman Gould and Bob Town were sailing *Imp*.

Page 80, "The introduction of this": White, "Yachters Thrill to Choosing of New Boats' Name, Color," *San Diego Union*, January 29, 1941; hull number 31 was fitted with an enlarged cabin created by carpenter Ben White, a relative of newspaper columnist Josephine Israel who worked for National Steel shipyard, though "not a yacht man," CAU, 12; Charlie fitted the new sink and toilet with covers, permitting more usable cabin space, Bailey Cook, "PC News of the Month," *Sea* (March 1941): 34; on the popularity of the new cabin, note that PC#30 was immediately retrofitted with doghouse and cabin for Balboa skipper Dorothy Davis, while conversion was proceeding on PC#8 and plans were afoot to convert *Half Moon* as well, Ed Giddings, "PC Association News," *Sea*, late 1941, SDYCHC; Zahn, "Yachting Notes," January 8, 1941.

Page 80, "Needless to say": CAU, 12; the ability to outproduce and undercut the price of the Rhodes was due to boatbuilding techniques Charlie would introduce in wartime, while new demand for the PC came from the postwar boats' much-improved interiors.

Page 80, "The first of very few": The December 1935 meeting was one of four the class had held to that date. Along with Genoas, they agreed to replace the rig's headstay arrangement and round the keel's leading edge. Options included extending the tiller through the deck, Jessop, "The Pacific Class is Ready for 1936," *Pacific Skipper* 13 (January 1936), SDYCHC scrapbook; DG, 2005, 7; genoas remained in use until September 1944, Roger Bryan, "PC Racing Bulletin #11," 1944 scrapbook, SDYCHC.

Page 81, "With more pressure": GT, 2005, 6; Springstead, interview with the author, April 14, 2006.

Page 82, "George Kettenburg had": "German Yacht Skippers Win in Bay Event," unknown newspaper, April 2, 1934, from 1934 scrapbook, SDYCHC; Israel, "Ahoy, Skippers!" *San Diego Union*, September 29, 1934; Germans sailed *Ni-Ni-Nie*, the Americans, *Scamp*. *Karlsruhe*'s career ended in 1940, tor-

pedoed by HM Submarine *Truant*. British sailors were from HMS *Norfolk*. Other multinational competitors who raced loaned PCs included Canadians from destroyers HMCS *Vancouver* and *Skeena* in January 1935; Jerry MacMullen, "University of Arizona Wins Pacific Coast Intercollegiates," *San Diego Union,* ca. 1936, Giddings scrapbook.

Page 82, "The finest publicity coup": Roosevelt was an active sailor in San Diego, flying in to race PC hull #29 frequently during 1940, see "Bubbly Splashes at Roosevelt Launching," probably *San Diego Union*, ca. 1938.

Page 82, "Travel to distant regattas": Jessop, interview with Ruth Held, November 10, 1990, 9, SDHS; Dauchy, "Pacific One-Design," 58.

Page 83, "The young racers": DG, 2005, 7.

Page 83, "The positive effects": JUJ, 3, and letter.

Page 84, "When another Kettenburg boat": DG, 1999.

Page 84, "Doug also was among": This PC belonged to "Bo" Heller and his brother, DG to Fetter, 4.

Page 85, "In 1939": GT, 2005, 11.

Page 85, "Newport Sailor Bob Allan": Trane, *Newport Harbor*, 361, italics added; Allan identified the injured crewman as Dick Fenton, but he is J. G. Kennedy in "Wave, Boat Breaks Leg," clipping from unidentified newspaper, August 25, 1939, SDYCHC.

Page 85, "The culprit?": DG, 1999, 17.

Page 85, "The original PC was lost": GT, 2005, 11.

Page 85, "Not long after that": "The All Purpose Racing-Cruising Sloop"; Zahn, "Yachting Notes," *San Diego Tribune-Sun*, April 23, 1941; construction was started on #32 in Hawaii before war broke out; the destruction of a PC on December 7 is noted in "PC Boats Open Regatta Here," *San Diego Union*, September 2, 1942; the fact that it was apparently PC #2, *Blue Jacket*, is suggested in an August 1945 Hawaiian newspaper article listing hull numbers of Hawaii's remaining PCs, found in SDYCHC's 1945 scrapbook; by 1947, however, *Blue Jacket* may have been restored, for she is listed as owned by Dr. Paul Withington in Honolulu, although it is possible the listing may not have been current, "List of PC (Pacific Class) Owners," August 25, 1947, SDYCHC; hull numbers #31-33 were intended to have been built in Hawaii, but were never completed.

Page 85, "Virtually overnight": Although hull #35 was the last completed before the war, she was the thirty-first PC built, since four designated hull numbers were never completed for various reasons, Pavelec, PC registry, 2006.

Page 90, "Gravel sprayed": The November date appears in Charles La Dow, "Kettenburg Marine: The Story of an Enterprise," unpublished typescript, 1988, 11.

Page 90, "When Paul had left": PK, interview with author, October 16, 2003, 5; PK, interview with Robert Wright, May 25, 1985, 6; PK, video interview by Steve Barber, Scott Wild, and "Rish" Pavelec, with TK, January 3, 2002, 4; that Paul worked for his father-in-law is attested by CAU in self-recorded reminiscences, October 1987, 36.

Page 91, "The Second World War": PK, quoted in Paul Lazarus, "Kettenburg Boat Works: Power and Sail for Southern California," *WoodenBoat* 116 (1994): 65; Josephine Israel White, "Yachting Society Prepares for Annual New Year Race," *San Diego Union*, December 31, 1941; "Yachtsmen to Christen New Penguin Fleet Here Today," *San Diego Union*, January 21, 1942; the Penguin was a 1939 Phil Rhodes design for Chesapeake Bay frostbiters that became very popular after *Yachting* featured it in May 1940, see Henderson, *Philip L. Rhodes and His Yacht Designs*; Kettenburg built these first 11-foot, 6-inch Penguins; other San Diego builders constructed many more.

Page 91, "By the time Paul returned": CAU, 15.

Page 91, "George had based": The Chicago business engineering firm of George S. May is identified as the consultant in La Dow, "Kettenburg Marine," 15; Charlie remembered hearing that they had been recommended by the office manager, and given authority over hiring and firing in exchange for waiving any fee unless they put the company "in the black"; ironically, the first person they fired was the office manager, CAU, 3-4; PK remembered that they had previously helped set up production lines for various types of construction equipment, PK, 2002, 5; GT, interview with author, March 10, 2005, 13.

Page 91, "Charlie continued": CAU, 5; Charlie was actually put in charge of production, not the plant itself, according to his future partners Bill Kettenburg and Morgan Miller.

Page 92, "As everyone who knew him": CAU, 6; CRU, quoted in Jeff McDonald, "Charles Underwood, 84; Yacht Designer," *San Diego Union-Tribune*, October 15, 1998; Wallace Springstead, interview with author, April 14, 2006, 4; BK interview with author, May 8, 2006, 5.

Page 92, "Pridefulness in his work": CAU, 3.

Page 92, "Any employee": CAU, 15, 28; Charlie continues that "we got all the boats" from those specifications; in the company's 1952 brochure, he is Superintendent of Navy Repair; courtesy TK.

Page 93, "To make your steam-bent frames": JUJ, interview with author, October 10, 2005, 4, 5.

Page 89, "Charlie remembered being": CAU, 10.

Page 93, "For starters": On precedents for upside-down production, see Thomas G. Skahill, "Cal 32s: Formidable Racers, Comfortable Cruisers," *WoodenBoat* 83 (1988): 44; Skahill noted the origin of the practice in Europe in conversation with author, October 9, 2006; CRU, however, recalls his father telling him proudly that their main innovation lay in building boats inverted on a jig that could be disassembled, CRU conversation, October 2006; PK, interview with author, November 21, 2003; inverted boatbuilding apparently began at Kettenburg shortly before March, 1941; Bill Smith, conversation with author, October 2005; "Building Another Beauty," *San Diego Daily Journal*, January 24, 1946, punctuation altered.

Page 94, "What Charlie introduced": CAU, 10-11.

Page 94, "Jim Underwood Jr.": JUJ, 4; Charlie also worked alongside crews, to push them further; The number of PRBs produced by Kettenburg has been variously recalled. Charlie remembered the boat's production rate as five per month, and that they were completed in two separate contracts of 30, CAU, 5; in 1985 PK probably incorrectly recalled the total built as 150, and later related that they were built in two contracts, the first for 20 boats, and the second for 40, PK 1985, 7; PK interview with Charlie Bishop and Ted Moskowitz, December 30, 1998, 20, SDYCHC.

Page 94, "George's crew mushroomed": JUJ, 4; Charlie gives the prewar figure of 12-14 men and over 100 during the war, CAU, 4, 10-11.

Page 96, "A generation of women": JUJ, 4; Charlie remembers their stepmother was hired originally to stuff boat bumpers with kapok.

Page 96, "Jim Underwood Jr.": CAU, 3.

Page 96, While working his way up": GT, interview with author, May 9, 2006, 6, 8; CAU, "Table of Contents," 1; JU, 5; BK is very specific about Charlie's feelings of being snubbed in interview, 7.

Page 96, "Charlie made room for Paul": Alex "Bud" Caldwell, interview with author, July 17, 2006, 2; PK, quoted in letter to Tom Fetter from La Dow, July 6, 1988, Tom Fetter coll.; PK, November 21, 2003.

Page 96, "The U.S. Navy was": Hershey, "Richard B. Hershey," undated typescript, 1987, 3, courtesy Harry Hershey, punctuation altered.

Page 96, "More important in developing": Mick Kronman, "The Kettenburg 38: The Story of a California Classic," *National Fisherman* (November 1987): 32; CAU, 20; PK, 1985, 7; PK, 1998, 20; the Interior Department actually had jurisdiction of fish boat construction, due to the fact that rivers and harbors were under their authority, CAU, 21.

Page 98, "George, Charlie and Kenny Baker": CAU, 20-21; see also Kronman, "Kettenburg 38," 32.

Page 98, "In the greatest single production run": Eighty-six 38-foot fish boats are mentioned in "Bob Higbee Retires," *The Ways Cable*, May 19, 1988, and in undated notes written late in life by CAU on reverse of photo of fish boat *Poggy*, where he also noted that each required 23 man-days to build; photo courtesy Susan Larkin; 80 fish boats, however, are listed in "Organization, Key Personnel and Facilities," (Whittaker document, ca. 1973), 4, and PK, 1985, 7; most fish boats were bought by major operators in the prewar tuna fleet; 50 were built after the war according to PK, 1998, 20; the first was built for the Lo Coco brothers in 1944, with 69 completed by spring 1949; Hegeman, "Kettenburg's," 29; four fishermen were the normal complement, with six on net boats; between 1947 and 1949 drawings were completed for a 46-foot fantail fish boat with greater range, ordered by new clients, but U.S. government subsidy for the Japanese fishing industry undercut financing, CAU, 27; Hershey, "Richard B. Hershey"; Miller, BK, and Miller, 11; hulls were identical, but buyers could choose between shorter or longer deckhouses; boats were first planked with cypress, with cedar and fir substituted later; a few 32-foot fish boats were apparently also constructed in early 1945, but discontinued because construction cost was almost equal to the 38-foot boat; cruising range was 600 miles; Kronman, "Kettenburg 38," 33; price quoted in PK, 2002, 5.

Page 98, "Fishermen thought very highly": PK, 2002, 5; Miller, BK, and Miller, 13; Steve Provdonovich and Walter T. Vestal, quoted in John Hegeman, "Kettenburg's of San Diego: A Pleasure Craft Manufacturer Begins Building Fishing Boats & Surprises All, Including Himself!" *Pan-American Fisherman* (May 1949): 29.

Page 99, "The design's only weak point": Kronman, 33; on a note card associated with photo P-11115 in the Maritime Museum of San Diego archives, Lou (Petranacci?) is quoted that *Baby Doll* "nearly tipped over at sea so it was loaded w/ chain for stability"; Charlie recalled the 20-ton catch, possible because sardine fishing's short durations at sea did not require ice, CAU, 20.

Page 100, "Demand continued well after": PK 1985, 8; Kronman, "Kettenburg 38," 33; Morgan Miller, conversation with author, February 9, 2005. Paying off within two seasons was more common. Kronman, "Kettenburg 38," 33.

Page 100, "Thanks to efficient production": Caldwell, conversation with author, January 23, 2005; PK remembered fish boats requiring ten days on the assembly line, PK, 1985, 7; in undated notes recorded years later on the reverse of a photo of the 1945 *Poggy*, CAU noted that a dozen man-days were devoted to set-up time, five man-days to planking, and six man-days to plugging, caulking, and painting: a total of 23 man-days, courtesy Susan Larkin.

Page 100, "The last station": PK, 1985, 7-8; "Building Another Beauty"; CAU, "Table of Contents," 1.

Page 100, "When V-J Day came": The launch of *Poggy*, their 34th fish boat, is noted in *Journal*, June 12, 1945, and detailed in *Pacific Motorboat* (August 1945), which notes that her 6-cylinder 80-h.p. Chrysler Marine diesel was the first of its kind installed in a fishing boat in Southern California; most boats received these or 4-cylinder Caterpillars, although some late boats housed 3-71 GM engines; boats sold for about $13,000 with gas engines, or $16,000 with diesel, Kronman, "Kettenburg 38," 32-33.

Page 103, "The same day found George": CAU, 12.

Page 103, "George was showing": BK, video interview with Fred Lewis for television program *The Heart of San Diego*, broadcast June 13, 2005; GT, 2006, 5; regarding the Island Clipper, see Skahill, "Fellows & Stewart Inc., Boatbuilders," *WoodenBoat* 173 (2003): 55; PK, 1998, 23.

Page 105, "The actual lines": Hershey, "Richard B. Hershey," 5; GT, 2006, 7.

Page 105, "I didn't want us to": CAU, 11, 10.

Page 105, "The war years taught": Miller, BK, and Miller, 14, 4, 11.

CHAPTER 6

Page 108, "I think I was the one": Norm Dawley, describing *Undine*, "*Selene* and *Undine*," 2006 manuscript courtesy Neil Atwood; the author is indebted to Mr. Atwood for generously sharing his research on the PCC.

Page 109, "Stock PCCs": "At sea, in big water, they will be especially sudden in their motions, and this is apt to wear the crew down," Henry E. Scheel wrote of the PCC in "The Light Displacement Ocean Racer," *Yachting* (January 1950): 85. To compensate for downwind handling eccentricities in extreme weather, some made temporary modifications. To control *Gossip* in the 1951 Transpac, Charlie Ross rigged a transom rudder, similar to a spade rudder, allowing her to carry a heavy spinnaker through squalls of close to 60 knots; Dawley fitted a spade rudder for the 1977 Transpac; BK states that Dawley's description of downwind handling is perhaps too extreme, but acknowledges it as "one of the tender spots" in the design, BK, conversation with author, September 28, 2006; others modified technique instead. Edward S. Barr, who crewed for his mother, Dennie, notes "in the early days … spinnakers were full shouldered. Solution to gyrations downwind was to choke the sail down near the deck, flatten it out by spreading, and increase halyard tension to the maximum. Another stabilizing 'trick' was to surf. PCCs had a flat bottom run off aft of the keel. This flat surface was excellent for surfing. On occasion I was thrilled … with the bow wave shooting up inside the mainsail. This breaking loose surfing technique would only be successful when positioning the vessel's heading directly down-wave," Barr, note to author, October 1, 2006; BK, interview with author, May 8, 2006, 7, some narrative details come from Barr, "Business Mixes with Pleasure as Kettenburg Heads for Canada–Part II," *MainSheet* (San Diego Yacht Club newsletter, October 1999): 31-32; in San Francisco, George handed *Mickey* over to owners Larry and Dennie Barr, see also Emily Devlin, "Mrs. Lawrence Barr Tells Beauties of Scenic Trip," scrapbook clipping from *San Diego Daily Journal* (1948), SDYCHC.

Page 109, "Smacked down momentarily": GT, interview with author, May 9, 2006, 6; Trepte won PCC Nationals in 1948, 1949, and 1950 in *Bolero* (#13), and participated in 1948 and 1950 trips north.

Page 110, "The three working vacations": JUJ, interview with author, October 10, 2005, 2; Barr, "Business Mixes," 31.

Page 110, "As the film whirred in George's camera": PCC #9 appears to have been launched in January 1948 for Gifford Ewing of La Jolla, but was quickly sold to Smith, "List of PCC (Pacific Class Cruiser [sic]) Owners," January 29, 1948, courtesy Deb Domenici; Ewing subsequently co-owned #10; It is unclear whether Smith purchased *Gossip* in advance of her delivery; authors Humphrey Golby and Shirley Hewitt state that Smith bought her after success in the PIYA regatta in *Swiftsure: The First Fifty Years* (Victoria: Lightship Press, 1980); BK notes she was shipped north on a flatcar, and that Smith bought her in San Diego, BK, conversation with author, September 28, 2006; Alex "Bud" Caldwell, interview with author, July 17, 2006, 3; Charlie and Ann Underwood joined them after the races for cruising in the San Juan Islands, GT, 2006, 6; the group's affection for "Jonesy" was recounted by Morgan Miller in a conversation with the author on February 9, 2005, while Bill Kettenburg remarked on him as "a real playboy" in a March 2007 conversation.

Page 111, "There, along with the hospitality": "New Type Racing Yacht Unveiled by Kettenburg," *San Diego Union*, May 19, 1946.

Page 112, "The Barrs rented a powerboat": The Petersen-Kettenburg prop is specified in "Here is Your Sailboat," Kettenburg Boat Works brochure, ca. 1948; TK states that his father, Paul, told him that Petersen played a relatively small part in developing the prop, although he patented it in his own name, conversation with the author, October 8, 2006; South Coast cast versions in several sizes and sold them as the South Coast-Petersen Folding Propeller, Tom Skahill, "South Coast Company: The Life of a Full-Service Yacht Yard," *WoodenBoat* 193 (2006): 86.

Page 112, "*Gossip* threaded tricky passages": CRU, interview with author, May 31, 2006, 2; Skahill was a valuable consultant on the preceding paragraph; GT, 2006, 3; *Bolero* was #13; Bill's "Lake Yottington" phrase came up in personal conversation in 2006.

Page 113, "For the last of their three trips north": "Liquid inspiration" noted in *Main Sheet*, San Diego Yacht Club newsletter, May 1946, SDYCHC; "The Pacific Cruising Class," *Sea* (November 1945): 18; crowd size is noted in "New Type Racing Yacht."

Page 113, "Just a few years before": This first postwar Kettenburg racer was soon renamed *Ray* by the skipper, Milt Wegeforth, and by January 1948 new owner Lewis Riley Jr. in Acapulco had renamed her *Nereida*, GT, 2006, 5; "List of PCC Owners."

Page 113, "The first PCC came out": BK, interviewed by Atwood, noted his father's opinion that *Ray* was faster; Jessop's involvement is noted in PK, video

interview with Steve Barber, Scott Wild, and "Rish" Pavelec, with TK, January 3, 2002, 5; CAU, however, seems to suggest that George himself did not like the bobtailed appearance of this first boat, CAU, self-recorded personal history, October 1987, 24; The 46-foot, 4-inch length is in Kettenburg brochure "Here is Your Sailboat"; A typographical error lists the PCC's beam as 6 feet, 6 inches in "Here is Your Sailboat" (also the source of the reference to dishes); beam is 9 feet, 4 inches in "Pacific Cruising Class."

Page 117, "At first glance": Tom Gwynne, "In this Corner," clipping from *San Diego Daily Journal,* 1946; displacement is in "Here is Your Sailboat"; estimates of other displacements are from Barr, conversation with author, October 1, 2006.

Page 117, "The principal distinction": John Springer, "'Greyhounds of the Sea': Sleek, Slick PPC [sic] Boats Have Startling Speed," *San Diego Union*, October 17, 1948; much of this article is also quoted, without credit, in John Hegeman, "Kettenburg's of San Diego: A Pleasure Craft Manufacturer Begins Building Fishing Boats & Surprises All, Including Himself!" *Pan-American Fisherman* (May 1949): 28-29; "The Kettenburg PCC Class," *Sea* (December 1951): 57; Springer, "Greyhounds"; A base price without sails of $16,500-$16,600 is given by CAU; the price on #14 was close to $20,000 in 1948, while a base price of $17,700 is listed in 1949, CAU, monologue recorded October 1987, 25; "The PCC: A Fast, New San Diego-Built Yacht is the Sensation of Pacific Coast Sailing," clipping, probably from *San Diego Magazine*, ca. 1948, courtesy TK; George Kettenburg Jr. to Henry duPont, December 13, 1949.

Page 118, "Bill Kettenburg remembered": George's price concerns are noted by CAU, 25; BK video interview with Fred Lewis for television program, *The Heart of San Diego*, broadcast June 13, 2005; Miller, BK, and Miller, 10; the Cal 32 featured 857 square feet of sail area to the PCC's 740, GT, 2; on the Cal 32, see Skahill, "Nick Potter: His Boats Won the West," *WoodenBoat* 83 (1988): 38-47; an eighth Cal 32 was built in Hong Kong.

Page 118, "One of these established boats": This race occurred in spring 1948, Barr, "The Last Sailboat Design by George Kettenburg: The PCC (Pacific Cruising Class)–Part I," *Mainsheet* (September 1999): 29.

Page 119, "Not long afterwards": CAU, 7; Springer, "Greyhounds of the Sea."

Page 120, "San Diego's own newspapermen": George speculated about entering the 1947 Transpac in "New Type Racing Yacht"; BK, with Miller and Miller, 11; *Selene*, PCC #3, finished 13th in the 1947 Transpac; *Life* photographer Ted Sierks fell overboard in heavy seas about 800 miles from Hawai'i; *Gossip* and four other racers detoured to search, but Sierks was rescued by the navy 29 hours later; figures are extracted from Atwood, "Kettenburg Transpac Race Results 1949-1971" (2006), with additions of *Selene* in 1947 and *Undine* in 1977; important victories include those by Gartzman "Gartz" Gould's *Ballerina*, #12, which won the SCYA Summer regatta in 1950, the

Lipton Cup in 1952, and the Coronado Island Race in 1952 and 1955; Pat Boldrick won the 1949 San Clemente Island Race in *Lani*, #11, while Fred Lyon's *Kitten*, #6, won the Ensenada Race in 1949; *Hussy*, #15, placed third in Swiftsure in 1964 and 1967.

Page 120, "As the shadow of war receded": PK, interview with Charles Bishop and Ted Moskowitz, December 30, 1998, 23, SDYCHC.

Page 120, "Paul Kettenburg crewed": Carl Ritter, "Fate Likely to End Kettenburg Reign," *San Diego Union*, May 25, 1952; 1947's San Clemente Island Race was won by Hal Ramser's *Antigua*, #5, of Voyagers' Yacht Club, Newport Beach; *Eulalie* also won SDYC's 1947 and 1948 opening day races, the 1949 Newport-Ensenada Race, took second in the 1950 Southern California Yachting Association (SCYA) Summer Regatta, won the Trepte Trophy as first finisher in the 1950 and 1951 San Clemente Island Races, another first in the 1950 midwinter Catalina Race, and was first to finish the 1951 Coronado Race, Atwood, "Kettenburg PCC Registry," unpublished man-uscript, 2006; although "Kettenburg PCC Class," 51 calls Irwin's PCC *Belle of the South*, BK remembers this boat's name as *Belle of the West*, and that name is confirmed in the yacht registers; duPont to W. L. Stewart Jr., April 28, 1950.

Page 120, "As the boats' racing reputation spread": Atwood, email to author, October 6, 2006; Watts made sails for all PCCs except #25, which featured the first set of sails made for a large boat by Lowell North, later famed as a sailmaker; Henry E. Scheel, "The Light Displacement Ocean Racer," *Yachting* (January 1950): 84.

Page 122, "The premier East Coast ocean race": William H. Taylor, "Light Displacement in the Bermuda Race," *Yachting* (August 1950): 38-39, 93-94.

Page 122: "In 1955 Hank duPont took *Cyane*": Alfred F. Loomis, "'Windigo' Wins the Gotland Race," *Yachting* (September 1955): 54; Alfred F. Loomis, "'Carina' Wins the Fastnet," *Yachting* (October 1955): 58.

Page 125, "In 1950, duPont entered *Cyane*": Olin S. Stephens, email to author, July 18, 2006; Taylor, "Light Displacement in the Bermuda Race," 39; *Cyane* was PCC #17.

Page 125, "Among the 1950 Bermuda Race's mix": Atwood, email to author, October 6, 2006; Watts made sails for all PCCs but #25; which featured the first set of sails made for a large boat by Lowell North, later famed as a sail-maker, BK; Lewis interview; Caldwell, 4.

Page 126, "One frustrated Pacific Coast competitor": BK, with Miller and Miller, 10; Lewis interview; Springer, "Greyhounds of the Sea"; Caldwell, 4.

Page 126, "After one Ensenada Race": Barr, "Dennie Barr O'Bryan: Dynamite Yachtswoman," *The Albatross* (Ancient Mariner's Sailing Society newsletter) 24 (February 1998); Debra A. Dominici, "Dennie Barr O'Bryan: A Pioneering Woman 'Big Boat' Sailor," *Mains'l Haul* (Winter 2005): 42-47.

Page 126, "A traditional yachtsman like Bogart": See Bud Desenberg, *The Ensenada Race: Thirty Years of Silver and Gold* (Newport, CA: Newport Ocean Sailing Association, 1978); PK, interview with author, October 16, 2003, 3.

Page 126, "The yacht club was almost entirely men": Barr, "Last Sailboat Design," 28.

Page 128, "Bound by her own code of honor": "Here is Your Sailboat."

Page 128, "After listening to the skipper": Iris Engstrand with Cynthia Davalos, *San Diego Yacht Club: A History* (San Diego: San Diego Yacht Club, 2000), 120; Bill Center, "Dynamite Dennie O'Bryan," *Sea* (September 1978): 107.

CHAPTER 7

Page 135, "Outside the circle of partners": Morgan Miller, conversation with the author, February 9, 2005; the January 1949 date is given in sales brochure, Kettenburg Boat Works: San Diego, Calif.," ca 1952, courtesy TK.

Page 135, "Morgan Miller": BK, video interview with Fred Lewis for television program *The Heart of San Diego*, broadcast June 13, 2005.

Page 135, "Bill Kettenburg found himself": BK, video interview with Fred Lewis for television program *The Heart of San Diego*, broadcast June 13, 2005; Bill became a partner after college in 1951; Miller, BK, and Jean (Kettenburg) Miller, interview with author, February 22, 2004, 12; 6-cylinder Chrysler engines powered these 16- and 18-foot tenders, also used by the pole-fishing fleet to catch anchovies for bait, TK, "Kettenburg Boats Timeline," unpublished typescript, 2003; one 18-foot power dory sold for $513 in 1946, "City of San Diego Leases and Contracts" (1946), 31, SDHS; under Whittaker ownership in the 1970s, Kettenburg operated another store on Harbor Island in San Diego, one in Dana Point, Balboa Marine and San Pedro Marine Hardware in the Los Angeles area, and a marine repair yard and store in Oxnard.

Page 136, "Upstairs behind his drawing board": "Kettenburg Boat Works"; the number is noted in CAU, "Table of Contents" for audio tapes, 1987, 3; PK, interview by Robert Wright, May 25, 1985, SDHS, 11; navy repair projects included whaleboats, buoy boats, LCPLs, LCPVs, plane re-arming boats, and life rafts, B. L. Stovall letter reprinted in "Kettenburg Boat Works"; A 63-foot prototype air-sea rescue boat was launched for the Air Force in 1953, *San Diego Evening Tribune*, March 26, 1953, it was essentially a modified version of the WWII rescue boat designed by Dail Long, powered by a pair of 12-cylinder Hall Scott 650-h.p. gasoline engines, and was designed by Thomas Lundy in San Francisco; Kettenburg's contract to build boats was cancelled, but they profited by being selected to manage the 101 boats built in yards at Seattle, Detroit, and Stonington, and to function as procurement center for the contracts.

Page 137, "Under George's usually watchful eye": CAU, self-recorded oral history, October 1987, 7-8.

Page 137, "This hull would be the basis": CAU, "Table of Contents," 2; "Bud" Caldwell recalled that a PCC was completed every dozen days, in conversation with author, January 23, 2005; Charles La Dow gives a figure of every 21 days in "The Kettenburg Story…" (1986); Charlie's account of building the sportfisher *Langosta* for Paul Berry of Michigan is from CAU to La Dow, ca. 1986; on Charlie's experiments with net boat construction, see CAU, 33-35; on his considerable dissatisfactions with the partnership as it evolved, see CAU, 37-39.

Page 139, "The supervisor of repair work": GK, interview with author, October 7, 2006, 5; The date of Kearns's hire appears in "Kettenburg Boat Works"—he replaced Jimmy Underwood, who retired during the war, and he and Charlie had known each other since 1930, CAU, 36; on land improvements, see PK to Karen Scanlon, June 19, 2003.

Page 139, "Bill Kearns also": CAU, 36; GT, interview with author, March 10, 2005, 13; Helen Kearns Sheverton, telephone conversation with author, January 4, 2005; the fire axe reference is from Bob Walters, "La Siesta: A Superlative Yacht," *Sea and Pacific Motor Boat* (December 1969): 49.

Page 139, "The well-liked, knowledgeable": Morgan Miller Jr. learned to surf from Bud, Alex "Bud" Caldwell, conversation with author, 2006; PK video interview by Steve Barber, Scott Wild, and "Rish" Pavelec, with TK, January 3, 2002, 12.

Page 139, "Bud later realized": Caldwell, interview with author, July 17, 2006, 3; Richard L. Palmer, interview with Betty Quayle, April 6, 1992, 8, SDHS; Palmer became a noteworthy sculptor and painter. His estimate of a work force of about 30 is borne out by the number in the 1944 company picnic and 1945 dinner photos, although in 1998 PK recalled that the wartime workforce reached 120. Palmer rejoined the company after 1968, when he was sent to manage the Channel Islands Harbor yard as vice president and general manager. He stayed for six years, primarily managing the construction of navy LCM-8s, until it was sold. According to Caldwell, the only exception to the rule of promoting from within the shop was a failure.

Page 139, "The spirit of cooperation": B. L. Stovall to Kettenburg Boat Works, January 9, 1952, reproduced in "Kettenburg Boat Works"; Caldwell, 1.

Page 141, "This unusual labor practice": CAU, 16.

Page 141, "And so even as the titans of labor": CAU, 3, 1-2.

Page 141, "Boatbuilders also had in-house incentive": PK, 2002, 12; CRU to author, July 17, 2005, 4; GT, interview with author, May 9, 2006, 7; he is describing the construction of his K 50.

Page 141, "We got the best of people": Miller, BK, and Miller, 10; Keller, 2. The carpenter in question was Bob Ballinger or Bill Smith, and the boat a K 40.

Page 142, "The final group on which success hinged": Robert McNeil, "The Story of *Zephyrus III* on the race Los Angeles to Mazatlan" (privately printed, 1966), 2; the boat was a K 40.

Page 142, "Customers frequently moved up": Keller, 4.

Page 142, "Since almost half of K 50 owners": Ten owners are cited as previous Kettenburg customers in "Jim Arness Goes from Gun Smoke to Sea Smoke," *Sea* reprint; CRU, revised transcript of interview, October 8, 2006, 2; Charlie started working part time in 1960, and worked full time from 1963 to 1970.

Page 142, "Among the new racers were women": Josephine White, "Feminine Yachters Encouraged over Giddings Trophy Winner," *San Diego Union*, November 26, 1941. Royce's boat was PC #27, *Zorra;* Peggy Slater with Shelley Usen, *Peggy: An Affair with the Sea* (Edens Publishing, 1992), 39; Slater had previously owned a PIC, which like her PC was named *Seventh Heaven;* changes made to the PC standing rigging included removal of the headstay (from bow to masthead), and the "diamond rig," replaced by a double jib forestay. The jib stay deck fitting was moved a foot aft–the stay now meets the mast near the new jumper struts. These strengthen the mast's top section, and the double jib stays act as a forestay without going to the head of the mast as the headstay had, thus reducing strain on the masthead. After 1944 the genoa was discarded in favor of the jib, but the hoist was raised higher on the mast. In order to keep within one-design rules on permissible sail area, the longer foot of the new jib was compensated for by shortening its luff, leaving the sail area of 385 square feet unchanged. A large spinnaker was added, with a fore triangle of 9'6", but a 12' pole. Postwar PCs were built with an elongated cabin and a hatch before the mast for light and ventilation, Rish Pavelec, personal communications, 2005.

Page 143, "Every champion praised the toughness": Wallace Springstead, interview with the author, April 14, 2006, 6.

Page 143, "Racing resumed with a vengeance": The added weight came to 500 pounds, although one of these "cruising" boats won the Coast Championship, *Yachting* Magazine eds., *Your New Boat* (New York: Simon & Schuster, 1946), 75; DG to Thompson Fetter, 3, Fetter coll.; interview with Doug Werner, Andy Bofinger, and Bishop, January 20, 1999, 7, SDYCHC; PK, quoted in Elaine Davis, "PCs if You Please: West Coast Woodies Have Found the Magic Formula for Longevity," *Waterfront* (December 1988): 18A.

Page 143, "Loyal customers quickly spread": The total number of PCs built was 79; "Organization, Key Personnel and Facilities," Whittaker document, ca. 1973, 4, courtesy Tom Fetter; PC hulls #56-59 were built in Vancouver, using a mold and patterns for keel and cabin parts sent from San Diego, PK, 2002, 13; hulls #80-83 were built in San Diego, decked, and primed, then shipped upside down via rail to Charlie Ross in Seattle where cabins were built and masts stepped–"We could ship four boats almost for the price of one" complete boat, PK, 2002, 8, 13; Carl Eichenlaub used original plans to build one more PC in 2006.

Page 144, "George Kettenburg Jr.'s business partners": Morgan Miller, conversation with author, February 9, 2005; obituary for George Kettenburg Jr., *San Diego Union*, December 21, 1952; CAU, 37.

Page 144, "George was a regional archery champion": Caldwell, 4; JUJ, interview with author, October 10, 2005, 2-3.

Page 144, "As an investment": Scanlon, "Creating an 'Island' Playground: San Diegans Recall the Development of Shelter Island" *Mains'l Haul* (Fall 2002/Winter 2003): 32-35.

Page 144, "Ironically, given George's swift decline": His father's cancer was discovered in February or March of 1952, BK, Miller, and Miller, 11; JUJ, 2-3.

Page 145, "Near the end of George's life": BK, Miller, and Miller, 13, 14.

Page 145, "Bud laughed uproariously": Caldwell, 4.

CHAPTER 8

Page 148, "Kettenburg Boat Works sailed smoothly": PK, interview with author, November 20, 2003, 12-13; PK, interview with Robert Wright, May 25, 1985, SDHS, 9; since the company apparently never officially decided whether "K" names should be hyphenated, they appear here without hyphens; CRU, conversation with author, April 22, 2005; this assessment of Paul and Charlie's respective design roles is also supported by GT, interview with author, May 9, 2006, 8, and by Dennie Barr's memories, related by her to Ed Barr; "Memo Re: K-38 design," October, 1 2006; CRU explains that "initially the design center was located in George Kettenburg's office in the main building. Later in the mid 50's it was situated in the corner building across the street from the store on Carlton Street. . . . In the mid 50's KBW significantly expanded the store and added executive offices on the second floor for Paul Kettenburg and Charlie. The design office was then relocated in a room connected to Charlie's office. It was in this location that the K 40, K 50, K 43, K 41 were designed," CRU, letter to author, July 17, 2005, 3; according to Charlie's reminiscences, George Moore was the primary designer of the K 40 and K 47. Among other work, Moore also perfected the fiberglass wrapped core construction system for an unsuccessful fish boat, and for pro- totype LCVPs (with Dick Palmer), and the fireboat *Shelter Island* in 1961;

"New Fire Boat is Christened by Mrs. Dail," *San Diego Union*, May 26, 1961; CAU, self-recorded personal history, October 1987, 26.

Page 148, "The racing/cruising market": Daniel Spurr, *Heart of Glass: Fiberglass Boats and the Men Who Made Them* (New York: McGraw Hill, 2004), 137; in 1945, San Diego had 1,481 registered pleasure boats, with 5,973 by 1957. At the end of 1958, that number had climbed to over 9,000: the highest per capita in the U.S., Iris Engstrand and Cynthia Davalos, *San Diego Yacht Club: A History* (San Diego: San Diego Yacht Club, 2000), 131.

Page 149, "In the meantime, however": *Los Angeles Times*, December 16, 1956, as quoted in Peggy Slater with Shelley Usen, *Peggy: An Affair with the Sea* (Los Angeles: Edens Publishing, 1992), 178. She replaced George Strom of Newport, who was advertised as Kettenburg's representative in 1946.

Page 149, "She was a *real good* sailor": PK, November 20, 2003, 3; Slater is identified as Woman of the Year for 1956 in *Los Angeles Times*, December 16, 1956; Slater, *Peggy*, 72; she represented Kettenburg sailboats until the end of production, and CRU notes her involvement in 1968 sale of K 46, CRU, conversation with author, January 12, 2007.

Page 149, "Their joy became her job": Robert McNeil, "The Story of *Zephyrus III* on the race Los Angeles to Mazatlan" (privately printed, 1966), 13; PK, November 20, 2003, 3; GK, interview with author, October 7, 2006, 5

Page 149, "A new trouble-free boat made": Slater, *Peggy*, 72, 73.

Page 150, "She decided she wanted a boat": PK, November 20, 2003, 3; Slater purchased the PC *Seventh Heaven* in 1947, K 38 #22 *Valentine* in 1954, and K 43 #9 *Valentine II* in 1965; the K 38 class racing organization was founded in 1953; TK, conversation with author, February 2, 2007; the 42- foot- long, 3-by-4-inch fir timbers, used also for PCC planking and PC masts, had been laid up by the navy at North Island to deck escort carriers; Philippine mahogany became available to construct K 38s from hull #17 on, PK 2002, 8; PCC #14 cost close to $20,000 in 1948, "The PCC: A Fast, New San Diego- Built Yacht is the Sensation of Pacific Coast Sailing," clipping, probably *San Diego Magazine*, ca. 1948; The K 38's 1949 price is given as $12,000 in 'Hitch,' "Anchor Watch," *San Diego Daily Journal*, February 21, 1949; Spurr discusses other contenders for the title of first production fiberglass sailboat in *Heart of Glass*, 30; "The Kettenburg 38," *Yachting* (August 1949): 51.

Page 151, "The one thing that George did was": Charlie Underwood noted that the K 38 hull was not drawn on paper, but the table of offsets was calcu- lated proportionally from the PCC and the lines were then lofted; CAU, 25.

Page 151, "Paul chose a name": PK, interview by George Wheeler, June 14, 1995; PK, email to Karen Scanlon, June 19, 2003; TK, however, never heard his father mention this P-38 connection, TK, February 2, 2007; Paul Lazarus, "Kettenburg Boat Works: Power and Sail for Southern California," *WoodenBoat* 116 (1994): 66; PK, 2002, 9.

Page 151, "Paul recalled the genesis": PK married Dorothy Johnson in Yuma in March 1947. He and his first wife divorced in 1946, after nine years of marriage. The event was the SCYA mid-summer regatta, Anderson, "Through Three Generations," 32.

Page 151, "I got back home": They also created the mold, or jig, on which K 38s would be built, PK, video interview with Steve Barber, Scott Wild, and Rish Pavelec, with TK, January 3, 2002, 7.

Page 151, "While we still hadn't launched": PK, 2002, 7, 10.

Page 152, "In addition to sales": CAU, 36; PK, November 21, 2003; CRU believes that their design method changed from full-size layouts on the loft floor to paper scale drawings after the K 38, CRU, conversation with author January 12, 2007.

Page 152, "In later designs": Tim Shepard, "Craftsmanship Rules: Violins, Racing Hulls Are Similar," San Diego Union clipping, ca. 1955; GK, 2.

Page 152, "In retrospect": CRU interview with author, May 31, 2006, 4; CRU letter to author, July 17, 2005, 4, punctuation altered for emphasis.

Page 152, "Charlie's father was sophisticated": GT, March 10, 2005, 14; BK, interview by Steve Barber and Neil Atwood, October 29, 2006, 2; Tom Gwynne, "In this Corner," Daily Journal clipping, ca 1946; BK agreed with this assessment of K 38 handling in conversation with author, September 28, 2006.

Page 152, "The challenges of downwind handling": K 38 #33 Crest voyaged to Hawaii, as noted in PK, 1995; the barracuda appear in Sea (May 1958).

Page 153, "Moments later, Ono's chilled": Anonymous Canadian sailor quoted in Humphrey Golby and Shirley Hewitt, Swiftsure: The First Fifty Years (Victoria: Lightship Press, 1980), 47; Dr. H. W. Day owned Ono; "L-36," Latitude 38 (May 2004): 132-36.

Page 153, "Yachting had informed its readers": "The Kettenburg 38," Yachting (August 1949): 51.

Page 153, "Americans had looked closely": "Sweet Sixteen" prototype date appears on photo in the Underwood family's collection, courtesy Susan Larkin; CAU, 9.

Page 153, "Kettenburg would sell more": The "Sweet Sixteen" sold for $900-$1,400, while the "Saucy Fourteen" sold for $700-$1,200, George Story, "Area's Boat Builders to Emphasize Luxury," (Part 2) San Diego Union, June 21, 1959; A 40-h.p. Scott-Atwater outboard was standard on the 16, but some were equipped with a 6-cylinder inboard-mounted Chrysler Ace; the boats came with trailers. TK, "Kettenburg Boats Timeline," 2003; "Sweet Sixteen" was 15 feet, 4 inches long with a 72-inch beam, and weighed 550 pounds; "Saucy Fourteen" was 13 feet, 7 inches long with a 68-inch beam

and weighed 400 pounds, "Sweet Sixteen" / "Saucy Fourteen" brochure, n.d., Tom Fetter coll.; the 1958 date for halting construction, and "more than 500" runabouts appear in Carl Plain, "Boat Builder Expands: Kettenburg Adds Santee Operation," San Diego Union, February 26, 1967; the success of the "Sweet Sixteen" design, however, led to a navy contract to build a fiberglass prototype of the steel 36-foot LCPL, which they designated the Mark II; Spurr, Heart of Glass, 89.

Page 156, "The K 47 Motorsailer": "The New K-47 Kettenburg Motorsailer," Yachting (June 1959): 80-81.

Page 157, "Nevertheless, on a summer's day": K 40 design was primarily by George Moore, working under Paul's direction, with minimal input from Charlie Underwood, CAU, 26; "New K-40 Type Yacht Launched," San Diego Union, July 26, 1959; PK notes that he tried a masthead rig on the K 38, but "it wasn't competitive," PK, 2002, 10; "K 40: Traditional Yachting in the Modern Manner," 1959 brochure; "K 40: The Boat with the Winning Ways," Sea (July 1960): 109; new distributors were Pohn Brothers Yacht Co., Chicago, and William Burchenal Jr., Florida, "NOW—represented in the Great Lakes and Florida," probably Sea, ca.1960; Story, "Area's Boat Builders," (Part 1) San Diego Union, June 14, 1959.

Page 159, "Peggy's best-known customer was": PK, 1985, 19.

Page 161, "Jim named both his Kettenburg sailboats": Jim Arness, quoted in McNeil, "The K-40 Story," (privately printed, ca. 1962); GK, 4.

Page 161, "When Jim moved up to a K 50": PK, 1985, 18; PK recalled that sailmaker Kenny Watts and his wife also went along.

Page 161, "One K 40 took the thousand-mile race": This was K 40 #25, Windspun; Fred Miller, "Bravata Wins Ensenada Race," probably Los Angeles Examiner, clipping, ca. May 1960, SDYCHC, italics added; Bravata actually finished tenth, but was corrected to first by handicap time, a very common occurrence, Mel Zikes, "Bravata Big Winner of Sail Classic," probably Los Angeles Times, clipping, ca. May 1960, SDYCHC; "Long Beach Boat Wins at Ensenada," San Diego Union, May 8, 1960.

Page 161, "We got down there and": GK, 7.

Page 163, "The results of the 1961 Transpac Race": The K 40s tracking problems are noted in Harry Monahan, "Now We Have 'Compact' Yachts: K-43's Improved Stern Design Seen as Aid to 'Tracking,'" San Diego Union, October 6, 1963.

Page 163, "While many yachtsmen were celebrating": The "many yachtsmen" who considered the K 40 Kettenburg's best boat are cited in Anderson, "Through Three Generations," 32; "Jim Arness Goes from Gun Smoke to Sea Smoke," Sea reprint, ca. 1963; naval architect George Moore assisted with design of the K 50, according to Anderson, "Through Three Generations."

Page 163, "Serious racers like Doug Giddings": DG, interview with Doug Werner, Andy Bofinger, and Charles Bishop, January 28, 1999, 6, SDYCHC.

Page 165, "For the first time, however": Trepte wanted to heighten the boat's rig and give it more ballast and better speed; Charlie Underwood resisted; Paul gave in, GT 2006, 7-8.

Page 165, "In the sad days at the end of 1963": PK, quoted in Peter Bohr, "Kettenburg 43: The Legend Lives On," *Sea* (September 1987): 47; Monahan, "'Compact' Yachts"; advertisement, *Sea* (February 1965): 39; the price of the first Mustang was $3,334; CRU, 2006, 3; Bohr, "Kettenburg 43," 47; two of these hulls were built by Yacht Dynamics in Torrance of aluminum, a material Paul preferred over fiberglass, Anderson, "Through Three Generations," 33; they considered building the K 43 of fiberglass, but decided to begin with the smaller K 41; sailmaker Kenny Watts was heavily involved in aluminum hull production; a third bare aluminum hull was shipped back to Detroit and made into a yawl, PK, 2002, 8, 11; the two aluminum-hulled K 43s had hulls 1,300 pounds lighter, with keels given more lead to compensate; spade rudders were installed as original equipment on these two.

Page 166, "Rolled up together": Both undated drawings are in Kettenburg Boat Works Coll., MacMullen Library & Research Archives, Maritime Museum of San Diego; Milt Wegeforth gave uncredited assistance with the lines of the K 43, CRU, conversation with author, January 12, 2007.

Page 169, "Bill Lapworth of Newport was": "Bill Built Boats You Could Love," *Sailing* (June 2006): 15. The two builders were Stephens, and Stone & Sons of Oakland; the customer quoted is George Griffith.

Page 169, "The Cal 40 was a pioneer": Katriana Vader, "An Afternoon With Bill Lapworth," *Latitude 38* (April 2002); Spurr, "Heart of Glass," 140.

Page 169, "The Cal 40's long winning streak": Lapworth quoted in Wendy Mitman Clarke, "Father of the Cal-40 disowns its offspring," *Soundings* (August 1995): A36; Lapworth had been sent to San Diego by the navy in 1945, then moved up to L.A. to assist Merle Davis, designer of the Island Clipper, until Davis's early death, where he became intrigued with light-displacement construction while sailing International 14s.

Page 169, "In those times of intense market": Tim Shepard, "Restores Cars—Sail Expert is Partial to Wheels," *San Diego Union*, June 29, 1964; PK, 1985, 9.

Page 169, "Unlike his gregarious brother": Bud Caldwell, interview with author, July 17, 2006, 4; PK, 2002, 10; Barr, "Memo"; TK, conversation with author, December 14, 2006; Shepard, "Restores Cars.

Page 171, "Others found different ways": Slater, *Peggy*, 71, 158; PK believed that this boat was Peggy's second K 43, built with fancy teak trimmings for an Eastern owner who died shortly after it was delivered, PK, 2002, 9.

Page 171, "While back in Los Angeles": Slater, *Peggy*, 1.

Page 171, "During her passage": Slater, *Peggy*, 7.

Page 171, "Her struggle paid off": Slater, *Peggy*, 158-59.

Page 171, "I was back aboard!": Slater, quoted in Bohr, "Kettenburg 43," 49, italics added.

Page 171, "Even a vessel as well built as a K boat": McNeil, "Story of *Zephyrus III*," 4.

CHAPTER 9

Page 175, "Eight years earlier": "Norman Rockwell-esque" is from Bill Ritter, "Local Owner to Keep Kettenburg Course Steady," *Los Angeles Times*, June 3, 1986.

Page 175, "I sailed on it once": Thompson Fetter, interview with author, October 7, 2006, 11. *Tradition*'s inaugural cruise was in April 1987. On her restoration, he notes that "one of the most difficult things is making sure that the time charged is time spent, and time that was *needed* to be spent. And having a 'house account' was probably a costly way to recondition that PC." The 1937 PC #26 has since been renamed *Water Wagon*.

Page 175, "Back in the late 1960s": Carl Plain, "Boat Builder Expands: Kettenburg Adds Santee Operation," *San Diego Union*, February 26, 1967; PK, quoted in Paul Lazarus, "KBW: Power and Sail for Southern California," *WoodenBoat* 116 (1994): 68; see "The New K 41 – A Fiberglass Hull," *Sea* (October 1966); MG's TF and Chevrolet's Corvette were both introduced in 1953.

Page 175, "The K 41 was": CRU, interview with author, May 31, 2006, 2; advertisement, *Sea* (May 1967): 59.

Page 177, "When interviewed four decades later": PK, interview with author, November 20, 2003.

Page 177, "Like every K boat": Bruce Crabtree, "Kettenburgs to Try New Venture Aboard Latest in Sailboat Hulls," *San Diego Evening Tribune*, July 1, 1966, in Underwood family scrapbook, reverse bears handwritten notes by CAU; CRU, letter to author, July 17, 2005, 4; Plain, "Boat Builder Expands"; on building in fiberglass, see PK, November 20, 2003, 6; the Santee shop also began construction by September 1973 on the "Kettenburg Retriever," a 57-foot-long fiberglass commercial fishing boat–the first was completed in March 1974 but was not commercially successful, "Santee," *The Ways Cable* (Kettenburg newsletter) (June 1973); "Bits and Pieces," *The Ways Cable* (September 1973); Ferrell Hawkins, "Santee," *The Ways Cable* (March 1974), courtesy TK.

Page 177, "Looking up from his drawing board": CRU, letter, 4; CRU, interview, 2.

Page 179, "Another controversy": GK, interview with author, October 7, 2006, 2; PK recalled that K 41 #29 was intended to be his personal boat and was assembled from leftover wooden parts, after Whittaker stopped production on the line. Instead of putting Charlie's 1- to 1 ¾-inch-thick fiberglass in the bottom, PK followed the practice of other fiberglass builders and replaced it with ½- to ¾-glass, dropping 1,000 pounds of lead into the keel to compensate, PK, video interview by Steve Barber, Scott Wild, Tom Kettenburg, and Rish Pavelec, January 2, 2002, 11.

Page 181, "Gary needn't have worried": CRU interview (Underwood's revision), 2; advertisement, *Sea* (May 1967): 59; an Underwood family scrapbook clipping lists the introductory K 41 price at $27,975; Frank Rhoades column, *San Diego Union*, ca. January 1966; The $28,000 Cal 40 price is from the late 1960s, and appeared on the *Latitude 38* Web site in September 2000; BK agreed that weight was a drawback to the K 41 in interview by Fred Lewis for television program *The Heart of San Diego*, broadcast June 13, 2005, 1; in a March 2007 email to the author, CRU notes that "weight was certainly a factor in that the Cal 40 was proportionally built with lighter weight construction. However, I believe that most competent yacht designers would agree that the most significant performance difference was that the Cal 40 was fundamentally a bigger boat than the K 41 with a considerably longer water line with more potential for speed and a bigger more powerful rig."

Page 181, "Ultimately, in Gary Keller's opinion": GK, interview, 2.

Page 181, "Increasingly, too": CRU, letter, 5.

Page 182, "The Kettenburg boatyard did": CRU, letter, 5, punctuation altered.

Page 182, "While these improvements added": The new hull design reduced drag by lowering the wetted surface, improved the water flow over the keel, enhancing directional stability, and improving the efficiency of the rudder, CRU notes this, along with Slater's involvement, in letter, 5; Gunnar C. Anderson, "Through Three Generations: The Kettenburg Log," *Sailing* (June 1974): 33, lists the owner as R. A. MacDonald of Long Beach, but incorrectly states that two were built; CRU corrected this in conversation with author, January 12, 2007.

Page 182, "Paul called all the employees": GK, notes on March 24, 2007 conversation appended to transcript of October 7, 2006 interview, 9; 1969 size and earnings estimates for Whittaker appear in "Whittaker Corporation," *International Directory of Company Histories*, vol. 48, (London: St. James Press, 2003); BK, interview by author, August 5, 2006, 6; BK, interview by Steve Barber, October 29, 2006, 1; PK, 1985 interview by Robert Wright, May 25, 1985, 10; Paul retired January 1, 1979 from Whittaker; Larry Miller took over as president.

Page 182, "The family firm that Whittaker absorbed": The partnership arrived at its final arrangement as Kettenburg Marine in 1965, as George's five former partners equally split 79 percent of the business, sharing the remaining 21 percent of ownership with their key men—Bob Ballinger, Herb Prior, "Johnny" Peterson, and Caldwell, who each held 4 percent; Controller Fred Neumeister held 5 percent; they also owned the management firm Kettenburg, Inc., Plain, "Boat Builder Expands"; an incorrect 1956 date for the reorganization appears in James Barthold, "B.I. Visits Kettenburg," *The Boating Industry* (September 1972): 83; Charlie's efforts included two 63-foot boats for Air Force rescue work launched in 1953, "Air Force Goes 'Navy'," *San Diego Evening Tribune*, March 26, 1953; this job proved crucial for the firm as prototype boats for many built around the country; according to Charlie, he and Paul exchanged responsibilities here–Paul gained responsibility for the overall job and its frequent travel, while Charlie focused on the prototypes, and on making their firm the central procurement agency; a 36-foot fiberglass naval personnel boat followed, CAU, 9-10; in 1967 they had a contract for 19 navy 35-foot workboats with aluminum hulls built in Chula Vista by Rohr Antenna, Plain, "Boat Builder Expands"; Plain, "Kettenburg, Rohr Team Up for Aluminum Boat Project," *San Diego Union*, undated clipping, 1967, courtesy TK; AM, interview with author, July 17, 2006, 3; in 1971 Fetter, Grimes and Miley founded an investment business as "FGM"–the first initials of their last names.

Page 182, "Art explained that": AM, interview with author, July 17, 2006, 2; Whittaker merged with Telecomputing Corp. in 1956 and absorbed a San Diego company, Narmco, in 1960, picking up executives Fetter and Grimes; Miley joined them in 1969; Grimes's goal, according to Fetter, was primarily to inexpensively acquire firms in transition from wood to fiberglass construction, assisting them by transfusing their industry with a shot of Whittaker's own aerospace materials technology, Fetter, 3; GK, notes appended to interview, 9; Coronado was founded by Frank Butler, who would develop Catalina yachts; Marine and Leisure Time companies included non-boating firms like hot rod parts maker Anson Automotive, and gym machine maker Universal Athletics Sales.

Page 183, "They bought us for": BK interview, August 5, 2006, 6; they were capable of handling boats up to 80 feet long and 100 tons weight, and could handle 50 to 70 boats at a time; profits of $1,261,127 recorded for 1960 reached $3,308,857 in 1967, David Grimes, handwritten notes marked "Name and Location," ca. 1968, 2, 5, Fetter coll.; "Organization, Key Personnel and Facilities," Whittaker, ca. 1973, 1, Fetter coll.; Anderson, "Through Three Generations," 32; Barthold, "B.I. Visits Kettenburg," 82.

Page 183, "Whittaker, however, wasn't": Grimes's 1968 Whittaker acquisition notes state that Kettenbergs [sic] "have three semi production yachts that apparently have a very good reputation and acceptance in certain markets. K. does not have sufficient national or local … marketing capability or line of boats to successfully sell," Grimes, "Name and Location," 12; Fetter interview, 7; Kettenburg's stores included Carleton St., a Harbor Island branch (discontinued by 1985), Dana Point, Oxnard, and Newport Beach, which Whittaker purchased in 1968 and added to Kettenburg; it retained its old name of Balboa Marine Hardware; the San Pedro store remained Marine Hardware of San Pedro, as did their warehouses in Santa Ana; exports were also made to Mexico, plus "a bit to Korea, and a very little to Riva in Italy," Morgan Miller, conversation with author, March 30, 2005; Bill's involvement in setting up overseas sales is noted in PK, 2002, 13; Fetter interview, 7.

Page 183, "Whittaker's primary purchasing technique": Fetter interview, 3, 9.

Page 183, "Whittaker stock": Whittaker bought Kettenburg for $1,250,000 in stock; stock price is from Grimes, "Name and Location," 8; BK mentions the potential usefulness of Whittaker certificates as a wallpapering material, August 5, 2006, 6; AM, interview, 3; CRU email to author, March 2007.

Page 183, "Not only was stock volatility": AM, interview, 3.

Page 184, "Just over a year after buying": Joseph Alibrandi replaced Dr. William Duke as CEO, *International Directory of Company Histories*, vol. 48; in 1970, Alibrandi planned to spin off Kettenburg with its other Marine and Leisure Time companies as "Recreation Resources, Inc.," but had to withdraw the stock offering, "Preliminary prospectus, Recreation Resources, Inc.," 1970, in possession of AM; In Miley's opinion, the stock market believed this spin-off stock offering was overpriced; Fetter interview, 6; the other boat companies had been bought by Investicorp; foreign-owned companies were barred from taking over firms like Kettenburg that held Master Ship Repair contracts, Michael Krey, "Tom Fetter Buys Kettenburg Marine," *San Diego Daily Transcript*, May 23, 1986.

Page 184, "Along the way, Whittaker": The exception was Bertram, purchased from a group of New York investors rather than from Dick Bertram.

Page 184, "Paul and Charlie were asked": The vice president was Fred Fletcher, CAU, 40.

Page 184, "These were kind words indeed": CAU, 42.

Page 184, "With great effort": PK, 2002, 1, 3.

Page 184, "The boats, renamed K 32s": GK, notes from March 24, 2007, conversation with author, appended to 2006 interview, 9; Payne intended his boat to function as a one-design class, see "The Columbia K 9.6," *Sea* (September 1977): 69; hulls were molded for Kettenburg by Survival Systems of La Mesa, priced at $32,000 without options; notable alterations to the rig included replacing its "really weird" big rudder with a conventional one, PK, 2002, 10; CRU, email to author, July 28, 2005; the boatyard was acquired in June 1973, *The Ways Cable* (June 1973); CAU, "Table of Contents," 3.

Page 185, "To Tom Fetter in 1986": GK, 9; Fetter, 8; the June 30, 1986, transaction involved $4.2 million supplied by the Bank of America, $3 million loaned by Whittaker, and the remainder from Fetter and his father-in-law, Fetter, "The Business Side of Kettenburg after the era of New Boat Construction," February 2007, 7; his daughter, "JJ" Fetter (Isler), was then a 31-year-old on her way to being a two-time Olympic sailing medalist and four-time Rolex Yachtswoman of the Year.

Page 187, "So, Art Miley asked rhetorically": Fetter, "The Business Side," 9. "One of the arguments that Whittaker used when I bought this was Kettenburg was not designated as a small business—because they were owned by Whittaker. And they said, 'As soon as you buy this, you can be classified as a small business, and you can get even more contracts.' None of us realized that about the same time the navy was trying to make their procurement more efficient," Fetter, 15; first-quarter profits for naval repair in 1986 came to $4.9 million, Ritter, "Local Owner"; as an added curse in a business climate of tight money and high interest rates, a 10 percent excise tax was imposed on sales of boats over $100,000 at the beginning of 1991, which dried up their wholesale sales to other builders.

Page 187, "One smart move": The percentage figure combines profits for the San Diego store and Balboa Marine, "Kettenburg Marine Corporation Briefing," May 1987, 4, Fetter coll.

Page 187, "By the end": Fetter, 9; Keller, perhaps because of his specialty in electronics, also believes that Kettenburg's lower volume of sales prohibited them from purchasing goods at West Marine's low price, GK, 10; Fetter's original lender was Bank of America, which transferred the loan to Security Pacific, which was in turn acquired by Bank of America; Kettenburg spent five years in the Special Assets Group.

Page 187, "A friend of Art Miley's": AM, interview with author, July 17, 2006, 4; other factors in Kettenburg's decline included the loss of the opportunity to support Italy's 1994 *America's* Cup team to Driscoll, which enriched the latter, plus attrition from the retirement of reliable longtime workers, BK and Miller, April 18, conversation; Fetter, 10.

Page 187, "Tom recalled, with a shudder": Fetter, "The Business Side," 10; Grimes, "Organization, Key Personnel and Facilities," lists the number of employees, including Mexicans, 1; 215 employees are listed in "Kettenburg Marine Corporation Briefing," 2; the padlocking appears in Rod Riggs and Michael Kinsman, "Kettenburg Marine Out of Business," *San Diego Union-Tribune*, February 3, 1994; the firm employed about 160 people when Fetter took over, Krey, "Executive Buys Kettenburg Marine"; sales slumped from a 1989 high of $29 million to $12 million; Mike Allen, "Kettenburg Owner Seeks to Put Condos on the Property," *San Diego Daily Transcript*, February 7, 1994.

CHAPTER 10

Page 190, "As the business itself": Miller, conversation.

Page 190, "In the early 1960s": GK, 4.

Page 190, "In the 1960s, two Southern Californians": Alex "Bud" Caldwell, interview with author, July 17, 2006, 4; Bud's PC was hull #40; PC owner Mike Lally has also been credited with applying this technique to PCs; Miller, email communication to author, March 28, 2007, punctuation altered.

Page 191, " But age and attrition still took": In 1972, there was a "resurgence" of 8-10 PCs racing, out of 15 boats still on the bay; Vern Griffin, "Craft of Memories: Ancient *Wings* Makes Big Comeback," *San Diego Union*, December 21, 1972; Richard "Rish" Pavelec recalls possibly only four PCs still sailing in the mid-1980s, conversation with author, February 7, 2007; in 1992, SDYC's fleet was composed of fewer than ten regulars, Pavelec, "PC Fleet News," *MainSheet* (April 1998): 22; PK, quoted by Elaine Davis, "PCs, If You Please: West Coast Woodies Have Found the Magic Formula for Longevity," *Waterfront* (December 1988): 14A-15A.

Page 191, "Of the people who like PCs": Pavelec, conversation with author, February 7, 2007; this was Mary Jo Riley's PC hull #16; Pavelec, "The Kettenburg PC: A Feast for the Senses," *Mains'l Haul* (Winter 2005): 22-23; Pavelec, quoted in Bill Center, "A Dream in Wood: Carl Eichenlaub is Bringing a Classic Boat Back to Life," *San Diego Union-Tribune*, March 8, 2004; *Puff* is hull #67.

Page 192, "The primary midwife": James Hebert, "Crafts Man – Wooden Boats Share Their Past and Return to the Sea Under Hands that Love Them," *San Diego Union*, August 5, 2001.

Page 192, "One of the invalids laid up": Center, "*Wings* Sailed Her Way Into Hearts of Many," *San Diego Union*, December 13, 1983; Pavelec notes that Koehler never charged him a dime for storing *Wings* for almost four years–though he was undoubtedly aware that Pavelec was a valuable customer, Pavelec, email to author, March 25, 2007, 4.

Page 193, "Along with Pavelec": These were the Cup races of 1980, 1983, 1987, 1992, 1995, and 2000; Center, "*Wings* Sailed her Way."

Page 193, "His first ride in a PC": Pavelec, "*Wings* and a Prayer," *Full & By* (Maritime Museum of San Diego newsletter); a photo taken by Ed Barr in 1950, now at MMSD, shows a crew of eighteen kids aboard.

Page 193, "Jack and Bud worked closely": Note on back of Sutphen's 1993 PC fleet group photo, punctuation altered; Kate Bast, "A Good Guess that Endured 65 Years: The Pacific Class," *Sailing* (November 1994): 69.

Page 193, "PCs are known for the fact": Bast, "A Good Guess," 69.

Page 193, "Joe Jessop, still sailing": GT, May 9, 2006, 11; Mike McCaffrey, owner of S-boat hull #8, brought her after the 1994 San Diego visit by his wife, Elizabeth Meyer, and her J boat *Endeavour*; The races were held April 2 and May 27, 1995; PC fleet members later competed in team races aboard the New York Yacht Club's S-boat fleet, Pavelec, email to author.

Page 196, "One more testament": Center, "A Dream in Wood"; see also Catherine French, "Carl Eichenlaub Takes Sailing to a New Level," *The Log*, November 11-24, 2005; the keel was from PC #25; Betty Sue Sherman is Eichenlaub's daughter.

Page 196, "The revival of interest in Kettenburg": Barber, in PK, 2002, 10; the dockmaster connected Steve and Scott Wild with K 38 owner Norm Schute and with PK; the Web site www.kettenburgboats.com began in 2000; Barber, email to author, March 25, 2007; George Wheeler, "Yachting World Rediscovering the Great Kettenburg Sailboats," *The Albatross* (newsletter, Ancient Mariners Sailing Society), 1996.

Page 196, "George Kettenburg's last design": Neil Atwood, email to author, 2006; Atwood, "Restoration of *Eulalie*, Kettenburg PCC, hull #1," 5; PC #83, *Mirage,* was his boat; there were 24 PCCs built, but 25 sail numbers assigned, a consequence of PCC#1 being sold in 1953 and becoming #20; PCC class regulations specified that the designer retained the right to sail # 1 (Atwood sails as #1 today thanks to special dispensation from BK); According to Atwood, the whereabouts of 16 PCCs are currently known; 10 are sailing, 3 are undergoing restoration, while the condition of 3 others is unknown; of the remaining eight, two sank, one was cut up after neglect, and one was extensively modified; credit should go, too, to PCC owner Deb Dominici for reviving the annual Kettenburg regatta in 1993; PCC yacht racing today remains governed by the PCCYRA (Pacific Cruising Class Yacht Racing Association), founded October 2, 1948; their last official championship race was held in 1990, according to a trophy engraving.

Page 198, " In the last decade of the 21st century": The PC Association continues to govern racing, and has approved very few changes and set down few rules. Specifying the location of the jib car track, limiting the use of modern sail materials (Kevlar, etc.), and controlling lead keel shaping and hull weight in an effort to keep competition between pre- and post-war boats fair. Much effort has gone into locating and identifying the vessels still in existence: 64 of the 83 hull numbers assigned have been identified as lost, sailing, or "on the hard": 19 boats are yet unaccounted for, while 17 hull numbers are classified as either never built, converted and no longer a PC, lost, or otherwise destroyed, Bast, "A Good Guess," 69; PK, interview, November 20, 2003, 2.

Illustration Credits

1: © Pat Kirkpatrick, Kettenburg Boat Works collection
2-3: © Kipp Soldwedel, courtesy G. W. "Bill" Kettenburg III
6: Courtesy G. W. "Bill" Kettenburg III
12: Courtesy G. W. "Bill" Kettenburg III
13: Author's collection
14: Courtesy G. W. "Bill" Kettenburg III
15: San Diego Historical Society
16: Maritime Museum of San Diego
18: Top, © Mystic Seaport, Rosenfeld Collection, 1984.187.99265F; Bottom, William H. Hand Jr., *Hand V Bottom Motor Boat Designs* (New Bedford, MA: William H. Hand Jr., 1921), 9.
20: Courtesy G. W. "Bill" Kettenburg III
21: Courtesy G. W. "Bill" Kettenburg III
22: *Yachting* (January 1927): 67
23: Top and bottom, courtesy G. W. "Bill" Kettenburg III
24: Courtesy G. W. "Bill" Kettenburg III
26: Courtesy Tom Kettenburg
27: Kettenburg Boat Works collection
28: Kettenburg Boat Works collection
29: Courtesy San Diego Yacht Club
30: © aerofiles.com
31: Courtesy Hershey family
32-33: Courtesy G. W. "Bill" Kettenburg III
34: Top, courtesy G. W. "Bill" Kettenburg III; bottom, courtesy Hershey family
36: Top, courtesy Larkin family; bottom, Kettenburg Boat Works collection
37: Courtesy Hershey family
39: Kettenburg Boat Works collection
40-41: Kettenburg Boat Works collection
42: Kettenburg Boat Works collection
43: San Diego Historical Society U-T
44: Top, courtesy Hershey family; bottom, courtesy Larkin family
45: Kettenburg Boat Works collection
46: Kettenburg Boat Works collection
47: San Diego Historical Society
48: San Diego Historical Society
49: Kettenburg Boat Works collection
50: Courtesy G. W. "Bill" Kettenburg III
51 Courtesy Larkin family
53: © Mystic Seaport, Rosenfeld Collection, 1984.187.34811F
54: Left, courtesy Hart Nautical Museum, MIT; right, "The Atlantic Coast One-Design Class", *Yachting* (November 1928): 78, original in Coll. 11, Burgess-Donaldson Collection, Daniel S. Gregory Ships Plans Library, Mystic Seaport
55: "The Atlantic Coast One-Design Class," *Yachting* (November 1928): 78, originals in Coll. 11, Burgess-Donaldson Collection, Daniel S. Gregory Ships Plans Library, Mystic Seaport

56: © Mystic Seaport, Rosenfeld Collection, 1984.187.47422F
58: Kettenburg Boat Works collection
59: Courtesy Richard S. "Rish" Pavelec
60: Courtesy Hershey family
61: Kettenburg Boat Works collection
62: Kettenburg Boat Works collection
63: Ruskauf Press Features photo, Kettenburg Boat Works collection
64: Courtesy Dr. Iris W. Engstrand, G. B. Worthington Jr.
65: Kettenburg Boat Works collection
66: Courtesy San Diego Yacht Club
67: Kettenburg Boat Works collection
68: Kettenburg Boat Works collection
69: *Pacific Coast Yachting* (July 1931)
70: Courtesy Doug Giddings
71: Kettenburg Boat Works collection
72: Courtesy Les Hamm, Maritime Museum of San Diego, P11507
73: Courtesy Dr. Iris W. Engstrand
74: Courtesy San Diego Yacht Club
75: Kettenburg Boat Works collection
76: Both photos courtesy Larkin family
77: Newport Beach Historical Society, Sherman Library, Corona Del Mar
79: 1980.127.3, Coll. 80, Philip L. Rhodes Collection, Daniel S. Gregory Ships Plans Library, Mystic Seaport
80: Courtesy Coates family
81: Kettenburg Boat Works collection
82: Kettenburg Boat Works collection
83: San Diego Historical Society
84: Maritime Museum of San Diego, P-11508
86: Maritime Museum of San Diego
87: Courtesy G. W. "Bill" Kettenburg IIII
88-89: Courtesy Larkin family
90: Courtesy Hershey family
92: Courtesy G. W. "Bill" Kettenburg III
93: Courtesy Larkin family
94-95: Courtesy Hershey family
97: Kettenburg Boat Works collection
98: Kettenburg Boat Works collection
99: Top, courtesy Hershey family; bottom, Kettenburg Boat Works collection
100: Courtesy Van Pelt family
100-01: Maritime Museum of San Diego
102: Courtesy Van Pelt family
103: Kettenburg Boat Works collection
104: Courtesy Tom Kettenburg
105: Top, *San Diego Daily Journal*, January 24, 1946, courtesy San Diego Yacht Club; left, Kettenburg Boat Works collection

106: Courtesy Barr family
107: Courtesy San Diego Yacht Club
108: Courtesy Dawley family
110: Courtesy San Diego Yacht Club
111: Courtesy G. W. "Bill" Kettenburg III
112: Courtesy San Diego Yacht Club
113: Kettenburg Boat Works collection
114: Courtesy Tom Kettenburg
115: Kettenburg Boat Works collection
116: Courtesy Coates family
117: Courtesy Coates family
118: *Sea* (February 1946)
118-19: Kettenburg Boat Works collection
121: Courtesy G. W. "Bill" Kettenburg III
122: © Mystic Seaport, Rosenfeld Collection, 1984.187.126999F
123: © Mystic Seaport, Rosenfeld Collection, 1984.187.128752F
124: Courtesy Tom Kettenburg
125: © Mystic Seaport, Rosenfeld Collection, 1984.187.127005F
126: Photo by Floyd McCarty / MPTV.net
127: Kettenburg Boat Works collection
128: Dennie Barr scrapbook, courtesy Debra A. Dominici
129: Courtesy San Diego Yacht Club
130: Courtesy Coates family
131: San Diego Historical Society
132: Courtesy G. W. "Bill" Kettenburg III
132-33: © Ronald F. Ross, Kettenburg Boat Works collection
134: Kettenburg Boat Works collection
135: Maritime Museum of San Diego, P-11529
136: Kettenburg Boat Works collection
137: Left, Kettenburg Boat Works collection; right, courtesy Larkin family
138: Cloyd F. Coates photo, Maritime Museum of San Diego, P-11534
140-41: Courtesy Philip Barber, Maritime Museum of San Diego, P-11546
142: Kettenburg Boat Works collection
143: San Diego Historical Society
144: Left, San Diego Historical Society; right, Kettenburg Boat Works collection
145: Courtesy San Diego Yacht Club
146: Kettenburg Boat Works collection
147: Kettenburg Boat Works collection
148: Maritime Museum of San Diego, P-11554
150: Courtesy Beckner family
151: Courtesy Beckner family
153: Courtesy Larkin family
154: Courtesy Larkin family
155: Kettenburg Boat Works collection
156: Both photos, Kettenburg Boat Works collection

157: Kettenburg Boat Works collection
158: Kettenburg Boat Works collection
159: Maritime Museum of San Diego, P-11547
160: Maritime Museum of San Diego, P-11517
161: Kettenburg Boat Works collection
162: Kettenburg Boat works collection
163: Top, courtesy Harry Merrick; bottom, Kettenburg Boat Works collection
164: Kettenburg Boat Works collection
165: Both photos, Kettenburg Boat Works collection
166: Top, San Diego Historical Society U-T; bottom, Maritime Museum of San Diego
167: San Diego Historical Society U-T
168: © Mystic Seaport, Rosenfeld Collection, 1984.187.176165F
170: *Sea* (June 1965)
172: San Diego Historical Society
173: Kettenburg Boat Works collection
174: Maritime Museum of San Diego, P-11520
175: Kettenburg Boat Works collection
176: Top, Kettenburg Boat Works collection; bottom, courtesy Larkin family
177: Top, San Diego Historical Society; bottom, courtesy Charles AquaViva, Maritime Museum of San Diego, P-11518
178: San Diego Historical Society U-T
179: San Diego Historical Society U-T
180: San Diego Historical Society U-T
181: Maritime Museum of San Diego, P-11519
183: Kettenburg Boat Works collection
184: Kettenburg Boat Works collection
185: All photos, Kettenburg Boat Works collection
186: Courtesy Charles AquaViva
187: Maritime Museum of San Diego, P-14895
188: © Bob Eichler
189: © John Bahu
190: © Laura Allen
191: Courtesy Richard S. "Rish" Pavelec
192: © Laura Allen
193: Courtesy Jack Sutphen
194: © Bob Eichler
195: © Bob Eichler
196: Left, © Bob Eichler; right, © Nick Lee
197: Top, © Laura Allen; bottom left, © Lynda Rosi; bottom right, © Laura Allen
198-99: © Valerie McClelland

Index

(Page numbers in italics indicate illustrations)

displacement of, 117-18, 122, 125; price of, 118; compared with California 32, 117-20; on East Coast, 122, 125-26; downwind steering of, 152; restoration of, 196, 198

Penguin Class, *90*, 91

Petersen, Werner "Pete," 113

Petersen-Kettenburg two-blade folding bronze propeller, 112-13

Pittsburg, Pennsylvania, 14

Plane-rearming boats, *86, 88-89*, 91, 96

Poggy, 19

Poggy II, *31*, 34

Poggy III, 28

Poggy (yard boat), *102*

Potter, Nick, 118

Prohibition, 35

Puff (PC), 192

R

Rhodes, Philip L., 79-80

Rhodes 33, 79

Robinson, Dick, 40

Roosevelt, James, *82*

Ross, Charlie, 113, 121, 157

Rum-running, 35, 37

Ruski, Joe, 45-46

Ryan, T. Claude, 30, 31

Ryan Standard, 30

S

S Class, 52, *53*, *54*-55, 60

San Clemente Island Race, 120, 163

San Diego, California, *13*, *15*, 17, 31, 50, 77; harbor dredging, 74, 76-77; growth of, 149

San Diego Yacht Club, 17, *29*, 44, 50-51, 52, 196, 198

San Francisco, California, 77, 78

Santana, *126*

Scamp (PC 1), *58, 60, 61, 63, 64, 66, 67, 72, 84*, 85

Sea Smoke, 161, *163*

Selene (PCC 3), *108, 197*

Shelter Island, 76, 144, *145*

Shock, Edson Burr, 57

Six Meter Class, 52

Skylark (PC 31), *1, 73, 75*

Slater, Peggy, 128, 142, *146, 148*-50, 157, 161, 165, 171

South Coast Boat Building Company, 78-79

Southern Ocean Racing Conference (SORC), 121, 122, 169

Spade rudder, *166*, 169, *177*

Sparkman & Stephens, 126, 182

Springstead, Charles, 45

Springstead, Wally, 61, 62, 143, *197*

Star Class, *44*, 45

Starlet, *45, 46, 47*

Stephens, Olin II, 122, 125-26

Star of India, *10, 189*

Sterling, Tom, *197*

Stose, Willis "Clem," 17, 22

Sun Class sloop, *22-24*

Sutphen, Jack, *192, 193, 197*

Sweet Sixteen, *153-55*, 157

Swiftsure Race, 109, 120, 121, 153

T

Tomboy (K 38), *150*, 151

Tomboy II (K 40), 157, *158, 160*

Tomboy III (K 50), 161, *162, 163*

Tomboy V (K 41), *174, 176*

Tradition (PC), 175

Transpac Race, 120, 163, 169

Trepte, Gene, *110*, 113, 119, 193, *197*

Tripp, Bill, 182

Tuna fishery, 17, 42, 96, 100

Tuna net tenders, *135*

22-Square –Metre boat, 57

U

Underwood, Charlie, 91, *92-93*, 94, 96-98, *105, 137*, 148, 152, 153, 165, *166, 172*, 176, *177, 179*, 184

Underwood, Charlie Jr., 176, *178*, 181

Underwood, James "Jimmy" Sr., *36*, 37-38

Underwood, Jim Jr., 72, 93

Universal Rule, 52, 54

Upside-down construction, 93-94

V

Valentine II (K 43), *170*, 171

Vee-bottom powerboats, 18

W

Waterhouse, Glenn, 77-78, 157

Watts, Kenny, 125, 165

Wegeforth, Milt, 47, 119

West Marine, 187

Wheeler, George, 196

Whittaker Corporation, 182-85

Wings (PC 8), *10, 64, 67, 71*, 189, 192-93

Women skippers, 126-29, *131*, 142